Introduction

Welcome and Thank You

Thank you for your purchase of the SIE Professor's SIE Exam Study Guide. The Study Guide was created to help provide those interested in passing the SIE Exam with a comprehensive, affordable resource. With more than 40 years of combined securities industry experience, including time with several broker-dealers and securities industry regulators SEC and FINRA, we have unique insights into the securities markets that drive the content of the SIE Exam. Our veteran securities market experience has touched all areas that the examination covers, from equity and fixed income securities, to AML, political contributions, 529 Plans, and everything in between.

As either current or former students of something, we have all had to study unfamiliar and familiar material alike. When creating the study guide, we looked hard at the guidelines that the exam's author and owner, FINRA put together. Both of us have also passed and now hold several different FINRA examinations so our expertise is not theoretical, but practical. After reviewing FINRA's outline, you will notice that our guide very closely mirrors the FINRA outline. This is on purpose of course – we have matched the material likely to show up in your examination as outlined by FINRA, to the material found in this study guide. Although no study guide is perfect, the content herein combines the items you need to memorize and learn with some discussion on why the securities industry works the way it does. By not focusing solely on memorization, as a student you will be better able to think through a question on the exam that you are not quite sure of the answer.

We are always looking for feedback, so please let us know at sieprofessor@gmail.com if there are ways we can be clearer, fix an error, add more detail, or make the study guide a better experience. If you find our study guide helpful, please leave us a positive review on our Amazon page! Look for regular updates on our website or on social media sites such as Facebook and our YouTube Channel. Study hard and best of luck!

Thank you for your patronage.

Best,

Eric and Ann

SIE Exam Study Guide 2020

Your Complete Guide to Passing the SIE Exam

Eric T. Field

Ann M. Griffith

ISBN: 978-0-578-66188-9

About the SIE Exam

The SIE Exam is divided into four sections:

Section 1 – <u>Knowledge of Capital Markets</u>

12 Questions or 16 % of the SIE Exam

Section 2 – <u>Understanding Products and Their Risks</u>

33 Questions or 44 % of the SIE Exam

Section 3 – <u>Understanding Trading, Customer Accounts, & Prohibited Activities</u>

23 Questions or 31 % of the SIE Exam

Section 4 – <u>Overview of the Regulatory Framework</u>

7 Questions or 9 % of the SIE Exam

Here are the facts on the SIE Exam:
- 85 total questions
- 75 questions are scored, 10 questions are unscored
- You cannot tell which questions are scored or unscored
- There is no penalty for answering an unscored question incorrectly
- Multiple choice format with 4 possible answers to each question
- 105 minutes, or 1 hour 45 minutes to complete the exam
- You must take the SIE Exam at a FINRA approved testing center
- The SIE Exam is taken on a computer at the testing center
- The passing score on the SIE Exam is 70%.
- Cost to take the SIE Exam is $60 and is paid directly to a testing center.
- In the testing center, you cannot bring in anything with you (pen, pencil, calculator, cell phone, smart watch, paper – NOTHING)
- FINRA takes cheating seriously (rightfully so), so DO NOT CHEAT. You could be permanently barred from the securities industry if you are caught cheating.
- Additional information about the SIE Exam is available on FINRA's website at http://www.finra.org/industry/essentials-exam.
- Our YouTube channel has an SIE Exam Overview video with more detail.

How to Pass the SIE Exam

Everyone learns a bit different – the resources you are provided by SIE Professor can be consumed in whatever order works best for you. However, as we have taken many FINRA and MSRB exams over the years, there are some best practices and a rough order to things that tend to work the best for most people. The 'How To' below is our attempt to make the study process for the SIE Exam as quick, practical, and retainable as possible.

How to Study for the SIE Exam Using the SIE Professor's Method

1. **Read FINRA's SIE Exam Outline** – FINRA's publically published outline is available at https://www.finra.org/sites/default/files/SIE_Content_Outline.pdf You can read page two of the outline for now so you are familiar with what FINRA expects out of SIE Exam candidates, but it also provides some good information on question depth and focus.

2. **Read our Study Guide** – Ok, so this is obvious, but important to check off the list. Read all of the material in this Study Guide front to back.

3. **Complete the End-of-Chapter Questions** – As you finish reading each of the chapters, answer each of the questions at the end of that chapter. If you have answered any questions incorrectly, be sure to go back and review that section of the study guide that aligns with the correct answer.

4. **Table of Figures Review** – Starting with the Table of Figures in the back of the study guide, go through each of the Figures contained within the study guide sequentially. Each of the Figures within the study guide are excellent summaries of information you are likely to see in some form on the SIE Exam.

5. **Videos** – Subscribe to our YouTube Channel to review practice questions, correct answer explanations and test taking strategies. We cannot fit enough practice questions here, so we add new practice questions every Monday on our YouTube Channel.

6. **Final Exams** – Once you have completed the entire steps above, take the practice examinations! To simulate the actual test conditions, do your best to complete an entire examination within the 105 minute time limit you will have on the real SIE Exam. If you are scoring in the mid-80's on your practice examinations, you are ready to move on!

7. **FINRA Practice Exam** – Take the FINRA Practice Exam on their website at https://www.finra.org/industry/sie-practice-test.

8. **Sit for the SIE Exam** – The last and final step – take the SIE Exam! To learn more about everything related to the SIE Exam and how to schedule an examination for yourself, check out our website at www.SIEProfessor.com.

Let's begin!

Table of Contents

SIE Exam Study Guide 2020

Section 1: Knowledge of Capital Markets

Chapter 1: Regulatory Entities, Agencies and Market Participants

The securities industry is made up of several different regulatory entities, agencies, and market participants. Each has their own unique role to play within the securities industry. Not all regulators have the same level of authority, influence, or control over the securities market. Some regulators also operate in a niche, or specific area of the market (and that's all they do). It is important that you understand the basic regulatory structure, who each regulator is, what each regulator does, and for what each regulator is responsible.

The Securities and Exchange Commission

When the Securities and Exchange Commission ("SEC") speaks, those involved in the securities industry listen. The SEC is the primary regulator for the securities industry. The purpose of securities regulation is to strike the appropriate balance between competing interests – self-regulatory organizations ("SROs"), exchanges, broker-dealers, investment advisers, traders, mutual fund managers, retail customers, and institutional customers.

Modern day securities regulation is based on a variety of securities laws – some created recently, and some passed into law many, many years ago. The securities laws to focus on are the following:
- The Securities Act of 1933
- The Securities Exchange Act of 1934
- The Investment Company Act of 1940
- The Investment Advisors Act of 1940
- Dodd-Frank Wall Street Reform and Consumer Protection Act from 2010
- Employee Retirement Income Security Act ("ERISA")
- Jumpstart Our Business Startups Act ("JOBS Act")

These are the key laws passed over the years that you will need to know. Although some of these laws were passed many years ago, the laws and regulations have been updated numerous times over the years. In fact, when new securities laws are passed by Congress and signed into law by the President, they are often done so as amendments to existing law and not as a brand new, stand-alone law. In addition, when the SEC makes new rule or regulations, they do so under the authority given to them in one of these existing laws, like the Securities Act of 1933. Let's go through each of these important laws at a high level.

The Securities Act of 1933

Also known as the '33 Act or Securities Act, it covers offerings of securities and new issues. The '33 Act was born out of the stock market crash of 1929 and subsequent depression. It regulates the registration, offer, and sale of securities and requires issuers to 'fully disclose' material or relevant information to potential investors prior to an investment decision.

The Securities Exchange Act of 1934

Also known as the Exchange Act or '34 Act, it has several key elements. The '34 Act governs the public sale of securities that have been previously offered to the public. In addition to governing the public sale of securities through exchanges, the '34 Act also deals with the governance of public companies and the regulation of broker-dealers. Although the '33 Act obviously came first in date/year sequence, the '34 Act actually created the SEC.

The Investment Company Act of 1940

The Investment Company Act was passed by Congress and signed into law in 1940. The Investment Company Act was another important law put into place by the federal government in response to the stock market crash of 1929. It granted the SEC the power to regulate open end mutual funds, closed end funds, hedge funds, private equity funds, and unit investment trusts. Specifically, the Investment Company Act requires that investment companies:

1. Register with the SEC
2. Have a Board of Directors, with at least 75% of the Board being independent directors
3. Maintain a cash buffer for customer redemptions
4. Make public filings of certain financial data, holdings, expense information, and conflicts of interest – all publicly available to investors at the SEC's Edgar website
5. Limit the use of leverage to drive returns

Some hedge funds are able to avoid some of the above Investment Company Act requirements, because they meet certain exemptions available under the Investment Company Act for having a small number of investors.

The Investment Advisors Act of 1940

The Investment Advisors Act ("Advisors Act") sets out the legal requirements for those individuals giving investment advice. The Advisors Act further requires individual advisors to act as the customer's fiduciary. Acting as a fiduciary means that the investment advisor must act solely in the customer's "best interest" at all times. This differs from the '34 Act where brokers have to meet only a suitability obligation with regard to their customers' investments. The Act further requires Investment advisors with more than $100 million in Assets under Management ("AUM") must register with the SEC. For advisors with less than $100 million in AUM, those advisors must register with their state of domicile and in those states in which they conduct business. For those advisors operating private funds with AUM under $150 million, they are permitted to operate under an exemption from full registration as an investment advisor.

Dodd-Frank Wall Street Reform and Consumer Protection Act from 2010

The Dodd-Frank Wall Street Reform and Consumer Protection Act ("Dodd-Frank) was passed by Congress and signed into law by President Obama in 2010. It was implemented by the federal government as a result of the Great Recession of 2008-2009, where many financial institutions had to be bailed out by the U.S. government.

ERISA

The Employee Retirement Income Security Act ("ERISA") was passed into law in 1974 and amended several times since. ERISA imposes a fiduciary duty on those who run employee benefit plans. Although ERISA has a wide-reaching impact to both employers and employees, the SIE is only focused on how ERISA impacts registered representatives and customer accounts. You should focus on the fact that the laws, rules, and regulations around ERISA impact tax-qualified retirement plans like 401(k)'s. Being a fiduciary for someone else, or for another group of people means that you have only their best interests in mind when making investment decisions for the account, not merely that the recommendations or actions you take are suitable for those same people or groups of people.

JOBS Act[1]

The Jumpstart Our Business Startups Act ("JOBS Act") was passed by Congress and signed into law by President Obama in 2012. The JOBS Act covered three main areas: emerging growth companies, access to capital for job creators, and crowdfunding.

Definition, Jurisdiction and Authority of the SEC[2]

At the top of the SEC are 5 Commissioners, of which no more than 3 can be from the same political party. The lead, or head Commissioner is known as the SEC Chairperson. Each Commissioner serves a 5 year term. The SEC Chairperson is chosen by the party that controls the White House, which gives that party a majority vote among the 5 total SEC Commissioners. 2 of the commissioners are from the political party that controls the White House; the other two Commissioners are from the party that does not occupy the White House. The SEC's Commissioners vote on approving new or amended rules, disciplinary actions, and hiring key staff. All commissioners are appointed by the President and confirmed by the U.S. Senate.

The SEC has jurisdiction over all U.S. exchanges, SRO's, broker-dealers, investment advisors, clearing firms, and municipal advisors. Jurisdiction over these entities is one of the SEC's key powers, as these entities have most of the dealings with the investing public. Through the SEC's jurisdiction over these entities, the SEC can perform their key functions – oversight of the entities themselves. When the President signs a bill passed by the U.S. Congress into law that pertains to the SEC, it either expands the SEC's authority or contracts that authority. The law will often be an amendment to an existing law. A good example of this is the Dodd-Frank law passed in 2010. Although not limited to the SEC, the law gave the SEC more authority in many areas, but also mandated that the SEC write new rules and regulations. The SEC is seen to enforce *congressional intent*, or said another way, enforce the law as Congress wanted it to be enforced. This is known as the SEC's enforcement authority.

The SEC has the power to enforce the federal securities laws. Where individuals or entities have been found to violate the federal securities laws (or agreed to a settlement with the SEC), the SEC can take a variety of enforcement actions for violating SEC or other industry rules, including:

- **levying a monetary fine** – requiring an individual, entity, or issuer to pay a fine.
- **removal of securities licenses** – removing an individual's securities licenses, such as the SIE Exam, Series 7, Series 24, etc. In order to act in a registered capacity again, the individual would be required to requalify with any necessary examinations.
- **temporary bar from the industry for registered employees** – under a bar from the industry, an individual would not be permitted to work in the securities industry for a specific period of time, (e.g., 6 months, 1 year, 2 years).
- **permanent bar from the industry for registered employees** - an individual would no longer be permitted to work in the industry unless they applied for and received readmission by the SEC.
- **bar officers and directors** – officers and directors of public companies can be barred from the industry just like registered employees who work in the industry.
- **issue cease and desist orders** – The SEC can issue these orders to industry participants to prevent future specific actions from occurring. A cease and desist order is specific in that it describes exactly what the recipient of the order is required to stop doing now and avoiding doing in the future.

The SEC can only levy civil (non-criminal) penalties through its enforcement powers. The SEC can also enforce laws under the anti-fraud provisions of the '34 Act. Although rule violations can be covered under specific FINRA, SEC, or MSRB rules, the anti-fraud provisions of the '34 Act are often used when there is not a clear rule violation, or if indeed an individual or entity has committed actual fraud. Charging an individual or entity with a violation of the anti-fraud provisions of the '34 Act is one of the most serious charges that can be levied.

SEC Mission
The SEC's Mission itself is rather straightforward and has three equally important parts – maintaining fair, orderly, and efficient markets, facilitating capital formation, and protecting investors. At any one point in time, one of these three parts of the SEC's mission might figure more prominently in rulemaking or enforcement actions. In addition to enforcing its own rules, the SEC can also charge individuals or entities with

violations of SRO rules. Although many view the SEC to have wide ranging powers, the SEC only has jurisdiction over matters relating to securities – orders, transactions, recommendations, companies issuing securities, etc. The SEC does not have jurisdiction over other financial products such as commodities, futures, bank loans, or bank deposits.

Figure 1: The Three Missions of the SEC

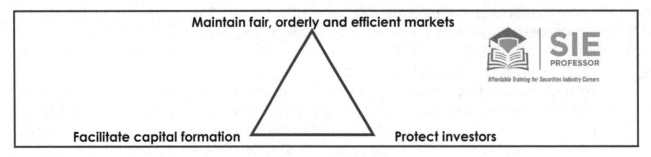

Role of the SEC[3]

Congress does not need to pass a new law and have that law signed by the President for the SEC to create new rules for the securities industry. Many of the new rules that the SEC creates are put into place after a law has become effective. The law often requires to take specific steps or to make new within certain areas of the market. For instance, the Dodd Frank law passed in 2010 mandated the SEC to institute rulemaking (i.e., making new rules) pertaining to Municipal Advisors. The law provided parameters and overall requirements about what the rules needed to address.

SEC Summary
• **Mission** – Threefold: Maintain fair, efficient, and orderly markets; facilitate capital formation; protect investors.
• **Core Duties** – The SEC is the top regulator in the securities market and oversees SROs and other market entities. They conduct inquiries and examinations of market participants, with the power to discipline both individuals and market participants for rule violations.
• **Jurisdiction** – The SEC is a U.S.-based Federal Government agency with jurisdiction over U.S. entities and those foreign entities operating within the U.S. In addition, the SEC only has jurisdiction over securities transactions, not commodities or depository institutions (commercial banks).
• **Board/Commissioners** – The SEC has five commissioners, with one commissioners designated as the Chairperson. All SEC Commissioners are appointed by the President. Three commissioners are from the President's political party with the remaining two commissioners from the party that does not control the Presidency.
• **Regulatory Entity or Government Agency** – The SEC is considered a Regulatory Agency and part of the Executive Branch of the U.S. Federal Government.

Self-Regulatory Organizations (SROs)

Self-Regulatory Organizations, or SRO's, perform an important function within securities market. SRO's have jurisdiction over their members and are overseen by the SEC. All SROs have several common purposes:

- Oversee conduct of their members
- Protect the investing public
- Establish rules of conduct for their members to follow and take appropriate steps to enforce their rules, including disciplinary actions
- Refer violations of their rules (or the SEC's rules) to other SROs or the SEC
- Exchanges have jurisdiction and enforcement authority over their members and activity occurring on their exchange - options, equities, other listed securities

The SEC oversees all regulators within the securities industry. FINRA is the largest of the self-regulatory organizations. However, there are three other regulators and agencies that should be familiar to you for this examination in addition to the SEC.

1. **FINRA**
2. **MSRB**
3. **Exchanges**

Let's first go through the largest SRO in today's security's market - FINRA.

FINRA – The Financial Industry Regulatory Authority[4]

FINRA regulates and enforces rules of the broad securities markets, focusing primary responsibility on over-the-counter-transactions. An over-the-counter transaction is any securities transaction that does not occur on an exchange (i.e., the third market). Many SROs actually have signed an agreement with FINRA to have FINRA regulate certain aspects of their exchanges on their behalf. FINRA collects vast amounts of regulatory reporting. By collecting information from the broader securities market, FINRA has a greater overall market view and is better able to see bad actors than exchanges could, as exchanges only look at their own exchange activity.

FINRA's Mission:

"FINRA is dedicated to investor protection and market integrity through effective and efficient regulation of the securities industry."[5]

FINRA Summary

- **Core Duties** – create rules for the over the counter market, review member firm conduct through examination and inquiries, discipline firms and individuals for rule violations, publish investor alerts notifying the public about market trends and issues, certify firms and individuals through examination programs
- **Jurisdiction** – Oversee member's activities within the securities markets
- **Board/Commissioners** – FINRA has a board that is made up of both industry and independent members
- **Regulatory Entity or Government Agency** – FINRA is a Regulatory Entity, not a government agency

MSRB – The Municipal Securities Rulemaking Board[6]

When you see MSRB, think municipal securities. Municipal securities are issued all the time by your local and state governments – school districts, towns and cities, water and sewer authorities, and states.

MSRB Mission[7]

The mission of the MSRB is to protect investors, state and local government issuers, other municipal entities and the public interest by promoting a fair and efficient municipal market through:
1. The establishment of rules for municipal dealers and municipal advisors,
2. The collection and dissemination of market information, and
3. Market leadership, outreach and education.

The MSRB's website is available at www.msrb.org. Market information, such as official statements, trading history, and information about specific municipal securities are available at the MSRB's EMMA site, available at emma.msrb.org.

The MSRB was created in 1975 through amendments to the Securities Act. Under the MSRB's original authority, it was required to regulate any financial company or individual that bought, sold, or underwrote municipal securities. As part of the Dodd-Frank legislation passed in 2010, the MSRB added responsibilities for Municipal Advisors, or financial professionals that provide advice to state governments, local governments, or other municipal entities. This advice must pertain to the issuance of bonds or other municipal financial products. MSRB has jurisdiction of all municipal securities activities in the marketplace. The MSRB does not actually enforce its own rules as it does not have the authority to do so – this is done by FINRA or the SEC.

MSRB Summary

- **Mission** – The MSRB established rules for dealers and municipal advisors, collects and disseminates market information and conducts outreach and educational activities.
- **Core Duties** – As noted in its mission statement, the MSRB makes the rules for dealers and municipal advisors, disseminations market information, and conducts outreach and educational activities.
- **Jurisdiction** – The MSRB makes the rules for municipal market participants. All non-municipal activity falls outside of the MSRB's jurisdiction.
- **Board/Commissioners** – The MSRB has a Board of Directors that approves new rules and revisions to existing rules. There is a mix of individuals on the MSRB Board, both from within the industry and independent of the industry.
- **Regulatory Entity or Government Agency** – MSRB is a regulatory entity, not a government agency.

The remaining SRO's – CBOE, NYSE Arca, AMEX, NYSE, and Nasdaq all operate as for-profit exchanges, in addition to SRO's.

Exchanges/SROs
- The Chicago Board Options Exchange ("CBOE")
- The New York Stock Exchange ("NYSE")
- Nasdaq ("Nasdaq")
- Others – NYSE Arca and AMEX

Companies that look to go public through an IPO usually want their stock to be traded on an exchange. Nasdaq like the NYSE, operates both as a SRO and as an exchange. The exchange component operates the platform where stock or options are traded by the exchanges members. Issuers must receive approval from the exchange to list their companies on the exchange for trading. The exchanges compete to win these listings. If an issuer is listed on an exchange, that company is generally considered less risky when compared to an unlisted company. That is because an exchange has listing standards, or rules that the issuer must follow. These rules have to do with a minimum price, minimum number of shareholders, standards for financial statements, and disclosure obligations, among others.

The NYSE is one of the oldest exchanges in the United States. It has two primary components – the listing side and the trading side. The listing side works with issuers to have their securities (primarily equity securities) represented on the exchange. The trading side facilitates actual trading of the securities. These are the exchange functions of the NYSE. The SRO side has jurisdiction over its members and their trading activities on the exchange. NYSE is owned by ICE. ICE also owns companion exchanges to the NYSE in the U.S. markets, including NYSE ARCA and the National Stock Exchange on the equity side, plus NYSE AMEX Options and NYSE ARCA Options on the options side of the market.

In 1971, Nasdaq created the world's first electronic stock market. Originally, Nasdaq was owned by the NASD (National Association of Securities Dealers), the precursor organization to FINRA. Unlike NYSE or other traditional bricks and mortar stock exchanges, Nasdaq never had an exchange floor, or floor brokers. Nasdaq has only had electronic-based traders, although the technology Nasdaq traders use today is much more sophisticated than in 1971. In that way, Nasdaq paved the way for the modern electronic securities markets.

Exchange/SRO Summary

- **Mission** – Each exchange is required to regulate and enforce their rules for activities that occur on their own exchanges
- **Core Duties** – enforce exchange regulations for activities that occur on the exchange or activities by the exchange members in general
- **Jurisdiction** – All activities that occur on the exchange or by the conduct of any of its members
- **Board/Commissioners** - Board
- **Regulatory Entity or Government Agency** – Exchanges are regulatory entities, not government agencies. They are owned and operated as for-profit entities.

Other Regulators and Agencies

In addition to the primary regulators described above, there are seven other regulators, agencies or market participants that should be familiar to you for this examination:

1. **IRS** – Internal Revenue Service
2. **State Regulators and NASAA -** North American Securities Administrators Association
3. **The Fed** - The Federal Reserve
4. **SIPC** - Securities Investor Protection Corporation
5. **FDIC** - Federal Deposit Insurance Corporation
6. **DTCC** – Depository Trust Clearing Corporation
7. **OCC** – Options Clearing Corporation

Each of these regulators performs a different function, and interact in different ways with the securities industry and securities industry participants. It is important to know when and how these regulators interact within the securities industry. First up is the Internal Revenue Service.

IRS – The Internal Revenue Service

The Internal Revenue Service ("IRS") is part of the Department of Treasury. The

Department of Treasury is headed by a cabinet-level secretary, which is appointed by the President and confirmed by the Senate. The IRS is responsible for collection of taxes, interpretation of U.S. tax laws and regulations, and enforcement of U.S. tax laws and regulations. According to their website[8], the IRS maintains the following mission and statutory authority.

The IRS Mission

Provide America's taxpayers with top quality service by helping them understand and meet their tax responsibilities and enforce the law with integrity and fairness to all.

- In the United States, the Congress passes tax laws and requires taxpayers to comply with these laws.
- The taxpayer's role is to understand and meet his or her tax obligations.
- The IRS role is to help the large majority of compliant taxpayers with the tax law, while ensuring that the minority who are unwilling to comply pay their fair share.

Statutory Authority

The IRS is organized to carry out the responsibilities of the Secretary of the Treasury under Section 7801 of the Internal Revenue Code. The Secretary has full authority to administer and enforce the internal revenue laws and has the power to create an agency to enforce these laws. The IRS was created based on this legislative grant. Section 7803 of the Internal Revenue Code provides for the appointment of a Commissioner of Internal Revenue to administer and supervise the execution and application of the tax laws.

IRS Summary:
- **Core Duties** – create and interpret U.S. tax laws, collect and enforce tax laws, assist taxpayers with tax questions
- **Jurisdiction** – Taxable activities dealing with any U.S. citizens or entities
- **Board/Commissioners** – One Commissioner
- **Regulatory Entity or Government Agency** – The IRS is part of the U.S. Treasury Department, which is technically neither.

State Regulators and NASAA – North American Securities Administrators Association[9]

State regulators play an important role in the regulations of activities that occur within their borders. NASAA membership includes 65+ separate U.S., Canadian, and Mexican states, provinces, and territories. State securities regulators are responsible for enforcing state securities laws and are primarily focused on retail investor issues. Each state has their own laws and state regulators enforce these laws by overseeing firms and registered representatives that conduct business within their state jurisdiction. NASAA attempts to provide a venue for separate state regulators to share information about market trends and changes, along with attempting to draft model legislation that can then be considered and passed by individual states into law.

According the NASAA Website:
THE ROLE OF STATE SECURITIES REGULATORS

NASAA members work within your state government to protect investors and help maintain the integrity of the securities industry by:
- **Licensing stockbrokers**, investment adviser firms (those managing less than $100 million in assets), and securities firms that conduct business in the state.
- **Registering** certain securities offered to the states' investors.
- **Investigating investor complaints** and potential cases of investment fraud
- **Enforcing state securities laws** by fining, penalizing, providing restitution to investors, prosecuting white-collar criminals, and imposing legally binding conduct remedies designed to correct specific problems.
- **Examining brokerage and investment adviser firms** to ensure compliance with securities laws and maintenance of accurate records of client accounts.
- **Reviewing certain offerings** that are not exempt from state law.
- **Educating investors** about their rights and providing the tools and knowledge they needs to make informed financial decisions.
- **Advocating** passage of strong, sensible, and consistent state securities laws and regulations.

State Regulators and NASAA Summary:

- **Core Duties** – license and examine individuals and firms conducting business with the state, along with enforcing laws and recommending changes to those state laws
- **Jurisdiction** – Each state has jurisdiction over securities activities that occur within their state, or conduct impacting investors within their state. NASAA has no formal jurisdiction itself, but has great influence on the direction of state and sometimes federal securities laws and regulations.
- **Board/Commissioners** – Each state typically has a state securities regulator role. NASAA has a president and Board selected by membership, or the state securities commissioners (or equivalent) from each state.
- **Regulatory Entity or Government Agency** – NASAA itself is neither, but the states that make up NASAA are considered Regulatory Agencies, as each state has some office that specifically handles securities, financial markets, insurance, etc...

The Federal Reserve[10]

The Federal Reserve is commonly referred to as 'The Fed'. The Federal Reserve has jurisdiction over large banks and bank holding companies. All bank holding companies and banks with assets over $50 million are within the Fed's jurisdiction. Typically, community banks fall under this $50 million threshold and are not within the Fed's jurisdiction. The Fed's powers were significantly expanded as a result of the Financial Regulatory Reform Act of 2010, a direct result of the Great Recession of 2008-2009. In addition to overseeing large banks and bank holding companies, the Fed sets monetary policy for the United States and reserve requirements for banks. In addition to overseeing banks and bank holding companies, the Fed also plays a key role in determining monetary policy. Monetary policy is discussed in Chapter 2.

Structure of the Federal Reserve

The **Federal Reserve has a Board of Governors** ("FRB") comprised of 7 individuals: five Federal Reserve Bank governors plus the Chairperson and Vice Chairperson. Each member of the FRB is appointed by the President and confirmed by the U.S. Senate. Under the Board of Governors of the Federal Reserve ("FRB") exists 12 regional Federal Reserve banks. The Board of Governors is financially and administratively independent of the President and Congress. The FRB members serve *14 year overlapping terms*. The U.S. President appoints the FRB members, and the U.S. President can serve a maximum of two, four-year terms for a total of eight years. The combination of the U.S. President's two term limit and the length of the FRB member terms prevent any one president from controlling the makeup of the FRB.

Makeup of the **Federal Open Markets Committee** ("FOMC")
- Chairperson of the Federal Reserve
- Other 6 members of the Board of Governors
- President of the New York Federal Reserve Bank
- Four additional Presidents selected from the remaining Federal Reserve banks, on a rotating basis.

The chairperson of the Board of Governors is selected from existing Federal Reserve Bank Governors and serves a four year term. The chairperson of the Federal Reserve ("Fed Chair") has significant amount of power over U.S. monetary policy. For instance, the Fed Chair controls the agenda of and chairs all Board of Governor and FOMC meetings, effectively determining what topics are permitted to be discussed.

Key Federal Reserve Duties
- Manage *systematic risk* in the financial system.
- *Oversee large banks and bank holding companies* – The Fed conducts examinations and stress tests these entities.
- Set *monetary policy*, such as conduct open market operations, adjust the discount rate, and determine reserve requirements.

There is a broader discussion on the Fed in Chapter 2.

Federal Reserve Summary:

- **Core Duties** – Manage systematic risk, execute monetary policy, be the lender of last resort, and oversee banks and bank holding companies.
- **Jurisdiction** – U.S. banks and bank holding companies.
- **Board/Commissioners** – The Federal Reserve has a Board, led by the Federal Reserve Chairperson.
- **Regulatory Entity or Government Agency** – The Federal Reserve is considered a Government Agency.

SIPC - Securities Investor Protection Corporation[11]

SIPC protects securities investors in the event a broker- dealer becomes insolvent or bankrupt. SIPC is not a true government agency or regulatory organization. Instead, it is a non-profit member-based corporation. However, all FINRA member firms are required to be SIPC members as well. When a broker-dealer becomes insolvent, is bankrupt, or is in some other financial trouble, SIPC steps in with a court-appointed trustee. SIPC and the trustee work to return customers' securities and cash. SIPC membership is mandatory for all broker-dealers and is funded by its broker-dealer members. SIPC does not have any authority to regulate, supervise, or investigate its broker-dealer members. That is the responsibility of FINRA and the SEC, generally.

There are a few important SIPC limits of which to be familiar. SIPC coverage is limited to securities and or cash holding within an investor's brokerage account. Coverage is tied to an individual or entity - one limit for that individual or entity regardless of the number of accounts at the broker-dealer. Joint accounts would be considered separate from individual accounts and have their own limits. The maximum coverage is $500,000 total for cash and securities and a separate limit of $250,000 limit for cash. Let's go through a few examples:

Example 1: John and Susan Investor have three brokerage accounts at Bankrupt Broker-Dealer – John's individual account, Susan's individual account, and John and Susan's joint account. Here is the balance breakdown:

John's individual account - $70,000 cash, securities valued at $110,000
Susan's individual account - $60,000 cash, securities valued at $90,000
Joint account - $265,000 cash, securities valued at $270,000

In the event Bankrupt Broker-Dealer is indeed, bankrupt, how much SIPC protection do John and Susan have for all of their accounts?

John's individual account - $180,000 total SIPC coverage
➢ securities at $110,000 and cash at $70,000

Susan's individual account - $150,000 SIPC coverage
➤ securities at $90,000 and cash at $60,000

Joint account - $500,000 total SIPC coverage
➤ securities at $250,000 and cash at $250,000

How did we get to those numbers, you ask? Let's go through them. John's individual account is straightforward. His cash position is below $250,000 so the total cash amount is fully covered. John's total securities are valued at $110,000, which combined with the $70,000 in cash keeps his account below the maximum account limit coverage of $500,000. Susan's accounts have similar math behind them. Susan's cash balance is $60,000, which is below the $250,000 cash limit. Susan's total securities are valued at $90,000, which combined with the $60,000 in cash put his total coverage at $150,000 which is below the maximum account limit coverage of $500,000. The trickier part of this example is the joint account. Why is the joint account only covered for $500,000? It comes down to the amount of cash in the account. Cash is only covered up to $250,000, regardless the value of the securities in the account. The total coverage for any single account is $500,000, with a cap of $250,000 cash for that account. The securities in this case will not be fully covered because the $250,000 cash limit plus the $270,000 securities value exceeds $500,000.

Let's go through another example, this time with only one account.

Example 2: Jane has $350,000 in cash and $150,000 in securities in her individual brokerage account. If her broker-dealer goes bankrupt, how much SIPC coverage does Jane have for this account?

The answer? $400,000. Why?

The cash limit is $250,000, so $100,000 of the cash is not covered under SIPC. All of the value of the securities is covered because the total value does not exceed $500,000. $250,000 cash plus $150,000 in securities = $400,000.

If you see a math-based SIPC coverage question on the SIE Exam, start with the cash limit of $250,000 first, and then work on the overall limit of $500,000. Any one account cannot be covered for more than $500,000, regardless of the cash and securities mix within the account. If there are multiple accounts involved though (joint and individual), then each account would need to be assessed separately.

SIPC Summary:
• **Core Duties** – When SIPC members become insolvent, SIPC steps in and makes securities investors whole, up to allowable limits.   • **Jurisdiction** – Any firm who is a SIPC member.   • **Board/Commissioners** – SIPC uses a Board to govern their operations.   • **Regulatory Entity or Government Agency** – SIPC is considered a regulatory entity, and not a formal government agency.

FDIC - Federal Deposit Insurance Corporation[12]

The Federal Deposit Insurance Corporation ("FDIC") covers deposits at insured banks. An individual or entity that deposits money into a bank is called a depositor. In the event of a bank failure or insolvency (i.e., bank goes bankrupt), FDIC coverage becomes effective. According to the FDIC's website, the FDIC's mission is as follows:

The FDIC is an independent agency created by Congress to maintain stability and public confidence in the nation's financial system by:
- Insuring deposits;
- Examining and supervising financial institutions for safety and soundness and consumer protection;
- Making large and complex financial institutions resolvable; and
- Managing receiverships.

For the SIE Exam, the role the FDIC plays in things like managing receiverships and supervising member institutions is less important. Instead, let's focus attention on the types of accounts and products covered and the limits of those coverages. FDIC covers many different types of accounts, including:
- Checking accounts
- Savings accounts
- Negotiable order of withdrawal ("NOW") accounts
- Money market deposit accounts ("MMDA")
- Certificates of Deposit (CD) or other similar time deposits
- Any other official item issued by the bank, such as a cashier's check or money order.

The primary goal is to protect bank deposit holders in the event of bank insolvency. What is exactly covered in these types of accounts? All of the deposits up to the insurance limit, including principal and accrued interest, up until the bank's closing.

The limits apply to each individual per bank. If an individual has two individual accounts at two separate banks, the coverage limits apply separately – $250,000 limit at each bank.

There are several things that the FDIC does not cover, including:

Stocks	Bonds
Mutual funds	Life insurance policies
Annuities	Municipal securities
Safe deposit boxes or their contents	U.S. Treasury bills, bonds, or notes

Even if you hold these products at an FDIC-insured institution, the products are not covered by the FDIC if the bank becomes insolvent. Why would the FDIC, a federally chartered organization, not cover U.S. Treasury bills though? These securities are not covered by the FDIC because the products are already backed by the full faith and credit of the U.S. Government. It is also important to know when FDIC coverage applies and when SIPC coverage applies. For instance, stocks, bonds and mutual funds are covered under SIPC and not the FDIC.

For a customer, it is important to understand how FDIC and SIPC coverage work together. If an entity is a member of both FDIC and SIPC, a customer is not 'double covered', but instead covered separately based upon the assets in question – securities (SIPC) or bank instruments (FDIC).

FDIC coverage is limited to cash within a deposit holder's bank account (i.e., checking, savings, cd, etc.). FDIC coverage is also tied to an individual or entity - one limit for that individual or entity regardless of the number of accounts at the institution. Joint accounts are considered separate from individual accounts and have their own limits. However, joint accounts for the same owners at the same institution are only protected up to $250,000 regardless of the number of accounts at the same institution. This same restriction applies to other accounts, such as individual, revocable trust, and irrevocable trust accounts.

Figure 2: FDIC Coverage Limitations[13]

Account Type	Coverage Limit by $	Coverage Limit by Person or Entity	Description
Single	$250,000	Per owner	
Joint	$250,000	Per co-owner	
Retirement	$250,000	Per owner	Applies when participants can direct the investments, such as IRAs, 401ks, Keogh plans
Revocable Trust	$250,000	Per each unique beneficiary	
Irrevocable Trust	$250,000	Typically total for the trust	
Employee Benefit Plan	$250,000	Per non-contingent interest of each plan participant	
Corporate, Partnership or Unincorporated Association	$250,000	Per entity	
Government	$250,000	Per official custodian	

Example 3: John and Susan Smith maintain several accounts at their local bank as follows:
- Joint savings account in both John and Susan's names, for $300,000
- Individual checking account in Susan's name only, for $100,000
- CD account in John's name only, for $50,000

How much coverage do John and Susan have in place with the FDIC?
- Joint savings account in both John and Susan's names: the $250,000 limit applies
- Individual checking account in Susan's name only: all $100,000 is FDIC covered
- CD account in John's name only, all $50,000 is FDIC covered

Example 4: Let's look at another example – similar to the above but with a slight twist!
John and Susan Smith maintain several accounts at their local bank as follows:
- Joint savings account in both John and Susan's names, for $200,000
- A second joint savings account in both John and Susan's names, for $200,000
- Individual checking account in Susan's name only, for $100,000

How much coverage do John and Susan have in place with the FDIC?
- Since both joint savings accounts in are in both John and Susan's names, the FDIC will limit protection to $250,000. The $250,000 limit will not be applied to both accounts separately, so they will not have 100 % coverage of their $400,000.
- Individual checking account in Susan's name only, will be covered for the full $100,000 account balance.

Example 5: Erin and Steve Johnson maintain several accounts at their local bank as follows:
- Joint savings account in both Erin and Steve's names, for $100,000
- Individual checking account in Steve's name only, for $200,000
- U.S. Treasuries of approximately $50,000

How much coverage do Erin and Steve have in place with the FDIC?
- Joint savings account in both Erin and Steve's names, the $100,000 is fully covered
- Individual checking account in Steve's name only is fully covered for $200,000 because it is only in Steve's name
- U.S. Treasuries of approximately $50,000 are not covered by the FDIC, as these securities are backed by the full faith and credit of the U.S. government

---

FDIC Summary:

- **Core Duties** – Insure deposits, supervise member institutions, making financial institutions resolvable, and manage receiverships,
- **Jurisdiction** – The FDIC has jurisdiction over all member banks. Almost all of the banks in the U.S. are members of the FDIC.
- **Board/Commissioners** – The FDIC has a Chairperson who leads the agency, along with a Board of Directors that provides additional governance and leadership
- **Regulatory Entity or Agency** – The FDIC is an independent agency of the US Federal Government

---

Market Participants

The term market participant is a broad term and covers many different types of individuals and entities. Below are the types of market participants you will need to be familiar with for the SIE Exam.

- Investors
  - Retail Investors
  - Institutional Investors
  - Accredited Investor
  - Qualified Institutional Buyer
- Brokers and/or Dealers
  - Introducing
  - Clearing
  - Prime Broker

- Investment Advisors
- Municipal Advisors
- Issuers and Underwriters
- Traders and Market Makers
- Custodians and Trustees
- Transfer Agents
- Depositories and Clearing Corporations

Let's start off with the easiest types of market participants to understand – **investors**. Under FINRA rules, there are two primary types of investors: institutional and retail Investors. Other terms can be more narrow or broad, or use security types to define qualifications for investment.

Under FINRA rules, the definition of a customer includes both institutional or retail account holders, but not broker-dealers. A broker-dealer is specifically excluded from the definition of a customer. So, a customer can either be a retail investor, or an institutional investor. Retail investors are most often actual people – Sally Smith, Judy Jones, or Tom Tuddel. Institutional customers are entities, in that an institution is not typically a person. For instance, **institutions** include, but are not limited to, the following types of entities:

- Insurance Company
- Hedge Fund
- Mutual Fund Company
- Pension Funds
- Venture Capital Funds
- Private Fund

So, an institution is typically an entity such as an insurance company. When might an entity not be considered a retail investor?

To meet the strict regulatory definition of an institutional investor, the customer must be one of the following:
- a bank, savings and loan association, insurance company, or registered investment company;
- an investment adviser; or
- *any other person or entity with total assets of at least $50 million.*

From a regulatory and industry rules perspective, a retail investor is any investor that does not meet the definition of an institution, as defined above. Retail investors are most typically individuals but can include smaller institutions that don't meet the definition of an institutional investor.

To meet the FINRA definition of an institution, that institutional must be one of the specifically listed entities above (bank, savings and loan association, insurance company, registered investment company, or an investment adviser) or have more than $50m in assets. Why is this necessary? Some entities, like hedge funds, partnerships, Limited Liability Corporations, or Limited Liability Partnerships are clearly not individuals. FINRA however requires these entities to have more than $50m in assets in order to be considered an institutional investor.

Qualified Institutional Buyer

A QIB (pronounced as "KWIB") stands for Qualified Institutional Buyer. An investor considered a QIB is a financially sophisticated investor. A QIB is not considered to need the protections that the securities registration process offers to investors. QIB status is required of investors when purchasing private placements, issues sold pursuant to SEC Rule 144a, or for purchases of below investment grade securities. To meet the QIB standard, an investor must meet one of the following thresholds for any of the following entities:
- acting for its own account or the accounts of other QIBs that in the aggregate owns and invests on a discretionary basis at least $100 million
- any investment adviser registered under the Investment Advisers Act
- any dealer acting for its own account or the accounts of other qualified institutional buyers, that in the aggregate owns and invests on a discretionary basis at least $10 million of securities of issuers that are not affiliated with the dealer
- any dealer acting in a riskless principal transaction on behalf of a qualified institutional buyer
- Accredited investor (see below)

Accredited Investor[14]

An Accredited Investor or AI is another level of distinction for investors. Similar to a QIB, an AI has specific rules-based definition and qualification process. The SIE Exam will not test you on the overly specific aspects of the AI standard. Stick to knowing things like:

- AI's are considered financially sophisticated investors
- AI's are considered not to need the protection that the securities registration process offers investors
- often used with private placements
- includes banks, savings and loan associations, broker-dealers, investment companies, business development company
- any director, executive officer, or general partner of the issuer of the securities being offered or sold, or any director, executive officer, or general partner of that issuer;
- any natural person whose individual net worth, or joint net worth with that person's spouse, exceeds $1,000,000. The person's primary residence is not included as an asset. If the natural person does not have $1,000,000 in net worth excluding their primary residence, **that natural person can still be considered an accredited investor if over the last two years that person has an earned income of over $200,000 (or $300,000 together with a spouse).** To meet the $200,000/$300,000 income test, the natural person must also expect to meet or exceed those income limits in the current year.

Brokers and/or Dealers

There are many different types of brokers and/or dealers. The three most common types of broker-dealers include an introducing broker-dealer, a clearing broker-dealer, and a prime broker. Each of these types of broker-dealers has a different purpose in the market.

An introducing broker-dealer is a broker-dealer that maintains direct relationships with customers. Customers of the introducing broker-dealer place orders and trades for securities through that introducing broker-dealer. An introducing broker-dealer does not clear or settle trades – this function is performed by a clearing broker-dealer.

The clearing broker or dealer clears and settles trades either for itself as a 'self-clearing' broker-dealer and/or another introducing broker-dealer. From the clearing broker-dealer's perspective, an introducing broker-dealer is also known as a correspondent firm or correspondent broker-dealer.

A prime broker is typically used by large institutional firms but is also used by large retail investors as well. An institutional client will have accounts open at multiple introducing firms where those institutional clients will place orders and execute trades. The institutional client does not however want to maintain separate positions at each of these introducing firms, or even at the introducing firm's clearing firm. Instead, the institutional customer will aggregate these positions at their Prime Broker. The Prime Broker is sent all of the trade information by the institutional client's introducing firm trading partners. This allows the institutional client to see all of their positions in one place. It also allows the institutional client's Prime Broker to do the same to manage various risks.

Figure 3: Retail and Institutional Customer

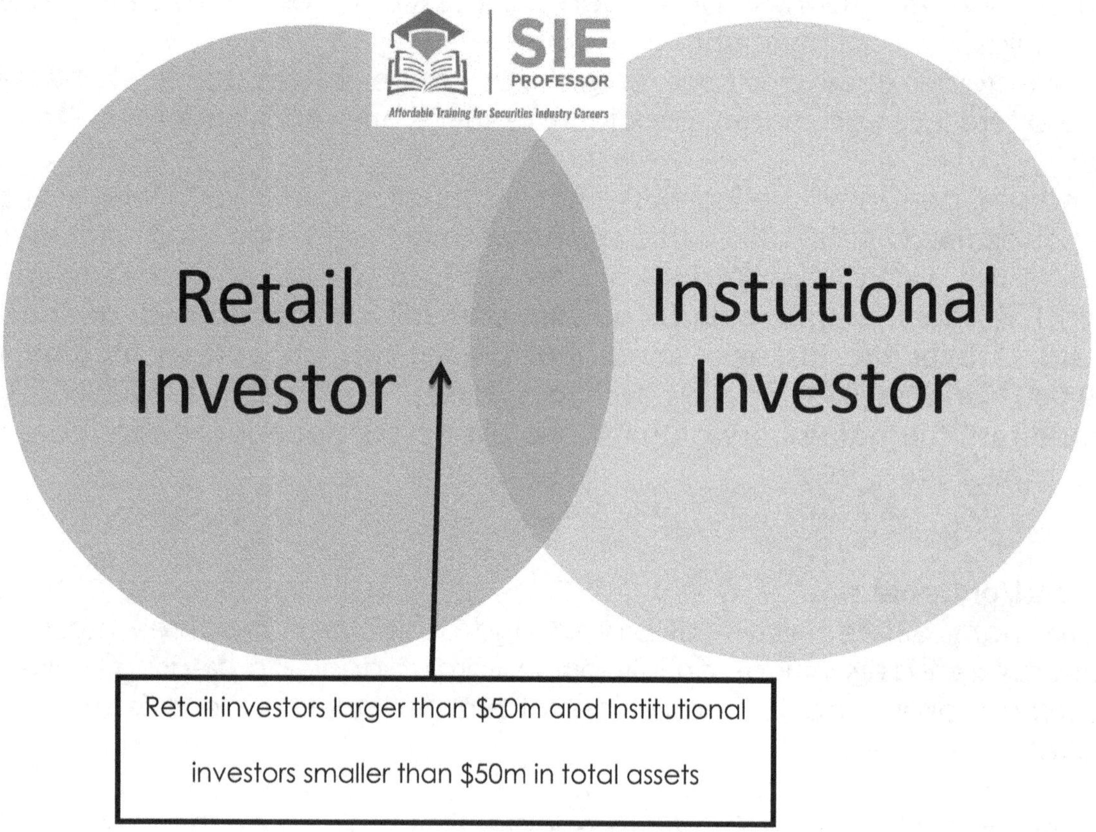

Retail investors larger than $50m and Institutional investors smaller than $50m in total assets

Investment Advisors

An Investment Advisor owes their customers a fiduciary duty. The SEC notes the following about investment advisors:

> An investment adviser is a person or firm that is engaged in the business of providing investment advice to others or issuing reports or analyses regarding securities, for compensation. Investment advisers may include money managers, investment consultants, financial planners, general partners of hedge funds, and others who are compensated for providing advice about securities.

Advice about securities not only includes advice about specific securities (such as stocks, bonds, mutual funds, limited partnerships, and commodity pools), but may also include advice about market trends, the selection or retention of other advisers, the advantages of investing in securities over other types of investments (such as coins or real estate), the furnishing of a selective list of securities, and asset allocation. Investment advisers generally must register with the Securities and Exchange Commission (SEC) or state securities authorities.[15]

Municipal Advisors

Municipal Advisors operate in a section of the market that you might expect – advising municipal issuers on capital raising activities. Municipal Advisors must be registered with the SEC by completing Form MA on an annual basis, and updating it when there are material changes. Municipal Advisors clients are entities such as cities, states, towns, and school districts. A Municipal Advisor owes their municipal clients a fiduciary duty. The SEC, on its Form MA instructions, defines a municipal advisor as "a person (who is not a municipal entity or an employee of a municipal entity) that

- provides advice to or on behalf of a municipal entity or obligated person with respect to municipal financial products or the issuance of municipal securities, including advice with respect to the structure, timing, terms, and other similar matters concerning such financial products or issues; or
- undertakes a solicitation of a municipal entity or obligated person."

Issuers and Underwriters

An issuer is an entity that offers equity or debt in exchange for ownership or a promise to pay a specified coupon or principal in return for the owner or investor's cash. A debt issuer receives cash from an investor in exchange for a promise to repay a future amount on a predetermined schedule. In the process, the debt issuer creates a security with the specified terms, conditions, risks, description of the business, etc.

An underwriter holds pricing risk, or the risk that the price paid for the securities from the issuer will be too high, resulting in the underwriter selling the securities to public investors at a lower price than what was paid, or a loss. Securities bought from issuer are intended to be sold quickly to the public, thus minimizing risk. If securities are sold in a public offering, a registration statement must be filed with the SEC for certain securities. More on that in Chapter 3.

Market Makers and Traders

Market makers are willing to buy and sell a particular security. Market makers are generally thought of working in the equity or options markets, but can exist really for any security. To be considered a market maker, the market maker must:
- Be willing to buy and sell on a continuous basis
- Publish a quotation reasonably related to the market

- Publish or post a two sided quotation
- Regarding equity securities, a market maker is permitted to sell short without obtaining a locate (find the stock or borrow the stock they are selling short). Normally, short sellers must perform a locate prior to effecting the short sale.
- A market maker makes money by selling at the ask and buying at the bid. The difference between the bid and the ask is the bid-ask spread. For some securities, the bid-ask spread is significant. For other securities, the bid-ask spread is very small, like $.01.
- A market maker may be a member of an exchange or only trade over the counter. Most market makers will likely be a member of an exchange.

A market maker cannot accept payments from an issuer in exchange for being a market maker in a security. A market maker is a type of a trader, but a trader may not necessarily be a market maker. Traders work in many different capacities within the securities industry. A trader buys and sells securities just like a market maker, but does not perform any of the key market making duties, like buying and selling on a continuous basis. A trader may be buying and selling on behalf of customers, the firm the trader works for, or perhaps even their own personal account.

Custodian and Trustees

A custodian is the entity that is responsible for the safekeeping of customer assets – stocks, bonds, and cash etc. In many cases, the custodian is the same entity as the customer's broker-dealer who is providing execution services (buying and selling of securities). Institutional customers rarely use any custodian outside of their Prime Broker. For firms that also clear their transactions in house, the broker-dealer and the custodian are typically the same firm. Introducing broker-dealers are however not typically custodians – the custodian is typically the clearing firm that the introducing firm uses to clear and settle trades.

Transfer Agents

Transfer agents play a specialized role in the securities industry. Transfer agents rarely have contact with customers. The SEC notes that transfer agents play an important role in the securities industry:

> Transfer agents record changes of ownership, maintain the issuer's security holder records, cancel and issue certificates, and distribute dividends. Because transfer agents stand between issuing companies and security holders, efficient transfer agent operations are critical to the successful completion of secondary trades.[16]

Depositories and Clearing Corporations

There are two primary depository and clearing corporations that operate within the securities industry and consequently, you will need to know about them on the SIE Exam - the Depository Trust Clearing Corporation ("DTCC") and Options Clearing Corporation ("OCC").

DTCC processes financial transactions related to several different types of securities products, including equities, corporate and municipal bonds, government and mortgage backed securities, derivatives, money market instruments, and mutual funds.

For these security types, DTCC provides the following services:

Clearing	Institutional matching
Settlement and Delivery	Asset servicing
Collateral management	Global data management
Information services	

Although DTCC performs many functions – the most important of these to remember for the SIE Exam is that DTCC handles the *confirmation, delivery, and settlement* of transactions on a daily basis. Broker-dealers join DTCC as members so they can receive DTCC's services. The DTCC is owned and governed by their members. DTCC seeks to reduce risk by streamlining securities transaction processes and disseminate information out to the market participants. For more information, please review the DTCC website at http://dtcc.com.

The OCC has a singular focus, as you might suspect – options! The OCC exists and performs many of the same functions of the DTCC, but with a more limited focus on U.S. listed options, futures, and options on futures. Given that the OCC handles both securities (options) and non-securities transactions, it operates under the jurisdiction of both the SEC and CFTC. For some background on the OCC, here is their mission statement:

> "We promote stability and market integrity through effective and efficient clearance, settlement and risk management services while providing thought leadership and education to market participants and the public about the prudent use of products we clear."

The OCC stands between market participants to help settle options trades on a regular basis. The OCC's role in settling options trades helps provide comfort to market participants that they will always be able to buy or sell options contracts without fear of delivery and settlement failures by other market participants. Like the DTCC, it is also owned and operated by its membership, which consist mainly of broker-dealers needing the services of the OCC.

For more information, please review the OCC website at https://www.theocc.com.

End of Chapter Quiz

Complete these end of chapter questions to assess your understanding of the subject matter discussed in this chapter. The answers follow on the next page. For those questions you have answered incorrectly, review the appropriate section of the chapter again to make sure you understand the concepts.

1. Transactions in municipal securities are the primary responsibility of which of the following regulators?
     a. NYSE
     b. FINRA
     c. FDIC
     d. MSRB

2. Which of the following is NOT one of the SEC's primary missions?
     a. Facilitate capital formation
     b. Preserve favorable market conditions
     c. Maintain fair, orderly, and efficient markets
     d. Protect investors

3. Which of the following market participants have a fiduciary responsibility to their customers?
     a. Municipal Advisors
     b. Broker Dealers
     c. Traders
     d. Market Makers

4. In the event of insolvency, which of the following would be fully covered by the FDIC in an individual account?
     a. Securities valued at $100,000
     b. CD worth $300,000
     c. Cash worth $200,000
     d. U.S. Treasuries worth $75,000

5. Which of the following is considered a Self-Regulatory Organization?
     a. SEC
     b. FDIC
     c. CBOE
     d. OCC

6. There are a total of how many SEC Commissioners?
    a. 5
    b. 7
    c. 12
    d. 14

7. The political party that controls the White House (U.S. President) gets to select how many SEC Commissioners?
    a. 1
    b. 3
    c. 5
    d. 7

8. FINRA Rules govern transactions in which of the following?
    a. Equities only
    b. Equities and corporate bonds
    c. Equities, municipal bonds, and corporate bonds
    d. Equities, municipal bonds, options, and corporate bonds

9. Which of the following penalties CANNOT be levied by the SEC?
    a. Monetary fines
    b. Jail/incarceration
    c. Bar from the securities industry
    d. Termination of licenses

10. Which of the following would be considered a retail investor under FINRA rules?
    a. Insurance Company with $30 million in assets
    b. Bank with $25 million in assets
    c. Individual investor with $40 million in assets
    d. Individual investor with $60 million in assets

End of Chapter Quiz Answers

1. D
The NYSE is both an exchange and a self-regulatory organization. The NYSE primarily lists and trades equity securities, not municipal securities. FINRA is a self-regulatory organization that does many things including rulemaking. FINRA however does not have authority to make rules for municipal securities or advisory transactions. FDIC is a bank regulator, and although may deal with municipal securities, but municipal securities are not considered their primary focus. The MSRB only deals with all aspects of municipal securities, nothing else.

2. B
Facilitating capital formation is one of the three SEC primary missions. The SEC is not charged with preserving favorable market conditions. Maintaining fair, orderly, and efficient markets are the three SEC primary missions. Protecting investors is one of the three SEC primary missions.

3. A
Municipal Advisors have a fiduciary duty to their customers, meaning they must always put the customer's interests ahead of their own. Broker dealers have a suitability obligation to their customers, not a fiduciary duty. Traders or market makers do not have a fiduciary duty. Market makers handle orders for customers, but typically do not help the customer to make investment decisions.

4. C
Securities are not covered by the FDIC, but coverage would exist with SIPC. A CD would only be covered up to $250,000, as that is the per account limit. Full coverage would exist in this case, as the cash is below the $250,000 account limit for full coverage. U.S. Treasuries are not covered by the FDIC, as they are backed by the full faith and credit of the U.S. government.

5. C
The SEC has 5 commissioners that are appointed by the President and confirmed by the Senate. It is not an SRO. The FDIC is a government organization, not an SRO. CBOE is an SRO and an exchange. The OCC is a government organization, not an SRO.

6. A

There are 5 total SEC Commissioners, including 1 chair. There are 7 members of the Federal Reserve Board of Governors who have 14 years overlapping terms. The Federal Reserve has 12 banks.

7. B

The U.S. President gets to select 3 SEC Commissioners, including the 1 SEC chair. There are a total of 5 SEC Commissioners, and 7 members of the Federal Reserve Board of Governors.

8. B

Of those items listed, FINRA Rules govern transactions in equities and corporate bonds, and options. Municipal securities are governed by the MSRB, even though FINRA may enforce the MSRB Rules.

9. B

The SEC cannot levy penalties that include jail or incarceration. These are criminal penalties, and the SEC can only levy civil penalties. The FBI however, can seek criminal charges if warranted.

10. C

An individual investor with less than $50 million in assets would be considered a retail investor. Although an insurance company and a bank are both entities and not individuals, they are small entities. Small entities below $50 million in assets would be considered retail (non-institutional) investors.

Chapter 2: Market Structure and Economic Factors

The structure of the securities market has evolved over time and will continue to evolve in the future. Changes in market structure result from things like technological innovation, changes to laws, rules, and regulations, market events, new market participants, and changing customer and market participants wants and needs.

Types of Markets

When you hear someone talking about the "market", what do they exactly mean? It really depends. The securities markets are for things like equities, most types of debt, and options. The SIE Exam is made specifically to test your knowledge of these markets. The market was up today? That probably means the equity market, as measured by an increase in the Dow Jones Industrial Average or the Standard and Poor (S&P) 500.

The commodities markets are for specific materials. Commodities include currencies, but also products like oil, corn, wheat, gold, and silver to name a few. The trading of commodities and regulation of commodities are not covered on the SIE Exam.

Now that you have a bit of background on a few market types, let's dive into the types of securities markets. There are four distinct types of securities markets:
- Primary Market
- Secondary Market
- Third Market
- Fourth Market

Each market involves securities transactions, but between different market participants. In the primary market, an issuer sells their securities to a retail or institutional investor or broker-dealer. In order to sell these securities to an investor or broker-dealer in the equity market, the issuer will typically list the securities on an exchange. The secondary market for securities involves selling the securities on an exchange where the security itself is listed (otherwise known as the listing exchange). In the third market, shares of stock are sold off of the listing exchange. A third market trade could occur on another exchange, or simply directly between two broker dealers. In the fourth market, no exchange or broker-dealer is involved at all – only (typically) two institutional firms (i.e., insurance companies) that decide to trade with one another.

Electronic -vs- Physical Markets

The electronic markets can refer to any type of securities or commodities – equities, bonds, options, currency, oil, gold, etc... It only means that some aspect of trading – orders, routing, or execution are handled in an electronic or automated fashion. Electronic markets are more of a recent phenomenon, taking root on a larger scale each year since the mid to late 1970's. Prior to that, markets were almost always described as physical, manual, or phone markets, meaning you needed to be standing next to someone or be able to reach them on the phone to place an order or execute a trade.

Figure 4: Market Types

Primary Market	transactions occurring between the issuer and investor or broker-dealer takes the form of IPOs, private placements, or other issuance of securities from issuers
Secondary Market	securities transactions executed on the securities listing exchange the issuer is not involved in the transaction
Third Market	securities transactions executed off the listing exchange, either between two broker-dealers or on another exchange
Fourth Market	securities transactions directly between two institutions occurs without the involvement of a broker-dealer or exchange

SIE PROFESSOR
Affordable Training for Securities Industry Careers

Think of the electronic markets like using your credit or debit card to buy something in person or online. The transaction occurs nearly instantaneously, transferring the payment from your credit card account to the merchant from who you are purchasing the goods or services. If electronic markets are akin to using credit cards, then physical markets would be similar to using cash to purchase goods or services. You can still use cash in many places – at a retail store or restaurant, for example. Cash, however, is not accepted for online transactions – you need a credit or debit card for this type of transaction! Physical markets work the same way – the same underlying currency is used to purchase goods or services in the real world, and securities in the SIE Exam world. Electronic market transactions settle much faster. If you hold securities in physical form, you can still sell them; it just takes a lot longer.

Consider this example for additional clarity – Twitter, Inc. is a publicly traded equity security. It trades under the stock symbol TWTR. TWTR is also listed on the Nasdaq exchange. To be listed, a company has to meet several listing requirements as set out by Nasdaq. The IPO of TWTR is a transaction occurring in the primary market, as the issuer is selling shares to a third party. Shares of TWTR being resold on Nasdaq by one of those third parties are considered a secondary market transaction. Shares of TWTR being sold on the NYSE or directly between two broker-dealers is considered a third market transaction. If an institutional investor decided to sell their TWTR shares directly to another institutional investor (without the use of a broker-dealer), that would be a fourth market transaction.

The Federal Reserve's Board's Impact

The overall background and general makeup of the Federal Reserve Board was discussed in Chapter 1. Before reading this section, make sure you have covered that chapter already, as it is important to understand the framework before diving into the specific role that the Federal Reserve Board plays in the economy. The Federal Reserve Board is also referred to as the 'FRB'.

The Fed has been charged with implementing something called monetary policy. But what is monetary policy? Monetary policy is defined as the managed increase or decrease in the supply of money in the economy.

Monetary policy focuses on the money supply and is designed to expand and contract the amount of money available in the economy. There are two important measures of the money supply, referred to as M1 and M2. M1 is the term used to define money as a medium of exchange and includes all moneys held in cash or in checking accounts. M2 is the term used to define money as a store of value, and includes moneys held in forms such as savings accounts, time deposits (e.g., Certificates of Deposits), and money market deposits. By keeping track of the overall levels of M1 and M2 in the economy, the Fed can determine if they should raise or lower the money supply.

Now that you have a basic understanding of what monetary policy is, let's move to what monetary policy does. What are some of goals of monetary policy – what is the point? The Fed implements monetary policy by focusing on six key goals of monetary policy. The first of these two Fed goals are the most important and are what the Fed refers to as its dual mandate - stabilizing prices and maximizing employment. Let's go through each of the six key goals of monetary policy in detail.

The first is price stability. The stability of prices gives consumers and businesses confidence to purchase goods and services when it makes good business sense to do so, without the fear of drastic changes in prices over the next few days. Price instability breeds uncertainty and fear, both enemies of a growing economy. Stabilizing prices means that although prices do typically increase over time, the rate of price change is targeted to be small.

The second is full employment. Full employment is NOT defined as 100% of adults working in a job. Economists consider full employment to be when 96% of those seeking employment have a job. Said another way, the unemployment rate is around 4% when the economy has reached full employment. The reason that full employment is not at 100% is because there are always people who are coming in and out of the workforce. It also often takes employers and employees time to both find and fill jobs that meet their needs. This also keeps the unemployment rate greater than zero. Maximizing employment means creating the conditions under which as many people are employed as want to be employed. The more people are employed in an economy, the more upward pressure there is on wages. This is called wage inflation. Although wage inflation is great for workers, it may not be good for businesses. As wages increase, businesses often must raise the prices of their goods and services. When customers have to pay more for goods or services, they purchase fewer of those goods and services. So although full employment is a goal of the Fed, the Fed will also monitor for the impact that full employment has in overheating the economy.

The third is economic growth. The growth of an economy is typically measured by that economy's Gross Domestic Product, or GDP. GDP measures the total value of all goods and services produced within a country over a distinct time period. If GDP grows, that implies that the economy is growing as well. If GDP is shrinking, that implies that the economy is contracting, or getting smaller. The Fed wants to see GDP increasing over time.

The fourth is interest rate stability. Although interest rates do move up and down over time, one goal of monetary policy is to keep interest rates relatively stable in the short and medium term. Stability of interest rates helps consumers and businesses have a reasonable estimate of where interest rates will be in the near future. If interest rates were unstable, then consumer and business behavior would reflect this uncertainty. Since a borrower would not know where interest rates would be tomorrow, their decision to borrow from a bank is also less predictable.

The fifth is the stability of the financial system. Although laws, rules, and regulations change on a regular basis, the U.S. financial system itself stays relatively stable over time. What makes a financial system stable? The rule of law does, or the ability for market participants to clearly understand what is legal and illegal, and the consequences of conducting illegal activities. Regulators help keep the financial system stable by identifying and rooting out bad actors (those who don't follow the law).

The sixth and final is the stability of the foreign exchange markets. The U.S. dollar is not only the currency used in the world, but it is considered the world's reserve currency and accepted as payment for goods and services in many parts of the world. Foreign exchange refers to the conversion of currency. If you hold U.S. dollars and want to exchange them for Japanese Yen, you could do so through the foreign exchange market. How many Yen you will receive in exchange for your U.S. dollars depends on the relative strength on that particular day of each of the currencies.

You now should have a basic understand of what the Fed's general purpose is and the mission it embarks on each day. How does it go about accomplishing the mission to maintain full employment and keep interest rates stable? How do you implement monetary policy and thereby change the money supply?

Figure 5: Six Goals of Monetary Policy

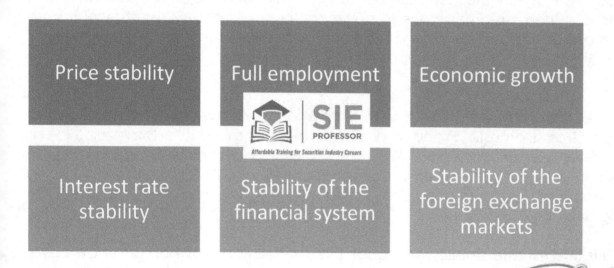

The Fed accomplishes this with four key tools of monetary policy:
1. Conduct open market operations
2. Adjust the discount rate
3. Adjust bank reserve requirements
4. Moral suasion

Changes to any of these items will either increase or decrease the supply of money.

Key #1: Conduct Open Market Operations – The Fed will buy or sell securities in the open market in order to change the money supply. Buying securities in the secondary market inserts money into the money supply or economy. Selling securities in the secondary market takes money out of the money supply or economy. The Fed conducts their activities through a group called the Federal Open Markets Committee ("FOMC"). The FOMC controls the money supply by conducting Open Market Activities, including the purchase and sale of government bonds. Purchase of government bonds like treasury bills increases the money supply because the Fed exchanges their dollars for the bonds, adding money to the economy, The sale of government bonds has the opposite impact - the Fed exchanges their bonds for dollars by selling bonds in the secondary market, effectively, pulling money out of the economy. This concept might seem confusing at first. Focus on the direction money is flowing from one party to another.

Figure 6: Fed Purchases Bonds

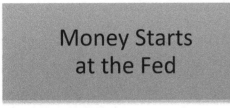

When the Fed conducts Open Market Activities, how do these activities impact the money supply and inflation? If economy is slowing, the Fed will want to increase the money supply by purchasing government bonds. With the money obtained from the sale of government bonds to the Fed, Banks loan out money to consumers and businesses. Consumers and businesses use the money for all sorts of things – purchase houses or cars, start new businesses, buy physical plants and equipment, or numerous other things.

On the flip side, if the economy is overheated or in the view of the Fed, the economy needs to be slowed down, the Fed will want to decrease the money supply by selling government bonds. With the money surrendered from the purchase of government bonds from the Fed, banks shrink their deposits and reduce the amount of money that they loan out to consumers and businesses, making loans more expensive.

Key # 2: Adjust the Discount Rate – The discount rate is the rate at which the Fed charges member institutions for use of Fed funds. When a member bank or depository institution borrows money from the Fed, it is said to have accessed the 'Fed window' or 'discount window'.

Key # 3: Determine Reserve Requirements – The Fed sets the amount of funds that banks and bank holding companies must hold in reserve either at the Fed or in their vault.   Banks prefer a lower reserve requirement because the banks can lend more funds and therefore make more money. The Fed likes a higher reserve requirement, as it makes the bank more stable and able to withstand unexpected events.

Figure 7: Fed Sells Bonds

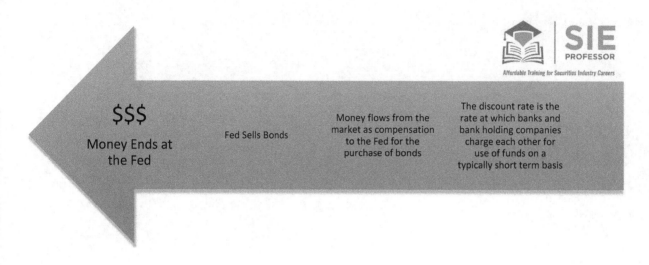

Key # 4: Moral Suasion - The Fed can influence market participants, and therefore the securities markets as a whole, by using moral suasion. Moral suasion is the ability of the Fed, through their words and statements, to push certain aspects of the market in one direction or another.   The Fed regularly holds meetings where they discuss policy decisions, analyze market data, and then try to predict or forecast what will happen next. These forecasts, executed through their written statements, are not binding but have great influence in the financial markets. Another type of moral suasion occurs when the Fed simply requests market participants to act a certain way or take certain actions. Market participants know this type of request is not required to be followed, but can often be followed up by formal rules, so it is often in the market participants best interest to follow the Fed's lead!

Impact of Monetary Policy on the Economy
What difference can effective monetary policy make within the economy? There are three main ways monetary policy can impact the economy:
- **Business investment** - purchases of new physical plants, equipment, technology, and inventory
- **Consumer Spending** – purchases of typical consumer goods such as automobiles, houses, travel and entertainment, dining at restaurants
- **Net Exports** – Imports into the country minus exports leaving the country

Do not confuse monetary policy with fiscal policy though. Fiscal policy is the responsibility of the U.S. Congress and refers to where and how taxpayer money should be spent. The decision on whether to and when to spend money on new road construction, defense spending, bank examiners, TSA airport screeners, etc... all comes under the category of fiscal policy. The Fed decides on monetary policy (expansion or contraction of the money supply). The U.S. Congress decides on fiscal policy (where and how to spend taxpayer money).

Different Types of Rates

Interest Rates
There are many ways to look at interest rates. Simply though, interest rates measure the cost of money. If you deposit money into a savings account, the bank pays you 'interest' at a pre-determined interest rate. The interest rate they pay you is the cost of you giving up your money (i.e., putting it in the bank and not using it). From the other side, the interest rate the bank pays you is the price they pay for using someone else's money. You can extend this line of thought to credit cards, mortgage loans, car loans, etc... Interest rates measure the cost of money. The higher the interest rate, the higher the cost of using someone else's money. The lower the interest rate, the cheaper the cost of using someone else's money.

Discount Rate
Remember from earlier - the discount rate is the rate at which the Fed charges member institutions for use of funds. The higher this rate, the more expensive it is to borrow funds. The lower the rate, the cheaper it is to borrow funds.

Federal Funds Rate
What is the Federal Funds rate? Often referred to more succinctly as the Fed Funds rate, it is the interest rate that depository institutions like banks or credit unions lend dollars to other depository institutions, typically on a short term basis. Changes in the Federal Funds rate provide insight to short term changes in monetary policy. The Federal Reserve cannot control the Fed Funds rate, but it does have influence over it by using its monetary policy tools.

Other Important Aspects About the Fed
There are a few other important things that the Fed does that you should be aware of for the SIE Exam. One, the Fed acts as the lender of last resort – When no one else will lend in the market, the Fed will. This usually comes into play during significant market downturns, like what was experienced globally between 2007-2009, where the U.S.

firms went to the 'Fed window' and borrowed significant amounts of money so they could stay liquid, solvent, and in business.

Now that we have a basic understanding of the Fed, various types of rates, the money supply, and monetary and fiscal policy – what does this mean for the economy? What are the basic effects on the bond and equity markets of monetary and fiscal policy?

There are a few key points here, but let's start with interest rates. Any action that lowers interest rates, whether the Fed intended to or not, lowers the price of money. If interest rates are lower, all market participants – banks, consumers, insurance companies, and other businesses can borrow money at lower rates. When companies who issue securities in the marketplace can borrow money at lower rates, they typically will do so and will look at taking on more business projects than they would otherwise. Think of it this way – if you were offered two car loans – one at 2.5% interest and one at 6% interest, all else equal, when would you more likely buy a car? When interest rates are at 2.5% or when interest rates are at 6%? The answer is obviously 2.5% - you are more likely to borrow when rates are lower, all things being equal. Think about what this simple decision has on the economy – more cars are likely to be sold when interest rates are lower – this increases the sales of the car manufacturing companies. But it doesn't just increase the sales of the car manufacturing companies; higher car sales fueled by lower interest rates also cause more tires to be sold that go on the car, more parts to make up the engine, etc… Lower interest rates are therefore considered expansionary or bullish for securities markets. The opposite, of course, is true for higher interest rates. With the cost of money higher, borrowing money becomes more expensive. Borrowers are more selective when they borrow money under a higher interest rate environment and therefore borrow less. Higher interest rates therefore cause the economy to slow down, or even contract, in some cases.

What about the money supply though? Think about the money in terms of supply and demand. Whenever there is a lot of supply of something, say pencils, the high level of supply typically drives the price of that good down. The opposite is true for a lower supply of pencils. A shortage of pencils? The price will typically then go up for pencils. The same concept holds true for money and the money supply. When the money supply is low, there is by definition less money available in the market. This tends to drive the price of money up. And what do we use to represent the price of money? Interest rates! A higher money supply means that money is more available to everyone in the market. Things that are in greater supply relative to their typical supply levels are less expensive. More supply means a lower cost of money and means interest rates are lower.

Figure 8: Expansionary and Contractionary Economic Factors

Expansionary Factors	Contractionary Factors
Lower interest rates	Higher interest rates
Increase in money supply	Decrease in money supply
Decrease in Fed Funds Rate	Increase in Fed Funds Rate
Decrease in Discount Rate	Increase in Discount Rate

SIE PROFESSOR
Affordable Training for Securities Industry Careers

Business Economic Factors

Financial Statements have a very important purpose for companies. Financial Statements allow both investors and company management to evaluate the overall financial health of the company. There are two distinct types of Financial Statements for the SIE Exam – the Balance Sheet and the Income Statement.

Balance Sheet

The Balance Sheet has three main classifications - assets, liabilities, and owners'/stockholders' equity. The Balance Sheet is intended to show the balance of specific items within each classification of assets, liabilities, or owners/stockholders equity. As a mathematical equation, the Balance Sheet is represented as Assets = Liabilities + Owners Equity.

- Assets include items such as cash, marketable securities, inventory, accounts receivable, physical plant and equipment, etc...
- Liabilities includes items such as accounts payable, accrued expenses, long term debt, notes payable, etc...
- Owners' or Stockholders equity includes items such as preferred stock and common stock, retained earnings (less treasury stock), etc...

The Balance Sheet, through items represented in the asset, liability, or owners' equity categories shows a picture of a company's financial condition at a specific point in time - end of month, end of quarter, end of fiscal year, etc... The Balance Sheet does not show the change in specific categories or the accounts that make up those categories over time. To determine the change in the level of assets for instance, you would need to review separate Balance Sheets from two different dates. For instance, comparing the Balance Sheet as of December 31, 2015 with the Balance Sheet as of December 31, 2016 would show you the changes in asset, liability, and owners' equity levels over the year 2016.

Furthermore, the Balance Sheet shows how the company's assets have been financed - either through borrowing (liabilities) or investments (owners'/stockholders' equity).

Figure 9: Balance Sheet Equation

Income Statement

The Income Statement is different than the Balance Sheet. The Income Statement is designed to show the income of a company. Unlike the Balance Sheet, the Income Statement covers a period of time, not a specific point in time. For instance, the Income Statement might be for the second quarter of 2018, or April 1, 2018 – June 30, 2018. The income shown on the Income Statement is typically broken out at three different stages - gross profit, operating profit, and net income. Depending on the company, income might be represented in different forms, such as:

- Revenue - expenses = net income
- margin
- earnings
- profit

In addition, below are some common terms you will find on an Income Statement:
- Revenue - includes sales, payments for services rendered, licensing fees, etc...
- Expenses - includes cost of goods sold, interest, taxes, depreciation, amortization, etc...
- EBIT - Earning Before Interest and Taxes
- EBITDA - Earning Before Interest, Taxes, Depreciation, and Amortization

Business Cycle

There are four stages within a business cycle:

1. Contraction
2. Trough

3. Expansion
4. Peak

No stage of the business cycle lasts for a specific period of time. The length of a business cycle though is typically measured from peak to trough. Changes in the cycle are determined based on what Gross Domestic Product ("GDP") does - grows, shrinks, or stays the same.

Figure 10: The Business Cycle

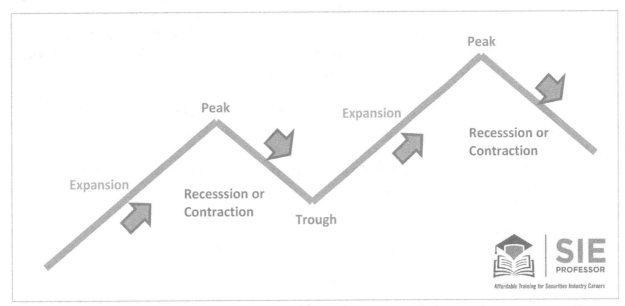

GDP measures the total value of all goods and services produced within a country over a distinct time period (more on GDP shortly). Here is a rough idea of the four business cycle stages:

1. **Contraction** - occurs after the peak; GDP level shrinks over 2 consecutive quarters means a recession; after contraction comes trough
2. **Trough** - occurs after the contraction; GDP stays relatively stable (decreasing or increasing minimally); depression; after trough comes expansion
3. **Expansion** - occurs after the trough; GDP begins to grow by more than a minimal amount; after expansion comes peak
4. **Peak** - occurs after the expansion, GDP stops expanding, but shows minimal change quarter over quarter

Take a look at Figure 10 for a visual description of the business cycle, but do not let the diagram fool you! The business cycle does not always move in a neatly graphed cycle. A business cycle can have multiple expansion and contractions before getting to peaks and troughs.

Indicators

Indicators are useful tools that predict future social, financial, economic, or political trends. There are four main categories of indicators on the SIE Exam - leading, lagging, inflation, and coincident. For the SIE Exam, you should know which indicators represent which category.

A leading indicator is an indicator that changes prior to the economic cycle moving towards a new phase. Simply put, a leading indicator signals future events. A good representation of leading indicators is published by an organization called The Conference Board[17]. The Conference Board publishes a composite index called the Leading Economic Index, which itself is comprised of ten individual leading indicators. These ten leading indicators are as follows:

1. Average weekly hours, manufacturing
2. Average weekly initial claims for unemployment insurance (jobless claims)
3. Manufacturers' new orders, consumer goods and materials
4. ISM® Index of new orders
5. Manufacturers' new orders, non-defense capital goods, excluding aircraft orders
6. Building permits, new private housing units
7. Stock prices (500 common stocks)
8. Leading Credit Index ™
9. Interest rate spread, 10-year Treasury bonds less Fed Funds
10. Average consumer expectations for business and economic conditions

Other examples of leading indicator are inventory levels, retail sales, and number of new business startups.

Another type of indicator is a lagging indicator. A lagging indicator is an indicator that changes direction after the economic cycle has moved into a new phase. The Conference Board maintains a lagging index as well. The components of the lagging index include:

1. Average duration of unemployment
2. Inventories to sales ratio in manufacturing and trade
3. Labor cost per unit of output for manufacturing
4. Average prime rate
5. Commercial and industrial loans
6. Consumer installment credit to personal income ratio
7. Consumer price index for services

The next type of indicator that you should be familiar with are inflation indicators.

Inflation is defined as the increase in the price of a good or service. Most commonly, inflation is measured through two indicators – **CPI and PPI**. **CPI** is the *Consumer Price Index*. **PPI** is the *Producer Price Index*. The CPI measures the increase in the prices that consumers pay for goods – everything from bananas to milk, bread, and cars (and lots of other goods in between). The CPI does exclude more volatile goods like energy prices (i.e., gasoline and oil) to help ensure a more consistent and fair representation of typical prices of everyday goods.

The last type of indicator is a *coincident indicator*. A coincident indicator is an indicator that appears to indicate a move to another phase of the economic cycle, but in reality only moves in tandem with the economic cycle. The Conference Board maintains a <u>Coincident Index</u> that includes the following components:
1. employees on nonagricultural payrolls
2. personal income less transfer payments
3. industrial production
4. manufacturing and trade sales

International Economic Factors

Gross Domestic Product ("GDP") and **Gross National Product** ("GNP") are two important economic measures. Both GDP and GNP measure a specific country's market/final sale value of all goods and services, or economic activity, but from slightly different perspectives. GDP measures the total value of all goods and services produced within a country over a distinct time period. GDP includes all domestic activity produced within the U.S., even if the producer is a foreign citizen or foreign corporation. GDP or GNP can be measured using either an income method or expenditure method. The income method simply measures all income earned within a country, where expenditure method measures all expenditures within the country. In theory, both methods yield the same result. GDP and GNP are measurements of the fluctuation in economic activity over a period of time. GNP's measure of economic activity includes all activity by American Nationals or American National-owned businesses all over the world.

GNP = GDP + income from foreign sources – income paid to foreign sources

When trying to remember the difference between GDP and GNP, focus on the two middle letters of the acronym – the 'D' and the 'N'. The word "Domestic" indicates something is *not foreign*. A domestic company is a company that is based in the U.S. or only has operations in the U.S. The word "National" implies something is of a particular nation. GDP's primary driver is geographic location. GNP's primary driver is ownership.

The usual time period for both GNP and GDP measurement is quarterly (i.e., Q1, Q2, etc...). GDP or GNP is compared to measurements over the prior period, or growth rate/contraction from the quarter one year ago. This past comparison helps us to understand what has changed in the economy, then diving deeper to figure out why the GDP or GNP is changing.

Figure 11: Comparison of GDP and GNP

There is certainly more detail to be learned here about GDP and GNP, but probably not for purposes of the SIE Exam.

A few quick thoughts about the U.S. balance of payments, which is a topic on the SIE Exam outline. The U.S. government over the last several decades has run a budget deficit, meaning on an annual basis, the U.S. government spends more money than it brings in each year. On an ongoing basis, the U.S. government has a national debt. The national debt is added to each year as past and current budget deficits continue to accrue and therefore add to the national debt. A big contributor to the national US Balance of Payments is the fact that the U.S. consumers and businesses purchases more goods and services from other countries than other countries consumers and businesses purchase from the U.S. Each of these scenarios cause the U.S balance of payments to be weighted toward deficits and debts, both from the U.S. country's budget perspective, but more specifically from a consumer and business perspective when compared to other countries.

Principal Economic Theories
There are two primary economic theories that you should be familiar with while studying for the SIE Exam – **Keynesian and Monetarist**. When you hear Monetarist Economic Theory, think of one of the most famous monetarist economists of all time - Milton Friedman. Keynesian Economic Theory was championed by John Maynard Keynes.

Figure 12: U.S. Balance of Payments

Monetarists believe that the *key to impacting the level of output in the economy (economic spending) is to alter the money supply*. Changes to the money supply impact spending and GDP/GNP. When people have more money than what they need for the basics (food, clothing, shelter), those people tend to spend money on other things as well (new cars, vacations, phones, etc...). This desired behavior helps to stimulate the economy in a positive direction, expanding the economy's output. When people have less money than what they need for the basics, those people tend to restrict their spending to the basics and not much else. This behavior acts to restrict or cool off the economy. Both expansion and contraction of the money supply are important at various points in the business cycle. Sometimes, the money supply may be expanded to grow the economic output or GDP/GNP. Other times, the economy might be growing too quickly or overheating. In this case, it might make sense to contract the money supply.

Unlike a monetarist economist, *a Keynesian economist disregards changes in the money supply*. Instead, a Keynesian economist focuses on changes in interest rates and their impact on economic spending. Further, Keynesian economists believe that changes in taxation or government spending are the primary fiscal policy levers the government officials can pull to obtain the desired future economic state. As the government spends money, it injects money into the economy. As the government levies taxes, it withdrawals money from the economy. An increase in government spending leads to an increase in GDP/GNP. Lowering of tax rates has similar impact on GDP/GNP. Why is this the case? Increasing government spending or lowering taxes causes what's called a *multiplier effect*. By increasing income for consumers, consumers spend money, which causes more and different consumers to spend money. All of this activity fits under the umbrella as expansionary fiscal policy. A decrease in government spending or an increase in tax rates has the opposite impact and ultimately decreases in the GDP/GNP. This is known as contractionary fiscal policy.

Exchange Rates

An exchange rate is the rate which you can trade one item for another. In most cases, the exchange rate involves currency. In the U.S., dollars are the currency used to purchase goods and services, but also to pay employees' wages. If you were to travel from the U.S. to France, you may want to purchase goods or services in the currency used by the French – the Euro. But how do you change from dollars to euros? This is where the exchange rate comes in. Let's say that $1 is worth .90 euros. This exchange rate is otherwise known as the spot rate. It is no more complicated than that.

So if you had $10,000, how many euros would you receive in exchange?

The answer: 10,000 dollars x .90 euros / 1 dollar = 9,000 euros

The same works of course in reverse. If you had 5,565 euros, how many dollars would you have?

The answer: 5,565 euros x 1 dollars / .90 euros = 6,183.33 dollars.

This answer makes sense, as the exchange rate indicates that you should have more dollars than euros when converting one currency into another.

To determine how many dollars you would receive in exchange for Euros (or vice versa) today, check out Yahoo! Finance's exchange rate calculator and plug either the dollars or Euros into the calculator.

It is important to note that currencies are not securities. Currencies can appreciate and depreciate just like securities do however. Currencies can overlap with securities in many areas, like a euro denominated corporate bond. If a U.S. investor wanted to purchase such a bond, the investor would first need to convert their U.S. dollars into Euros, and then purchase the euro-denominated bond with their converted Euros.

End of Chapter Quiz

Complete these end of chapter questions to assess your understanding of the subject matter discussed in this chapter. The answers follow on the next page. For those questions you have answered incorrectly, review the appropriate section of the chapter again to make sure you understand the concepts.

1. Which of the following is considered the Federal Reserve's dual mandate?
   a. Maximum employment and low inflation
   b. Stable prices and maximum employment
   c. Economic growth and stable prices
   d. Interest rate stability and maximum employment

2. A trade in a listed equity security occurring over the counter would be considered to be in the:
   a. Primary market
   b. Secondary market
   c. Third market
   d. Fourth market

3. M1 defines money as a:
   a. Store of value
   b. Price of good and services
   c. Medium of exchange
   d. Value of employment

4. Monetary policy is the responsibility of _____, where fiscal policy is the responsibility of _____.
   a. Federal Reserve, U.S. Congress
   b. U.S Congress, Federal Reserve
   c. Federal Reserve, U.S. President
   d. U.S. President, Federal Reserve

5. Which of the following is considered an expansionary economic factor?
   a. Lower interest rates
   b. Decrease in the money supply
   c. Increase in Federal Funds rate
   d. Increase in the discount rate

6. The purchase or sale of securities in the market by the Federal Reserve best describes which of the following?
   a. Primary market activity
   b. Profit taking
   c. Open market operations
   d. Store of value

7. Which of the following is NOT one of the key tools of monetary policy?
   a. Measuring the amounts of M1 and M2
   b. Adjusting the discount rate
   c. Moral suasion
   d. Conducting open market operations

8. The rate at which the Fed charges member institutions for the use of funds is:
   a. Interest rate
   b. Discount rate
   c. Federal Funds rate
   d. 10 Year Treasury Bond Rate

9. Which of the following is considered contractionary economic factor?
   a. Increase in Federal Funds rate
   b. Increase in the money supply
   c. Decrease in the discount rate
   d. Lower interest rates

10. Which of the following is NOT one of the six goals of monetary policy?
    a. Interest rate stability
    b. Economic growth
    c. Full employment
    d. Budget surplus/deficit

End of Chapter Quiz Answers

1. B
Although the Fed does have other goals, stable prices and maximum employment are known as the Fed's dual mandate.

2. C
Listed means that security already trades on an exchange, so primary market is incorrect. A secondary market trade occurs when a listed security is traded on the same exchange where the security is listed. Listed securities traded over the counter occur in the third market. A fourth market trade would not occur on an exchange, and instead would occur between two entities off-exchange.

3. C
M1 is a medium of exchange and includes things like physical currency and checking accounts. A store of value better describes M2, not M1. The prices of goods and services help influence inflation, but do not define M1. M1 is the most liquid form of money. The value of employment is not within the definition of M1 or M2.

4. A
The Federal Reserve has responsibility for monetary policy, while the U.S. Congress has responsibility for fiscal policy. The U.S. President nominates people to the Federal Reserve.

5. A
Lower interest rates help encourage investment, which aids economic expansion. Decrease in the money supply contracts money available for investment, making investments more expense through higher interest rates. Increasing the Federal Funds rate makes borrowing between institutions more expensive. Increasing the discount rate makes borrowing from the Federal Reserve more expensive.

6. C

When the Fed purchases or sells securities in the securities market, they are conducting open market operations. Primary market activity refers to the initial sale of a security from the issuer to an underwriter or investor. A store of value is one of the key aspects of M2.

7. A

Although measuring M1 and M2 are important, they by themselves are not one of the key tools of monetary policy. The remaining items, with the addition of adjusting bank reserve requirements, are all key tools of monetary policy.

8. B

The Fed charges member banks funds at the discount rate. Other banks charge each other the Federal Funds rate when borrowing funds overnight. Interest rate is a generic type of rate which would need more specifics to be applicable.

9. A

Increasing the Fed Funds rate makes borrowing more expensive, and therefore attempts to slow down the economy. The remaining items are all expansionary economic factors, as they encourage investment by adding money into the economy or lowering interest rates, which is an incentive for individuals and businesses to expand.

10. D

The six goals of monetary policy are price stability, full employment, economic growth, interest rate stability, stability of the financial system, and stability of the foreign exchange markets.

Chapter 3: Offerings

Participants
There are several different participants involved in securities offerings. One of the primary participants is a group of individuals called investment bankers. Investment bankers help to sell an issuer's securities to public or private investors. Often, investment bankers maintain specialized knowledge within specific sectors of the economy. The restaurant sector is a good example of sectorization and includes publicly traded companies such as Red Robin, Panera Bread, Dominos, P.F. Changs, McDonalds, Wendy's, and Chipotle. Even within the restaurant sector, there are sub-sectors like 'fast casual' (McDonalds, Wendy's, Chipotle, Domino's) and 'full service' (P.F. Changs, Red Robin). Although not all investment bankers operate with a sector based approach, a sector based knowledge often helps the investment banker fulfill their client's (the issuer of the securities) needs.

What does an investment banker actually do though? At the most basic level, an investment banker in the equity markets helps the issuer determine how many shares to sell to investors and at what price to sell those securities. An investment banker makes money by the difference in price the investment banking firm pays for the securities and the price at which those securities are resold to the public. This compensation is called the underwriting fee, or spread, and is disclosed to investors in a prospectus, offering document, official statement, or other such similar document.

Underwriting Syndicate
There are four distinctive roles within an underwriting syndicate – **Lead Manager or Bookrunner, Co-Manager, Syndicate Member, and the Selling Group**. Collectively, the first three entities are known as the *Underwriting Syndicate*. Generally speaking, these types of syndicate members must be broker-dealers.

Not all offerings have all four roles within the securities offering. Some securities offerings only have a Lead Manager; others have Lead Manager, Co-Managers, and Syndicate Members but no Selling Group. All securities offerings have a Lead Manager, however. A Lead Manager, Co-Manager and other Syndicate Members are all considered underwriters of the securities offering. The higher up an entity is in the syndicate, the greater economics that the entity will receive. In other words, the Lead Manager will typically make more money on the transaction than the Co-Manager, and the Co-Manager will typically make more money on the transaction than a general syndicate member. With more potential reward comes additional risk, however. If the offering does not go well and there is less interest than expected, the Lead Manager will take most of the financial hit, with less of a financial hit being for the Co-Manager, etc... The Lead Manager does most of the direct interaction with the issuer. Typically, the Lead Manager is also the book runner, responsible for building the order book (list of orders) and the allocation of institutional stock in the offering, basically, who gets to buy shares in the offering. Allocation of shares for retail accounts would typically be the responsibility of the individual member of the syndicate or selling group who receive shares to allocate those shares in the offering.

Figure 13: Underwriting Syndicate Roles

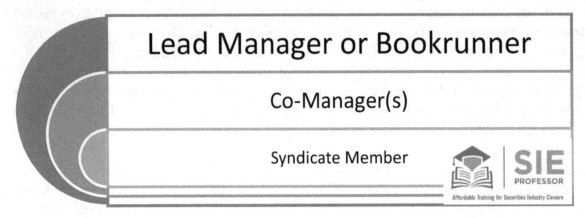

The fourth role in a securities offering is a Selling Group member. A Selling Group member is an investment bank that helps sell a securities offering but is not a member of the underwriting syndicate. A member of the selling group does not have the responsibilities or liabilities of an underwriter.

Another type of market participant is a municipal advisor. As the name implies, municipal advisors provide advice to municipal market entities, such as cities, towns, school districts, states, water and sewer authorities, etc... Municipal Advisors were covered in Chapter 1. A few important facts to remember about Municipal Advisors:
- Municipal Advisors *have a fiduciary duty* to their municipal entity clients. Underwriters, investment bankers, banks, and the underwriting syndicate do not.
- Municipal Advisors *do not actually buy securities in an offering* by their municipal entity client. Instead, municipal advisors assist their municipal entity client with the terms, structure, and timing of a securities offering. The municipal advisor will work with an underwriter, who will buy the issuer's securities in the offering.
- Municipal Advisors cannot be *both the Municipal Advisor and the underwriter* in the same offering of securities.

Types of Offerings
Both public offerings and private offerings are sold to members of the investing public at large. To be considered an official public offering, however, the securities must be sold to a wide investor base. The fewer investors who purchase the offering, the more likely the offering is not actually a public offering but a private offering. If the security

is registered with the SEC, this will mean that the offering is public. However, not all securities offerings are registered – municipals and Treasuries are exempt, for instance. If the offering is registered however, you can assume that the offering is a public one.

Private placements involve the sale of securities in a transaction that is exempt from SEC registration requirements. Let's review some important information about Private Placements. Private Placements are:
- only sold to investors who meet the Accredited Investor test
- limited to sophisticated investors that do not need the protection that the securities registration process provides in a public issuance of securities.
- conducted using a transactional exemption (e.g., each transaction is different)
- sold to a limited number of investors, with restrictions placed on the resale of the privately placed security

What are some benefits and costs to private placements?

Benefits
- *less costly* than registering shares with SEC
- *less time consuming* to get shares registered with SEC
- private placements *do not have to reveal private information*, like they would in the SEC registration process

Costs
- *no active public market* to trade private placement shares, which means less liquidity than public offerings
- *resale restrictions* prevent private placement owners from freely selling shares
- *potential investor pool is smaller* due to qualification standards
- public offerings have *more investors* and private placements have *fewer investors*
- public offerings have *better pricing* due to more investors and public markets

Once securities are sold in a private placement, they cannot be resold unless the shares become registered with the SEC, or they are resold again as a private placement under SEC Rule 144a to a Qualified Institutional Buyer (QIB). Private placements often have restrictions on the actual shares of stock to prevent their resale unless specific conditions are met. In this sense, a private placement might be conducted with restricted stock.

Public Offerings

When private or public companies either need capital to grow, or owners want sell parts of their ownership positions to others, the company will often use a public offering of equity securities. In exchange for an owner's share of the company, the new shareholder will pay a specified price. There are four types of public offerings:

1. IPO - Initial Public Offering
2. Secondary Offering
3. Follow On Offering
4. Stocks Rights Offering

Initial Public Offering - IPO stands for Initial Public Offering. As the name implies, the offering of securities is the initial or first offering of securities made by the issuer to the general public. In common parlance, an IPO is referred to as a 'new issue' or 'going public'. New issue or IPO shares must be registered with the SEC in order to be sold to the public in the IPO transaction.

IPO's are priced by the issuer themselves, with advice from underwriters the issuer hired to conduct the offering. The underwriters should have expertise on how to conduct an IPO, assist with valuing the company for sale to the public, and assist the company with helping potential new investors understand who the company is and what the company does.

For the issuer, there are many benefits to going public through an IPO. The first benefit to issuing an IPO is that an IPO generates new capital for the company. In exchange for an ownership stake in the issuer, the issuer sells shares for a specific dollar amount to an investor. The investor gets shares in the issuer and the issuer receives cash as compensation for selling a fractional ownership interest. The issuer can then use this cash to pay down debt, invest in new business projects, open new offices, etc...

A second benefit to issuing IPO stock is that a stock that is publicly traded can be used in acquisitions of other companies. When one company buys another company, the buyer unusually pays in two parts – cash and stock. The mix of cash and stock is up to the buyer and seller to determine. These types of deals happen all the time. A good example of this is the 2016 buyout of LinkedIn by Microsoft[18].

A third benefit to issuing IPO stock to the public is that it allows owners to cash out when selling part or all of their company. Similar to the exchange of cash for stock that benefits the company; individual owners of stock can also sell all or part of their shares in the company in what is sometimes referred to as a liquidity event.

The benefits to an IPO are substantial – both to the company and to individual owners of the company. There are however costs to conducting an IPO.

The first major cost of an IPO is IPOs are expensive. IPO's have high underwriting and administrative costs. To go public in an IPO, an issuer has to work with an underwriter, who charges a fee for their services. The underwriting fee is typically between 4-7%, depending on the size of the offering. The smaller the offering, the greater the fee as a percentage of the gross transaction. The larger the offering, the smaller the fee as a percentage of the gross transaction. As an example, let's say an issuer sells 1,000,000 shares in an IPO at $10/share. If the underwriter charges 5% for their services, the issuer only receives $9.50. Mathematically this looks like 1,000,000 shares x $10/share = $10m gross sale. Then, the underwriter must be paid, so from the gross sale of $10m the underwriting costs of $500,000 must be subtracted, for a net amount to the issuer or sellers of $9.5m.

The second major cost of an IPO is the higher level of scrutiny that the issuer will be subject to due to their new status as a publicly traded issuer. Often, a company that has issued stock in an IPO is listed on an exchange like Nasdaq or NYSE. These exchanges have specific listing requirements that must be met (e.g., board makeup, minimum share price, minimum number of board members, corporate charter, etc...). This increased scrutiny means that the company will have to answer to public investors and the media about company performance.

The third major cost of an IPO is the new pressure that the company and company management have to meet public expectations. A publicly traded company has a lot of pressure put on it to meet research analyst and shareholder expectations. Often, this presents as a focus on beating the projected or expected quarterly earning number instead of a taking a more long term (multiple year) view more available to private companies. Public companies must typically hold quarterly earnings call for investors where they answer questions and discuss the company's overall financial performance. Private companies do not need to conduct public earnings calls with the investing public at large. Private companies only need to inform their relatively small number of investors about the important financial numbers and metrics.

The fourth major cost of an IPO is the need to comply with various regulatory requirements, such as Sarbanes Oxley or SEC filing requirements.

A primary offering of securities always raises new money for the issuer through the issuance of new shares. The first primary offering (or distribution) of securities to the public is the IPO. Any further offerings of securities with newly issued shares sold to the public would be considered seasoned offerings.

Follow on Offering - A follow on offering is an additional equity issuance by a company or issuer when that company or issuer already has shares trading in the public markets. This type of offering generates new capital for the company.

Secondary Offering - A secondary offering is an offering of securities that allows existing owners to sell their part or all of their position in the company. A secondary offering does not however raise new capital for the company whose shares are being sold. This type of offering should not be confused with a secondary market transaction, which describes a trade between two investors that generates no new capital for the company or issuer of the security. Secondary offerings (or SEOs) are for a company with shares or stock already trading in the public markets. Therefore it is easier to price the offering because the market is constantly pricing the company equity stock each and every day. Secondary offerings are priced as a discount to the market closing price of the security. The same market participants are involved in this offering type as an IPO – underwriters, syndicate, etc.

Stock Rights Offering vs. Secondary Offering - Stock rights offering are a type of public stock offering that allows existing shareholders to purchase additional shares in the company, typically in proportion to their current holdings. For instance, if a shareholder currently owns 1% of the outstanding shares of Google and Google executes an offering, existing shareholders will see their ownership proportion (the percentage of the GOOG that they own) decrease because of the new shares being issued.   In a stock rights offering, the existing owners of GOOG would have the opportunity to buy additional shares at the offering price so they can maintain their current percentage of ownership. Existing shareholders would have the opportunity, but not the obligation to buy. The public would not have the opportunity to buy these shares unless an existing shareholder sold their rights to do so themselves.

Methods of Distribution

Buying securities from the issuer for a fixed price is also known as a 'fixed price offering'. Securities offerings occur at specific price for a reason. This gives the issuer and the underwriter certainty on the sale price for sure, but also prevents the underwriter for charging more for an offering that is in high market demand, potentially disadvantaging or providing an advantage to various customers. Outside of an offering typically being a fixed price offering, there are two general types – *best efforts underwriting and firm commitment underwriting.*

In a *best efforts underwriting*, the underwriters do exactly what the term implies - use their best efforts to sell the securities to the public at the agreed upon price. In a best efforts underwriting, the underwriter only purchases the amount of shares it can sell to its institutional and/or retail clients. Best efforts underwritings are typically conducted for transactions that are small in size or larger in risk.   Underwriters will typically insist on this type of offering structure due to the increase risk the underwriter takes in reselling the higher risk securities.

In a *firm commitment underwriting*, the underwriter actually purchases the securities from the issuer at a specified price, then resells them to investors.   In a firm commitment underwriting, the underwriter buys all of the securities in the offering and sells as many of those securities as it can to the underwriter's clients. These types of underwritings are conducted for more liquid offerings that have less risk and greater size. Underwriters are willing to agree to conduct a firm commitment underwriting precisely because there is reduced risk in selling those specific securities to the public.

For **both types of offerings**, the difference between the price the underwriter acquires the shares, or net price and the price the underwriter sells the shares to investors (and the offer price) is called the underwriting spread.

Shelf Registrations and Distributions

Shelf registrations allow an issuer to quickly access the market when needed to, without having to go through registration process. The shelf registration can be used over a three year period using the Automatic Shelf Registration (S-3) process. The shelf registration is only available to issuers that can file Form F-3 or Form S-3. Below are some important characteristics of shelf registrations:

- a master registration statement is filed with SEC
- a shelf is a 2 year plan filed with the SEC to issue more shares to the public
- only available for issuers with $150m or less in outstanding company stock
- allows firms to issue securities in response to changing market conditions
- avoids a lengthy and costly registration process each time an issuer wants to raise capital or sell shares
- underwriting expenses typically lower
- more common with debt than equity, although can be used with both

Offering Documents and Delivery Requirements

The Prospectus is the document given to potential investors in a new offering of securities and has all essential facts and details about the offering. The Preliminary Prospectus is an initial draft document and is used to market the transaction. The SEC reviews the Preliminary Prospectus as part of the Offering Registration Process. Also known as a 'red herring', the Preliminary Prospectus is the vehicle used by the SEC to provide feedback to the entity or individual selling shares. The SEC provides multiple rounds of feedback on the Preliminary Prospectus, with the Final Prospectus including all SEC changes. Both the Preliminary and Final Prospectuses are detailed documents that must be provided to all investors in the transaction. The Final Prospectus is sent to investors by hard copy or electronic link.

Typical Prospectus Contents

- Title page – number of share offered, underwriting participants, terms, where shares will be listed
- Company operational information
- Risk factors
- Financial information
- Insider ownership
- Business strategies
- Key markets and customers
- Management
- experience/competence
- Board of Directors makeup
- Ownership by Board of Directors, management, officers and directors prior to and after offering
- Type of offering - seasoned, secondary, IPO, mixed
- Share count before and after the offering
- Comfort letter by auditors

Official Statement ("OS")

An OS is similar to a Prospectus in many respects, but is used for municipal securities. Preliminary Official Statements ("POS") must be sent to any investor who is being solicited in the municipal securities offering. Once the POS is final, it is referred to as the Final Official Statement, or simply the OS. An OS must be sent either in hard copy or electronic form to any investor who purchases securities in the municipal offering no later than settlement date. The MSRB has stated the following about an OS[19]:

"Information in an official statement includes, but is not limited to, the terms under which bonds can be redeemed prior to maturity, the sources of money pledged to repay the bonds, and the state or local government's covenants for the benefit of investors. The following information is typically included in an official statement:

- The interest rate or, if the interest rate is variable, the manner in which such rate is determined
- The timing and manner of payment of the interest on and the principal of the bonds
- The minimum denomination in which the bonds may be sold
- Whether the bonds can be redeemed by the state or local government prior to maturity and, if so, on what terms
- Whether the investor has the right to require the state or local government to repurchase the bonds at their face value
- The sources from which the state or local government has promised to make payment on the bonds
- Whether any bond insurance, letter of credit or other guarantees have been provided for repayment
- The consequences of a default by the issuer
- A description of outstanding debt, the authority to incur debt, limitations on debt and the future debt burden of the issuer
- A description of basic legal documents such as authorizing resolution, indenture and trust agreement
- Legal matters such as pending proceedings that may affect the securities offered, legal opinions and tax considerations"

Registration and Filing with SEC

Typically speaking, an offering and the shares to be sold in the offering are required to be registered with the SEC for all public offerings of securities. Shares are registered with the SEC through the use and filing of a Registration Statement. The entities or individuals looking to sell their sell their shares to the public must have their shares registered through this Registration Statement and do so by submitting information to the SEC, including a copy of the Preliminary Prospectus. The Registration Statement itself must be filed and approved with SEC. This is an important step for two reasons:

1. *Investors can be solicited only after the Registration Statement has been filed*, and
2. *The Registration Statement must be approved by the SEC before the offering can be sold to investors.*

Once approved by the SEC, the Registration Statement is deemed effective. Only after the Registration Statement is deemed effective may the broker-dealer accept payment from the customer for the purchase of offering related securities.

Potential investors who are being solicited in the offering must receive a copy of the preliminary prospectus immediately. After the Registration Statement is approved by the SEC, the Preliminary Prospectus becomes the Final Prospectus, or simply the Prospectus. The SEC does not make statements on the quality or investment potential of an offering of securities. The SEC in fact goes out of its way to make sure parties know that the SEC's approval is <u>not</u> an approval in the sense that 'this is an excellent offering and investors should buy shares.' Once the SEC approves the Registration Statement, the offering is declared effective. **There are some securities that are exempt from the SEC registration process:**

- Municipal securities
- Securities issued by non-profit entities
- Offerings with maturities of less than 270 days
- Securities guaranteed by a bank
- U.S. Government or Agency securities
- Eurodollar bonds

Remember:
- *Bank loans are not securities* so they are not within the SEC/SRO's jurisdiction.
- Securities offerings can be public or private.
- An offering of municipal securities or government securities is not subject to SEC registration rules.
- Offerings of municipal securities can be public or private offerings; but the municipal securities themselves are not subject to registration with the SEC.
- No securities are exempt from the anti-fraud provisions of the SEC rulebook.

Other Offering Related Terms

Oversubscribed – This term is used to describe an offering that has more interest than perhaps expected, as measured in terms of number of shares. If the issuer is interested in selling 500,000 shares, and investors are interested in purchasing 1,500,000 at the expected offering price, the offering is said to be oversubscribed. In our example, this offering would be 3x oversubscribed.

Price stabilization – One underwriter, typically the lead underwriter, is permitted to engage in price stabilization. This means that the underwriter is permitted to buy securities in the open market to help keep the market prices somewhat level and not allow the market price to fall below the offering price for a period of time. What the underwriter cannot do, however, is promise to purchase offering securities back from a customer who originally bought offering securities from the issuer. This would be considered fraud and manipulation.

Green shoe option – The issuer grants this option to the underwriter prior to commencement of the offering. The green shoe allows the underwriter to purchase an additional 15% of stock from the issuer. The green shoe is exercised by the underwriter when the offering is oversubscribed as a way to fill additional demand. The underwriter likes this option because the underwriter can make an additional underwriting spread on the green shoe option. For deals that are undersubscribed, the underwriter would not typically exercise the green shoe, as this would likely mean the underwriter would be stuck with the additional shares with no interested buyers!

Due diligence – An underwriter is required to conduct due diligence on the issuer and its officers ahead of commencing with an offering of securities. Due diligence is basically research; research on recent audits performed, outstanding litigation, who owns the issuer, the makeup of the Board of Directors, the issuer's finances, and any other item that would present a material risk to the offering or may be contained the Registration Statement and Prospectus or Official Statement. The underwriter is said to possess 'underwriters liability' when conduct an offering of securities, and the due diligence obligation helps to reasonably ensure that the underwriter has met their duties to the potential investing public. The due diligence process helps to flesh out any problematic areas prior to the public or private offering.

Issuer buy-backs under SEC Rule 10b-18 – This is an SEC safe harbor that allows issuers to buy back their securities. Think of a buy back as a reverse IPO – instead of selling shares to the public in exchange for cash, the issuer exchanges their own cash for investor's securities. A buy back helps to reduce the number of outstanding shares that the issuer has sold to the public in prior offerings.

Blue Sky Laws

When you hear Blue Sky laws, think new issue registration with individual states and state securities regulators. For those equity new issues listed on an exchange, those new issued are automatically 'Blue Sky'd'. An underwriter may need to register non-listed equities and fixed income securities with specific states where they plan to be sold. The registration process helps to ensure that securities are legitimate, reducing fraud and other serious issues for investors.

End of Chapter Quiz

Complete these end of chapter questions to assess your understanding of the subject matter discussed in this chapter. The answers follow on the next page. For those questions you have answered incorrectly, review the appropriate section of the chapter again to make sure you understand the concepts.

1. Which type of securities offering allows existing shareholders to purchase additional shares in the company, typically in proportion to their current holdings?
   - a. Private placement
   - b. Initial public offering
   - c. Secondary offering
   - d. Stock rights offering

2. An underwriter and issuer have priced a new IPO at $15 a share. The IPO had an initial range of $14-16 leading up to the IPO. The underwriter has agreed to purchase the new IPO stock from the issuer at $14.75. In a hot market, what is the maximum price the underwriter can sell the IPO shares to the public?
   - a. $14.00
   - b. $14.75
   - c. $15.00
   - d. $16.00

3. Which of the following is TRUE about private placements and public securities offerings?
   - a. Private placements are less costly than registering shares with SEC in a public offering
   - b. Private placements are more time consuming to get shares registered with SEC than in a public offering
   - c. Private placements are more liquid than public offerings
   - d. Private placements have more investors than there would be in a public offering

4. An official statement is provided to buyers of what type of securities in a new issuance offering?
   - a. Municipal bonds
   - b. Corporate bonds
   - c. Equity securities
   - d. Private placements

5. Which of the following roles in a new securities offering is not considered an underwriter?
   - a. Lead manager
   - b. Selling group
   - c. Co-manager
   - d. Syndicate member

6. Which of the following is TRUE regarding municipal advisors
   a. Municipal Advisors cannot be both the Municipal Advisor and the underwriter in the same offering of securities under any circumstance
   b. Municipal Advisors can be both the Municipal Advisor and the underwriter in the same offering of securities as long as they disclose both roles to the issuer.
   c. Municipal Advisors can be both the Municipal Advisor and the underwriter in the same offering of securities as long as the issuer provides their express, written consent.
   d. Municipal Advisors cannot be both the Municipal Advisor and the underwriter in the same offering of securities that occur in the same calendar year.

7. Which of the following has a fiduciary duty to the municipality who is planning to issue new bonds?
   a. Municipal underwriter
   b. Transfer agent for the municipal bonds
   c. Municipal advisor
   d. Underwriter's counsel

8. Which of the following is TRUE about private placements and public securities offerings?
   a. Private placements are more costly than registering shares with SEC in a public offering
   b. Public offerings have worse pricing due to more investors and public markets than private placements
   c. Private placements are less liquid than public offerings
   d. Private placements have equal number of investors than there would be in a public offering

9. Underwriter ABC is contractually obligated to purchase all of the agreed upon shares from the issuer. This type of arrangement is known as what type of underwriting?
   a. Best efforts
   b. Firm commitment
   c. Fixed price
   d. Stock rights

10. Which type of offering allows existing owners to sell all or part of their ownership position in the company?
    a. Follow on offering
    b. Stock rights offering
    c. Secondary offering
    d. Warrant offering

End of Chapter Quiz Answers

1. D

A Private Placement is an offering of securities to a limited number of purchasers, typically large institutions. An IPO, or Initial Public Offering is an issuer's first sale of securities to the investing public. IPO investors can be existing or new owners. A secondary offering of securities offers additional shares of an issuer to the public. Both new and existing owners can purchase shares in a secondary offering. A stock rights offering is an offering of securities available to existing owners. An owner has the right to purchase shares of the issuer in proportion to their existing ownership, allowing that owner to keep a proportional ownership interest.

2. C

The underwriter could sell at $14, but this is not the maximum they could get for the stock in the market. The underwriter could sell at $14.75 but this is not the maximum they could get for the stock in the market. The difference in price between $15 and $14.75 is the underwriter spread. The underwriter will sell the stock at $15, the level where the IPO priced. The underwriter must sell the stock at a price no greater than $15. The underwriter could not sell the stock above where the IPO priced at $15.

3. A

Private Placements typically cost less than do similar size public offerings. This is primarily because there is no registration with the SEC. Private Placements are actually less liquid than public offerings, as there are fewer security holders. Private Placements have fewer overall investors than there would typically be in a public offering of securities.

4. A

An Official Statement, or OS, is available to investors in most municipal offerings. For corporate bonds, investors receive a Prospectus, not an Official Statement. For publicly traded equity securities, investors receive a Prospectus, not an Official Statement. Investors in Private Placements typically receive a Private Placement Memorandum, similar to a Prospectus.

5. B

The lead manager, co-manager, and syndicate member roles are all considered an underwriter. A selling group member sells securities to the public as part of a securities offering, but is not an underwriter.

6. A

A firm must choose to be either a Municipal Advisor or an underwriter in the same issuance of municipal securities. Playing both roles and disclosing that fact to the issuer is insufficient. In practice, a firm could be an underwriter for one issuance, then be a Municipal Advisor for a separate issuance in the same calendar year.

7. C

Only the Municipal Advisor has a fiduciary duty to the municipality issuing the bonds. The underwriter must provide required disclosure to the municipal issuer and deal fairly, but must also sell securities to the public. The transfer agent and underwriter's counsel do not have a fiduciary duty to the municipality under MSRB and SEC rules.

8. C

Private placements are less liquid than public offerings because private placements are not registered with the SEC are not listed on exchanges, and have fewer investors. Registering shares with the SEC makes a public offering more costly.

9. B

When an underwriter is contractually obligated to purchase all shares in an offering of securities, this is referred to as a firm commitment underwriting. Without a contract to purchase all of the shares, the underwriter typically acts in a best effort capacity. Best efforts underwriting is typically used for smaller issuers. Part of the underwriting is offering the securities to the public at a fixed price for a period of time.

10. C

In a follow on offering, a company sells part of itself to the investing public. In a stock rights offering, existing owners are given the right to purchase additional shares in proportion to their current ownership. Existing owners of the company, not the company itself, sells shares in a secondary offerings. In a warrant offering, existing owners may receive warrants, but this has nothing to do with the party selling shares in the offering.

SIE Exam Study Guide 2020

Section 2: Understanding Products and Their Risks

Chapter 4: Equity Securities

Equity securities are the securities that most people are already familiar with on some level. Equity securities are the ownership positions in many of the companies whose products and services we use on a daily basis – Apple's *iPhones*, Verizon's *cellular and data services*, Amazon's *everything*. Apple, Verizon, and Amazon are publicly listed common equity securities and although the most commonly known, represent only one aspect of the broader equity security landscape. As a definition, an equity security is a type of security that represents an ownership stake in an entity. An owner of a company holds an equity stake in that company. Equity stakes can be full stakes (100% ownership) or partial stakes (less than 100% ownership).   Ownership stakes in entities can vary amongst equity securities. Some, like Apple, Verizon and Amazon, are publicly traded common equity securities and the most well-known, but certainly not the only, type of equity security. There are six primary types of equity securities that will be covered in this section. Equity securities include:

1. Common Stock
2. Preferred Stock
3. Control and Restricted Securities
4. Penny Stocks
5. Rights and Warrants
6. American Depositary Receipts

Common Stock

The term common stock refers to the shares held or owned by investors of the issuer company of that stock. Common stocks are also referred to as common equity. Said another way, common stock refers to the general ownership interest in a firm. Shares represent the partial ownership of that issuer company. Issuer is used to describe a company in this way because the company itself, through the Board of Directors, decides to when and how to issue, or sell, that common stock to the public. Publicly traded companies are not the only types of companies that issue common stock. Private companies also issue common stock, most often to company founders and employees. Publicly traded stock may be listed on an exchange, but not necessarily. An exchange will have listing requirements, such as a minimum number of publicly traded shares, shareholders, share price, and pre-tax income as a few examples. Most companies start out as private companies (Facebook, Google, and LinkedIn are all excellent recent examples of this), then move to become publicly traded companies by listing their shares to trade on an exchange like Nasdaq or the New York Stock Exchange (NYSE).

Common stock often pays dividends to their investors that ideally represent their share of the profits. An issuer in financial trouble may borrow money to pay dividends, which is obviously less desirable. In the U.S., if an issuer pays a dividend, it will typically pay out on a quarterly basis. For foreign firms, dividends are more typically paid out on an annual or semi-annual basis.

In addition to the benefits of capital appreciation and dividends, owners of equity securities also have the right to vote on important corporate matters. These corporate matters include the election of the Board of Directors, voting on binding or non-binding corporate resolutions, and proposed mergers and acquisitions.

For voting rights of common stock, there are two possible methods of counting the votes--statutory voting and cumulative voting. Under statutory voting, each shareholder is entitled to one vote for each share of stock owned (e.g., you own 20 shares of stock and are voting for 5 board members, you can vote 20 votes for each board member). Under cumulative voting, shareholders can weight their votes toward a particular candidate (e.g., you own 20 shares of stock and are voting for 5 board members, you can cast 100 votes for one board member and none for the rest or 60 votes for one board member and 40 total for the rest). Depending on where the issuer is incorporated, there may be additional state specific laws that the issuer must follow with regard to common stock owners. Common stock owners have residual claims against the issuer's assets in the event of liquidation. These residual claims sit behind the firm's debt holders and preferred stockholders, if any.

An equity security's market capitalization, or "market cap" is used to describe the overall size of an equity issuer. The calculation to determine an issuer's market cap is simply the share price times the number of outstanding shares.

Share price x number of outstanding shares = market capitalization

Generally, equity securities are broken into three categories – Small, Mid and Large Capitalization. Although there is no universally agreed upon definition of market capitalization, we will use the below numbers to represent a rough estimate of market capitalization delineations:

1. **Small Cap** – under $4 billion
2. **Mid Cap** – $4-$10 billion
3. **Large Cap** – above $10 billion

In real life, these ranges often overlap and are interpreted differently by different mutual fund companies, investors, and regulators. In fact, many market participants use the terms 'mega cap' or 'micro-cap' to better describe securities larger than or small than large and small cap securities respectively. However, let's use the ranges above to better understand some of the basic common stock characteristics. Memorizing the market cap numbers is not important. Instead, make sure you understand that large cap stocks denote a larger and more expensive company when compared to mid-cap stocks. First, start by accessing the market quote page on www.cnbc.com and enter each stock ticker/symbol into the quote box at the top of the page. Otherwise, follow the links below and complete the information for each security.

Flower Foods (stock ticker/symbol – "FLO")
https://www.cnbc.com/quotes/?symbol=flo

_____Last sale price (top left of screen, above chart)
x _____Number of shares outstanding
= _____Market Capitalization
Is Flower Foods considered a small, mid, or large cap security based upon our defined ranges above (circle one)?

PepsiCo (stock ticker/symbol – "PEP")
https://www.cnbc.com/quotes/?symbol=pep

_____Last sale price (top left of screen, above chart)
x _____Number of shares outstanding
= _____Market Capitalization
Is PepsiCo considered a small, mid, or large cap security based upon our defined ranges above (circle one)?

Based on our definition, Flower Foods is likely to be considered a mid-cap stock, whereas PepsiCo is considered a large cap stock. New companies often start out as small cap stocks, then grow over time into the mid and large cap categories. The components of market cap should also be explained a bit. The last sale price is simply the last price at which the stock traded. During normal U.S. market hours between 9:30 a.m. – 4 p.m. ET, the last sale price changes constantly. Outside of those hours (generally speaking), the last sale price is the last price that the stock traded at during normal market hours.

The number of shares outstanding is the number of shares held by all investors except the issuer. However, the number of shares outstanding that an issuer has may be different than the number of authorized shares. Authorized shares are the number of shares that the issuer's Board of Directors has approved, or authorized, to be sold to third parties. The number of authorized shares will always be equal to or greater than the number of shares outstanding. This is true because the issuer may hold back, or buy back some of the shares outstanding from investors. These shares are not retired in some cases, just held by the issuer. On the balance sheet, this may show up as treasury stock (which is stock that has been issued but subsequently reacquired by the issuer) under owner's equity.

The par value of a stock is usually $1.00. An issuer is prohibited, usually under the laws of the state of the issuer's incorporation, from issuing shares below the par value of the stock. This limitation comes from state law (typically in the state of Delaware) where the issuer is formally incorporated if the issuer is structured as a corporation. The par value does not have any impact on the actual market price of the equity security however. Rules that prohibit the issuer from selling new shares below $1.00 help to protect existing shareholders from being diluted. When an investor is diluted, this means that the investor sees their ownership position weakened by having to divide up corporate ownership (and therefore potential profits) amongst a larger group of owners. When incorporating, however, an issuer gets to determine the par value as part of the incorporation process. From an issuers' perspective, the issuer wants the par value as low as possible, so if necessary, it can issue additional equity shares. If the issuer set the par value at $10, this would in some cases negatively impact the issuer's ability to issue new shares under dire circumstances, forcing the issuer to go to the debt market or sell off productive assets instead.

Preferred Stock

This type of stock still represents an ownership position in the company, but logistically works a bit different than common stock. When reviewing common stocks, we noted that common stocks may pay dividends to investors. Preferred stock is more likely to pay a dividend than common stock, as that is one of the key reasons an investor purchases preferred stock. In addition, some versions of preferred stock may be convertible into common stock based on a prescribed formula. Preferred stockholders also have a contractual payment of dividends that must be paid ahead of common stock dividends. In most ways, preferred stockholders more closely resemble bond/debt holders, however, preferred stockholders cannot force an issuer into bankruptcy if it does not make scheduled payments; bond/debt holders can.

There are five different types of preferred stock that you should be familiar with for the SIE Exam – **Senior Preferred, Preference Preferred, Cumulative Preferred, Participating Preferred, and Convertible Preferred**. Although some of them are self-explanatory, let's go through some detail on each type of preferred stock, with the goal being to understand the differences between them. Note however that although these are the high level categories of preferred securities, in reality a preferred issuance can cross into multiple types – Cumulative Convertible Preferred, Participating Senior Preferred, etc...

Senior Preferred is the 'highest ranking' preferred security. When an issuer has multiple issuances of preferred stocks, it is important know which is more senior compared to another preferred issuance. This is important when an issuer only has enough money to pay dividends to one of its preferred issuances. The Senior Preferred issuance always gets paid first.

Preference Preferred is the next type of preferred. A Preference Preferred gets paid ahead of all preferred issuances, with the exception of the Senior Preferred.

A **Cumulative Preferred** issuance 'keeps score' every time a preferred dividend payment is expected. If the cumulative preferred dividend is paid, the 'score' stays even. However, if a cumulative preferred dividend is missed, the deficit accumulates with each subsequent missed cumulative dividend payment. Future cumulative preferred payments must be made for the current period PLUS all of the cumulative preferred dividends payments that were 'missed'.

Participating Preferred securities are another type of preferred securities. Participating Preferred securities have an 'upside' feature built into them. Instead of just paying out the typical preferred dividend payment, Participating Preferred securities can also pay out more to the holder! Each Participating Preferred will have some key metrics or threshold that the issuer must exceed in order for the 'participating' part of this preferred security to be activated. For instance, the threshold might be that any time the company earns more than $5 per share in profit and has gross revenues in excess of $100 million, the Participating Preferred shareholder will receive an extra $.10 per share.

Convertible Preferred securities are also not difficult to understand. Basically, some security types, like bonds or preferred stocks, sometimes have a convertibility feature attached to them. This convertibility feature allows the owner of Convertible Preferred to convert a predetermined number of preferred shares into common equity stock. This conversion can be exercised at any time, but the number of shares is typically fixed. For instance, for every 100 share of convertible preferred you own, you can convert those 100 shares into 50 shares of common equity stock. Each Convertible Preferred will have a different ratio of Convertible Preferred to common equity stock. Convertible bonds work exactly the same way, except of course you have the option to convert the bonds into a predetermined number of common equity stock.

Common and Preferred Stock on the Balance Sheet

If you have taken an accounting class, this will be very familiar. If not, let's go through the basics of a balance sheet to help understand one of the key differences between common and preferred stock. A typical summary put together by any type of business is a balance sheet. Please see the sample balance sheet for reference and review.

The basic calculation is this: Assets = Liabilities + Owners Equity/Capital

You will note that both common stock and preferred stock show up in the Owner's Equity section of the balance sheet. That is because the shares are (hopefully) worth something, as simply turning the equation around gives you: Assets - Liabilities = Owner Equity. If the company were to go into bankruptcy, the assets would be sold off first to pay against any outstanding liabilities (bondholders and debt holders). In this way, those investors who hold the company's bonds (Company ABC Bonds), have first right to the cash that the assets generate, or to the assets themselves under the typical U.S. bankruptcy scenario.

Figure 14: Sample Balance Sheet

ABC Company, Inc. Balance Sheet December 31, 2018	Total ($ in millions)
Assets	
Current assets:	
Cash	10.16
Investments	6.40
Inventories	4.80
Accounts receivable	5.20
Pre-paid expenses	1.08
Total current assets	$ 27.64
Fixed assets:	
Property and equipment	5.00
Leasehold improvements	0.50
Equity and other investments	1.50
Less accumulated depreciation	
Net fixed assets	$ 7.00
Total assets	$ 34.64
Liabilities and owner's equity/capital	
Current liabilities:	
Accounts payable	3.30
Accrued wages	1.70
Accrued compensation	1.89
Income taxes payable	5.20
Unearned revenue	2.20
Other	-
Total current liabilities	$ 14.29
Long-term liabilities	
Mortgage payable	11.70
Total long-term liabilities	11.70
Owner's equity/capital	
Preferred stock	1.50
Common equity 4.50	
Accumulated retained earnings	2.65
Total owner's equity	$ 8.65
Total liabilities and stockholders' equity	$ 34.64

If there is anything left over, the owners of the company get to divide it amongst themselves based upon their proportional ownership. The preferred stock owner has higher bankruptcy rights than the common stock owner does, and therefore receives any leftover bankruptcy proceeds first, but after bondholders. If there is anything leftover in the bankruptcy after both the bondholders and preferred stock owners have been paid out, the common stock owners receive whatever is left, which is not usually much, if anything. If you hear someone describe the common stock or equity owners of a company being 'wiped out', this is what it refers to. Being wiped out though only means that your equity stake in the company worthless.

The most you can lose, as an equity owner, is your equity ownership position. If the company owes money even after all of the assets have been sold, creditors cannot come after the equity or preferred stockholders personally. For instance, creditors could not garnish your wages, seize bank accounts that you hold in your name, or anything else. The concept that equity and preferred stockholders can only stand to lose their investment and nothing more is referred to as limited liability.

Back to the bankruptcy concept; generally speaking, here is the order of payout in the event of a bankruptcy:
1. **Bond/debt holders** (or other liabilities) paid first. Within this category, senior debt holders will have priority over other debt holders, like subordinated or convertible debt. More on this in the next chapter.
2. **Preferred stockholders** – paid out after all bond/debt holders
3. **Common stockholders** – if there is anything left, common stockholders get the rest.

Figure 15: Characteristics of Common and Preferred Stock

Common	Common and Preferred	Preferred
Voting rights	May receive a dividend	No voting rights
More potential risk and reward	Sit behind bond/debt holders in bankruptcy claims	Must be paid a dividend before common stock
Last in bankruptcy claims	Limited indvidual liability	First right of bankruptcy after bond/debtholders
		Could be convertible into common stock

Control and Restricted Securities

Control and restricted securities are actually different forms of common or preferred stock. Investors come to own these securities due to private placements, holding executive positions within the company, or for being an early stage investor. The common or preferred stock has what is called a 'legend' on the restricted security. The legend is placed upon the stock for a certain period of time, where the owner of the restricted stock is not permitted to sell or trade those shares. In industry terms, these types of stock therefore are called "legended" or restricted securities. Control securities are often used as compensation to key employees of a public or private company in lieu of or in addition to cash compensation. Control and restricted securities have specific rules attached to them, notably SEC Rules 144 and 144a.

To resell restricted or control securities once you have acquired them, you must either register the shares with the SEC or find a valid exemption from the registration requirements. Rule 144a stock can typically only be sold to QIBs!

Selling restricted or control shares under SEC Rule 144[20] is possible if the seller complies with five key obligations:
1. **Holding Period** – sellers must have held the stock for 6 months if the issuer is a reporting company, or 12 months if the issuer is not a reporting company.
2. **Current Public Information** – There must be adequate information about the company available to the investor. The level of information required differs depending on whether the issuer is a reporting company or a non-reporting company.
3. **Trading Volume Formula** – This has some nuance to it, but basically remember the 1% cap. You cannot sell more than 1% of the outstanding shares during a quarter or 1 % of the average weekly volume for the 4 weeks prior to the sale. This requirement only applies to affiliate sales. An affiliate is an entity related to or under common control with, the issuer. An issuer will often have a parent company corporate owner, which owns many other companies in addition to the issuer. These other companies would be considered affiliates.
4. **Ordinary Brokerage Transaction** – This requirement only applies to affiliate sales. The broker or dealer handling the sale must only charge normal compensation charges.
5. **Filing Notice with the SEC** – within 10 days, the seller must file a notice of sale with the SEC if the sale totals more than 5,000 shares or $50,000 in the prior quarter. This only applies to affiliate sales.

These requirements do NOT apply if the securities are purchased in the secondary market (on an exchange or over the counter).

Penny Stocks[21]

Penny stocks are a specific type of common stock equity securities. Like other common stock equity securities, they are considered to be publicly traded. If you recall from earlier, equities can be publicly traded in one of two ways – listed on an exchange and traded on the exchange or over the counter, or unlisted and traded over the counter. An equity security that is listed on an exchange must meet listing requirements to list on the exchange and remain listed on the exchange. Penny stocks are a subset of equity securities and are considered highly speculative. Penny stocks are not listed on an exchange and therefore only trade over the counter. Typically, penny stocks have some degree of financial difficulty or uncertainty attached to them. The penny stock may just be coming out of bankruptcy, or perhaps headed towards bankruptcy. In other cases, the penny stock could be a start-up without customers, revenues, or other items necessary to maintain a business for very long into the future. Since penny stocks are speculative, they are appropriate for very few investors and typically trade at less than $5 per share[22]. Many penny stocks will go out of business, and the investors who own shares in these companies will lose all of their money. Given the level of speculation that penny stocks have, penny stocks attract a large amount of fraud and market manipulation – things that are harder to accomplish with a listed equity security.

Rights and Warrants

FINRA has published a couple of simple definitions that explain rights and warrants, which should be sufficient for the SIE Exam. You need to be able to recognize the definition of each of these, plus be able to distinguish rights and warrants from other types of equity securities. Under FINRA Rule 11840, rights and warrants are defined as follows:

Rights - The term "rights" or "rights to subscribe," as used in this Rule is the privilege offered to holders of record of issued securities to subscribe (usually on a pro rata basis) for additional securities of the same class, of a different class, or of a different issuer as the case may be. Transactions in rights to subscribe shall be on the basis of one right accruing to each share of issued stock and the unit of trading in rights shall be 100 rights (unless otherwise specified).

Warrants - The term "warrants" or "stock purchase warrants" as used in this Rule is an instrument issued separately or accompanying other securities, but not necessarily issued to stockholders of record as of a specific date; i.e., warrants issued with or attached to bonds, common stock, preferred stocks, etc. The instrument represents the privilege to purchase securities at a stipulated price or prices and is usually valid for several years. Transactions in stock purchase warrants shall be on the basis of one warrant representing the right of the purchaser to receive one warrant in settlement of such transaction and the unit of trading shall be 100 warrants.

Owners/holders of warrants allow the potential opportunity to make an immediate profit, if market prices are favorable. A warrant is exercised against the issuer, not into the secondary market. The warrant will also have specific terms and conditions that dictate at what price the issuer will sell common equity shares to warrant holder. So, how does a warrant holder make a profit? Let's say the current market price of Coca-Cola (symbol "KO") is $50 per share. The warrant allows the holder to purchase a set number of shares, say 100 from the issuer (in this case Coca Cola) at a price of $40. All the warrant holder has to do is exercise their warrant against the issuer and buy the shares at $40. Since the now former warrant owner is now the direct owner of 100 shares of Coca Cola common stock, they can turn around and sell all 100 shares in the secondary market at a price of $50. The difference between the buy and sell prices is $10 per share, times 100 shares equals a gross profit of $1,000!

Warrants have a defined life span, usually between 5 and 10 years. Once the warrants are expired, they are worthless. Although the valuation of warrants is beyond the scope of the SIE Exam, you should know that warrants with more time between today and when they expire will typically have more value, all other things being equal. Also, the more volatile the equity security is that the warrant is written on, the more valuable the warrant.

American Depositary Receipts

American Depositary Receipts[23] or ADR's were created to easily allow U.S. - based investors to invest indirectly in foreign listed securities in U.S. dollars. Not having to trade and settle in foreign currency is a big plus for U.S. investors. In the U.S., foreign listed securities are referred to as Ordinary Shares or ORD's.

An example of a non-U.S. listed foreign security is Adidas. In order to access the U.S. capital markets, Adidas decided to create a U.S. ADR under the symbol ADDYY. Symbol ADDYY is listed on the NYSE, just like Apple (AAPL). In a typical ADR situation, the ADR shareholders own an indirect interest in the ORD shares, held in trust at a U.S. bank. ADR's and ORDs are not considered fungible securities, meaning they are not technically equivalent to one another. ADRs are exchanged for ORDs and vice versa through a settlement and conversion process. There is typically a conversion formula set up and managed by the U.S. bank and the foreign issuer. In some cases, one ADR is worth one ORD. In other cases, the ADR can be exchanged for a multiple or fraction of the ORD. Each ADR is different[24]. In summary, remember that ADRs are equity securities at their core, although ADRs do represent indirect ownership interest in a foreign security.

End of Chapter Exercise

Pull up CNBC's website at www.cnbc.com. Once on the main CNBC page, search for the name of a well-known public equity company, like Coca Cola (KO), Facebook (FACE), Twitter (TWTR), General Electric (GE), or one you come up with on your own. The search bar appears at the top of the page.

Find the company and look at:
- Company information
- Bid and ask
- Dividend amount, if any

- Dividend yield, if any
- Number of shares outstanding
- Last sale/trade price
- Compute market capitalization

End of Chapter Quiz

Complete these end of chapter questions to assess your understanding of the subject matter discussed in this chapter. The answers follow on the next page. For those questions you have answered incorrectly, review the appropriate section of the chapter again to make sure you understand the concepts.

1. Holders of which one of the following security types typically have the right to vote on issuer matters?
    a. Equity
    b. Preferred
    c. Debt
    d. Warrants

2. An equity security with a market capitalization of $10 billion is likely to be considered a:
    a. large cap stock
    b. mid cap stock
    c. small cap stock
    d. micro cap stock

3. Which of the following is TRUE about American Depositary Receipts ("ADRs")?
    a. ADRs cannot be listed on U.S. exchanges
    b. One share of an ADR is typically equivalent to 1 share of the underlying foreign security
    c. ADRs allow U.S. investors to buy and sell indirect ownership interest in a foreign company
    d. ADRs trade in the same currency as the foreign listed company does

4. Which of the following is a common characteristic between common and preferred stock?
    a. Voting rights
    b. Convertible into equity stock
    c. Limited liability
    d. Paid dividends before bondholders

5. Which of the following accurately describes the balance sheet equation?
    a. Liability + Assets = Owner's Equity
    b. Assets – Liabilities = Owner's Equity
    c. Owner's Equity – Liabilities = Assets
    d. Assets + Owner's Equity = Liabilities

6. Of the following, which is the highest ranking type of preferred stock?
    a. participating
    b. preference
    c. convertible
    d. cumulative

7. Which of the following types of preferreds has an upside feature built in, allowing preferred holders to receive a higher dividend if the issuer beats certain metrics?
    a. participating
    b. preference
    c. convertible
    d. cumulative

8. An equity security with a market capitalization of $50 billion is likely to be considered a:
    a. large cap stock
    b. mid cap stock
    c. small cap stock
    d. micro cap stock

9. A warrant gives the holder a right to purchase equity shares
    a. in the secondary market
    b. in the IPO
    c. at a set price from the issuer
    d. whenever new shares are issued

10. Which of the following is a common characteristic between common and preferred stock?
    a. Voting rights
    b. Convertible into equity stock
    c. Sit behind bondholders in bankruptcy
    d. Paid dividends before bondholders

End of Chapter Quiz Answers

1. A
Typically only equity holders have the right to vote on issuer matters. Preferred holders sit between equity owners and bondholders in the bankruptcy chain. They do not typically get to vote on issuer matters outside of bankruptcy proceedings. Debt holders do not get to vote on issuer matters. The warrant owner can trade or exercise their warrant, but they do not get a vote on issuer matters just because they hold the warrant.

2. B
Although there is no official definition market capitalizations would break down as follows: a large cap stock is usually above $10 billion in market capitalization, a mid-cap stock is usually between $4 and $10 billion in market capitalization, a small cap stock is usually below $4 billion in market capitalization, and a micro-cap stock is usually below $1 billion in market capitalization.

3. C
ADR's can be and often are listed on U.S. exchanges. The conversion rate between the ADR and the underlying foreign security varies from ADR to ADR. Owning an ADR provides investors with an easy way to purchase foreign securities, owned indirectly through the ADR. An ADR may trade in the same, or different currency than the underlying foreign security. In most cases, the ADR and foreign security trade in different currencies.

4. C
Voting rights typically only are allowed with common stock ownership. Equity stock cannot be converted into the same equity stock, but preferred stock could be converted into equity stock. Both preferred and equity stock have limited liability, meaning both sets of stockholders can only lose their investment, nothing else. Bondholders get paid before preferred stockholders, and preferred stockholders get paid before equity stockholders.

5. B
The correct balance sheet equation is Assets - Liabilities = Owner's Equity. The Owner's Equity therefore is what is left over after liabilities are paid off in the event of bankruptcy.

6. B
Preference preferred is the highest ranking type of preferred stock listed. Preference preferred provides the owner of this type of stock the right to get their dividends paid out first ahead of other preferred stock owners. Convertible preferred allows the owner to convert part or all of their preferred shares into another security, typically equity. Cumulative preferred allows owners to catch up on past missed preferred dividend payments. Participating preferred gives owners the ability to share in the upside profitability of the issuer within specified limits.

7. A
Participating preferred gives owners the ability to share in the upside profitability of the issuer within specified limits. Preference preferred provides the owner of this type of stock the right to get their dividends paid out first ahead of other preferred stock owners. Convertible preferred allows the owner to convert part or all of their preferred shares into another security, typically equity. Cumulative preferred allows owners to catch up on past missed preferred dividend payments.

8. A
Although there is no formal definition, a stock with a $50 billion market cap (outstanding shares x share price) would be considered a large cap stock. Large cap stocks would generally be above $10 billion market cap, while mid cap stocks would be between $4-10 billion market cap. Small cap stocks would be below $4 billion and microcap stocks below $1 billion.

9. C
A warrant gives the holder the right to purchase equity shares at a price set by the issuer. A warrant is executed against the issuer, not in the secondary market. Rights offer owners the ability to purchase additional shares in the secondary market, proportional to their existing ownership percentage. Warrants are often given to underwriters as part of their compensation for their role in the securities offering, but this does not typically give them the right to purchase shares in the IPO.

10. C
Common and preferred stocks both sit behind bondholders in bankruptcy. Preferred stock does not have voting rights, but common/equity stock does. Preferred stock can be convertible into common/equity stock.

Chapter 5: Debt Securities

Debt securities play an important role in the U.S. capital markets. Like equity security owners, debt security owners have a claim on the future revenues of the entity issuing the debt. The size of the debt markets exceeds the size of the equity markets by a huge factor. Unlike an equity security however, a debt security holder does not have an ownership claim in the entity.

What exactly is a debt? For an individual, a debt might be a car loan, home mortgage, or the unpaid balance on your credit card. None of these examples, however, are considered securities. A debt security is issued by an entity, just like an equity security. An entity can be a for-profit entity, like a company, or a not-for-profit public entity like a city, town, or state. The entity is loaned money from investors in exchange for a promise to repay that money at a future date. The loaning of money and the promise of repayment occurs alongside a very specific agreement that lays out the specifics of the debt securities transaction. These obligations of the issuer and rights of the purchasers hold true even if the debt security is resold by the original purchaser. On top of that, there are several different types of debt securities that you will need to understand for the SIE Exam.

Before discussing the unique aspects of specific types of debt securities, it is important to understand some general information applicable to all or many types of debt securities. This general information is broken up into three distinct groups:
1.   Common Characteristics of Debt Securities
2.   Bond Ratings and Ratings Agencies
3.   Common Terms and Conditions of Debt Securities

After understanding these three general areas of knowledge about debt securities, we will then move on to reviewing and understanding specific types of debt securities.

Common Characteristics of Debt Securities

Debt securities have several characteristics that are common to all forms of debt, but some characteristics that are unique to specific types of debt. At the core, the initial transaction is the same; in exchange for money today from the investor/purchaser of the bond, the company issuing the bond-the issuer- promises to either:
- Pay the stated coupon on a defined schedule (monthly, semiannually, annually, etc.) to the investor, and/or
- Sell the bonds at a discount (i.e., less than what they would be redeemed for at maturity).

Bonds that are initially sold at a discount without offering a coupon payment are known as zero coupon securities. The most recognizable example of a zero coupon security are U.S. Treasury Bills.

Holders of debt securities have at least one big advantage over equity holders issued by the same issuer as well – debt securities holders get paid first in the event of a bankruptcy. Debt securities holders are at the front of the line in a bankruptcy – they go ahead of both equity and preferred stock owners. Review Figure 16, which shows the bankruptcy hierarchy. Further, a secured debt holder will typically be paid ahead of an unsecured debt holder. When borrowing money from a lender, a company will often be required to pledge assets in exchange for the debt as collateral. This puts the lender in a secured position, and higher on the bankruptcy order than an unsecured lender would be. An administrative claim holder would also sit below a secured debt in the order of bankruptcy.

In fixed income securities, there is an inverse relationship between the bond's price and its' yield, or coupon rate. As a bond's price goes up, the yield goes down. As a bond's yield rises, the price goes down. This makes sense if you think about it some. Here is an example to illustrate the point.

Let's say you bought a brand new bond with a maturity in 10 years that pays a 5% coupon. After you hold the bond for one year, a new bond with similar characteristics comes to the market, now paying a 6% coupon. Both bonds mature in nine years and are rated similarly. Which bond would you want to own? As an investor, you would want to own the 6% coupon bond because it pays a higher coupon. The issuer of the 5% coupon bond cannot change the coupon amount after issuance without going into default. So, who would buy a 5% coupon bond in a market with 6% coupon bonds?

The answer?

No one, unless the owner of the 5% coupon bond were willing to sell the bond at a discount to where the 5% coupon bond was purchased.

This means that if the owner of the 5% coupon bond sold the bond in the market, they would in all likelihood take a loss on their principal investment.

Falling interest rates benefit issuers, who can issue debt securities at progressively lower and lower interest rates. Falling interest rates also can benefit bond holders (assuming their bonds are not called by the issuer – more on that later in this chapter), as the bonds that they own are more valuable, i.e., could be resold in the market for more than par value. Rising interest rates negatively impact debt issuers, as it become more expensive for these issuers to borrow money. Rising interest rates also negatively impact bond owners, as the bonds that they own become less valuable in the market. Rising interest rates do impact new bond purchasers in a positive way, as they receive higher coupon payments or a discounted bond, allowing them to realize a higher yield than they would otherwise in a lower yield environment.

Figure 16: Hierarchy in a Bankruptcy: Who Gets Paid First?

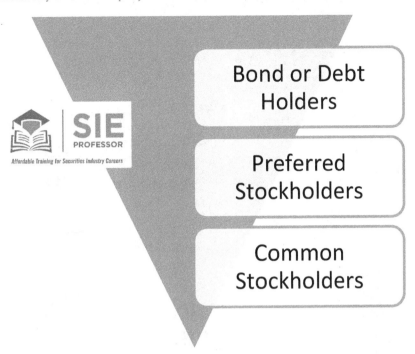

Review Figure 17, which shows the inverse relationship between price and bond yield.

How do bonds actually get to the market? Equity securities are issued by a company and are often (but not always) listed and traded on an exchange. In the debt securities world, there is no exchange listing or exchange trading. All debt securities trade in the over-the-counter market. Like new equity securities offerings, debt securities offerings often use an underwriter to get new issue securities into the marketplace, and therefore into the hands of institutional and retail investors. There are three primary ways new debt securities make their way to the market: negotiated, competitive, and auction.

Negotiated offer: A negotiated offer is just as it sounds – the issuer or financial advisor to the issuer negotiates with an underwriter on the price that the underwriter will pay to acquire the newly issued stock or bonds. A negotiated offer process makes sense for smaller offerings if there is expected to be few bidders in a competitive offer process, based on prior experience and market convention.

Competitive offer: In a competitive offer, an issuer, or a financial advisor representing the issuer, announces to the market that a new offering of securities will be made on a specific date. Underwriters then go through a process to evaluate the new offering of securities based on that debt security's characteristics. Each underwriter submits a bid, or a specific dollar amount to purchase all of the debt securities. Whoever has the highest bid for the debt securities gets the securities. When there are a sufficient number of bidders, this process helps the issuer to get the highest possible price available in the market.

Figure 17: Inverse Relationship of Bond Price and Bond Yield

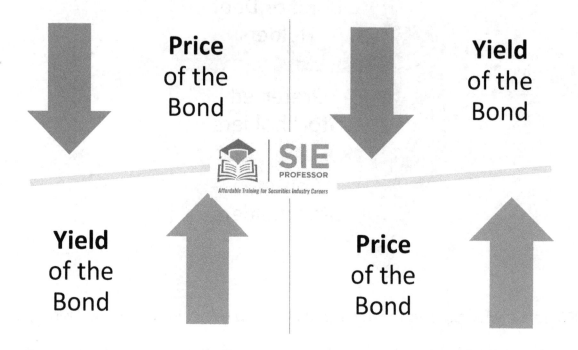

Auction: The most common type of auction is for treasury securities. Treasury auctions are run by the U.S. government and have some unique aspects. They include elements of competitive bidding within the auction, but the auction is not only competitive bidding. According to www.TreasuryDirect.gov[25] website:

"Marketable securities can be bought, sold, or transferred after they are originally issued. The U.S. Treasury uses an auction process to sell these securities and determine their rate or yield. Annual auction activity:

- Offers several types of securities with varying maturities
- Conducted 263 public auctions in 2016.
- Issued approximately $8.1 trillion in securities in 2016.

To finance the public debt, the U.S. Treasury sells bills, notes, bonds, Floating Rate Notes (FRNs), and Treasury Inflation-Protected Securities (TIPS) to institutional and individual investors through public auctions. Treasury auctions occur regularly and have a set schedule. There are three steps to an auction: announcement of the auction, bidding, and issuance of the purchased securities.

The auction announcement details:
- Amount of the security being offered
- Auction date

- Issue date
- Maturity date
- Terms and conditions of the offering

- Noncompetitive and competitive bidding close times
- Other pertinent information

When participating in an auction, there are two bidding options - competitive and noncompetitive:
- Competitive bidding is limited to 35% of the offering amount for each bidder, and a bidder specifies the rate, yield, or discount margin that is acceptable.
- Noncompetitive bidding is limited to purchases of $5 million per auction. With a noncompetitive bid, a bidder agrees to accept the rate, yield, or discount margin determined at auction.
- Bidding limits apply cumulatively to all methods that are used for bidding in a single auction.

At the close of an auction, Treasury awards all noncompetitive bids that comply with the auction rules and then accepts competitive bids in ascending order of their rate, yield, or discount margin (lowest to highest) until the quantity of awarded bids reaches the offering amount. All bidders will receive the same rate, yield, or discount margin at the highest accepted bid.

All auctions are open to the public.
- On issue day, Treasury delivers securities to bidders who were awarded securities in a particular auction. In exchange, Treasury charges the accounts of those bidders for payment of the securities.
- Treasury bills are issued at a discount or at par (face amount) and are paid at par at maturity. The purchase price is listed on the auction results press release and is expressed as a price per hundred dollars.
- FRNs have quarterly interest payments and are issued with a par, discount, or premium price and a stated spread. In some cases, the purchaser may have to pay accrued interest.
- Treasury notes, bonds, and TIPS are issued with a stated interest rate applied to the par amount and have semiannual interest payments. For TIPS, the interest payments and the final payment at maturity are based on the inflation-adjusted principal value of the security. In some cases, the purchaser may have to pay accrued interest."

Bond Ratings and Ratings Agencies

Debt securities are also often rated by third parties, called rating agencies. These rating agencies are specifically authorized by the SEC to conduct their activities within the debt securities markets. There are 3 primary rating agencies that operate within the securities markets – S&P™, Moody's™ and Fitch™. The rating agencies assign ratings, based on the issuer's relative risk. A higher rating means lower overall risk. A lower rating means generally higher risk. Prior to a new issue bond being sold to the public, the issuer will submit the bond to the rating agency for an initial bond rating.

The rating agency will require several key pieces of information from the issuer, including (but not limited to):

- Financials such as balance sheet, outstanding debt, income statement, statement of cash flows
- Debt covenants
- Proposed structure (length of debt), yield, terms and conditions

Not all bonds are submitted for rating, however. These bonds are (cleverly) called non-rated bonds. Why would a bond not submit to a rating agency for a rating? An issuer must pay the rating agency to obtain a rating on a securities offering, which increases expenses for the issuer. Almost any type of debt has the potential to be rated by a rating agency, include such debt as municipals, corporate bonds, asset-backed securities, and mortgage backed securities. If their rating is going to cost the issuer money, why would the issuer spend the money to obtain the rating?

Figure 18: Credit Scale by Rating Agency

Investment or Non-Investment Grade	S&P ™	Fitch ™	Moody's ™
Investment Grade	AAA	AAA	Aaa
	AA+	AA+	Aa1
	AA	AA	Aa2
	AA-	AA-	Aa3
	A+	A+	A1
	A	A	A2
	A-	A-	A3
	BBB+	BBB+	Baa1
	BBB	BBB	Baa2
	BBB-	BBB-	Baa2
Non - Investment Grade	BB+	BB+	Ba1
	BB	BB	Ba2
	BB-	BB-	Ba3
	B+	B+	B1
	B	B	B2
	B-	B-	B3

Investors, right or wrong, take comfort in the rating on a debt security when they are making a decision to purchase it. For a new debt issuance, if the issuer decided not to obtain a rating, investors as a group would be less likely to purchase the security. If investors are less likely to purchase the new issue security, investors will demand a lower price (and therefore higher yield) from the issuer. Sometimes, it can be more cost effective to simply pay to have the security rated.

The rating agency will evaluate the potential securities issue for the following risks:

1. **Default or Credit risk** – The overall risk that the issuer will either be unable to pay to coupon or principal as agreed. This risk becomes higher if the issuer already has a lot of other debt or has decreasing revenues or increasing expenses. Bankruptcy is a component of this risk, but an issuer does not need to file for bankruptcy to default on the bond.
2. **Cash Flow Level and Predictability** – Cash flow that is less predictable would be viewed as riskier, and the bond would therefore be assigned a lower rating.
3. **Likelihood of Adverse Conditions** – Adverse conditions would include loss of a major employer in the area or a market recession/downturn.
4. **Senior/Subordinated Level of Debt** – Senior debt holders will be paid first in the event of a bankruptcy, so senior debt is typically rated higher than subordinated debt. Subordinated debt holders are paid after senior debt holders, so there is more risk that the subordinated debt will not be paid in the event of bankruptcy or default.

Bonds rated below BBB or Baa2 are considered below investment grade or non-investment grades. Some in the industry use a more colorful term to describe these debt securities – junk bonds. The lower the grade or rating, the higher the risk of bankruptcy or default is. When bankruptcy or default occurs, there is a clear order as to who gets paid out first. See Figure 18 for the credit scale by rating agency.

In some cases, an issuer with a lower credit rating may decide to purchase credit enhancement to raise their rating. A credit enhancement can be given by a bank or insurance company for a fee. The bank or insurance company reviews the issuer's financial and may choose to offer the credit enhancement. The credit enhancement is sought by lower-credit quality issuers as a way to make their bonds more attractive to a wider investor base, as some investors would choose not to invest in lower credit quality issuers. The bank or insurance company providing the credit enhancement substitutes the issuer's credit quality for their own credit quality. Why do this at all? A higher credit rated bond means a lower interest cost to the issuer. If the interest cost drops enough, the issuer will pay to have the credit enhancement. If the cost is too high, the issuer will not have the bond's credit enhanced and will issue them at the lower credit rating.

Common Terms and Conditions of Debt Securities
If you have had any finance classes to date, some of these characteristics will look familiar - they are all components in the Present Value calculation. There are some characteristics of debt securities that are unique and not found in all bonds. The list below reviews the terms and conditions likely part of the SIE Exam.

Par Value – This refers to the face value or the value of the bond at maturity. Most bonds have a par value of $1,000. Bonds that sell below the par value are said to trade at a discount. Bonds that sell above par value are said to trade at a premium.

Discount – Bonds that trade below par value in the secondary market. For instance, if par value is $1,000 and the bond trades at $980, this bond is said to trade at a discount, or discount to par.

Premium - Bonds that trade above par value in the secondary market. For instance, if par value is $1,000 and the bond trades at $1,100, this bond is said to trade at a premium, or premium to par.

Maturity - This refers to the length of term of the bond. Said another way, the maturity is how many years the investor will need to hold the bond until the investor is repaid the principal.

Coupon - The company issuing the debt has agreed to pay a specific amount of interest per year, twice per year, quarterly, or by month to the investor. The coupon payment is the income a bondholder receives for purchasing the bond. To determine the coupon value, you need to know how often coupon payments are made per year and the coupon payment as a percentage of face value. As an example, assume you have purchased a twenty year corporate bond that pays a coupon twice per year. The coupon on the bond is stated as a 4.5% coupon. If there is a coupon to be paid on the bond, it is always explicitly listed. If the bond had face value of $1,000, each bond would pay out $1,000 x 4.5% = $45 in coupon payments annually. However, if the bond paid out coupons twice per year as is customary, each coupon payment would be $45/2 = $22.50.

Call Feature - A debt security is considered 'callable' when the issuer has the option, but not the obligation, to return the debt security holder's principal PRIOR to the maturity date of the bonds. A call feature gives the option, but not the obligation, only to the issuer of the securities. The option allows the issuer to call all or portion of the outstanding securities in the market at a specific price (call price) and at a specific time (call date). Why would the issuer put a call feature in bonds that they sell to investors? The issuer does this to give themselves future flexibility in the event market interest rates become lower. Another way an issuer could use a call feature is if the issuer's rating improves. This would allow them to issue new debt at a lower rate. In these cases, the issuer is likely to call the bonds, issue new bonds using their improved rating at the lower interest rate, and use the money received through the new bond issuance to refund the old bond issue that was called. Call features will always favor the issuer. Given bondholders know this, bondholders will seek to limit the ability of the issuer to call bonds, by having specified in the bond indenture a call schedule, or list of call dates and call prices on which the issuer can execute the call. Limiting the call provisions in this way provides the bondholders with call protection. Call protection is most valuable when bond prices are increasing (meaning the issuer is more likely to call the bonds if the issuer was permitted to do so!).

Put Feature – A put feature works exactly like a call feature, but in reverse. Instead of the company or issuer being permitted to buy back the bonds from an investor, the investor has the opportunity at a future date to place (or put) the bonds back to the issuer at a specific price. A company issuing fixed income securities may offer this feature to entice investors to purchase their bonds in the first place. Put features favor the investor/lender/bondholder.

Convertibility - A debt security is considered convertible if the security can, at some future date in a prescribed formula, convert from a debt to an equity security. Typically, the debt converts to the same issuer's equity security but not always.

Yield – There are several different types of yield calculations for fixed income securities. For bonds that pay a coupon, the yield is a combination of the coupon payment and any potential price appreciation/depreciation in the price of the bond itself. If an investor is intending to hold or own the bond until it matures, the yield calculated is the *yield to maturity*, whereby the years that the investor owns the bonds is the difference between the date that the bond was purchased and when the bonds mature. *Yield to call* is another common yield calculation. Like yield to maturity, yield to call uses a specific date when the investor would receive their principal returned or another specified amount. This specific date used is the first call date of the bonds. Finally, *yield to worst* is also a common yield calculation. *Yield to worst* assumes the worst return possible, whether that is either the yield to call or yield to maturity. This way, an investor knows the minimum yield they should expect, regardless of whether they hold it to maturity or it is called by the issuer. *Yield to worst* is also required to be disclosed to customers on a broker-dealer's trade confirmation.

Short Term – vs – Long Term – Investors can purchase bonds of almost any length of maturity, anywhere from a few days to 30 years. Short term bond investing has much less risk and therefore much more price stability, as there are fewer days that stand between your purchase of a bond and when you will receive your principal back at maturity. Therefore, short term investing has less risk, all things being equal. *The value of a bond or bond portfolio is going to be more stable the shorter the time to maturity.*

Figure 19: Three Yield Curve Shapes

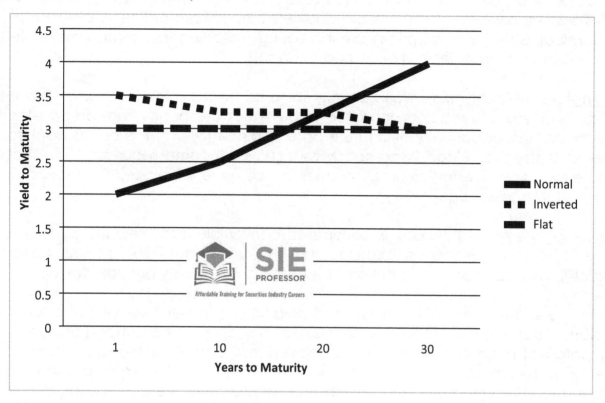

Long term investing has more risk for the exact same reason – with more time between the day you purchase your bond and when the bond is set to mature, making a bond or a portfolio of longer term maturing bonds much less price stable. These factors help determine the shape of the yield curve. The yield curve shows, in graphical representation, the differences in short term and long term rates. When long term rates are higher than short term rates, the yield curve is said to be normal. When long term rates are the same as short term rates, the yield curve is said to be flat. When short term rates are higher than long term rates, the yield curve is said to be inverted.

For a visual look at this concept, please check out Figure 19.

No Coupon - These types of debt securities do not pay any interest or coupon payment to the debt security holder. Instead, the debt securities are sold at a discount, or lower price, to investors than will be returned as principal when the debt security reaches maturity. These types of debt security are also referred to as Zero Coupon bonds.

When learning about debt securities, remember one of the basic principles - the price of the bond and the yield on the bond are INVERSELY related. If the bond price goes up, the yield must go down. If the yield goes up, the price goes down.

Now that we have reviewed the general information about fixed income securities, there are some specific things that you will need to know about the primary types of debt securities. Overall, there are seven primary types of debt securities that are covered in this chapter:

1. U.S. Treasury Securities
2. U.S. Agency Securities
3. Securitized Products
4. Municipal Securities
5. Corporate Bonds
6. Variable Rate Demand Obligations and Notes
7. Money Markets Instruments

Let's review these seven types of debt securities, with the goal of understanding a little bit about each of them. For each type of debt securities, the characteristics are noted along with a description of their unique features.

U.S. Treasury Securities

U.S. Treasury securities are issued by the United States Federal Government through the Department of Treasury. The Treasury Department issued U.S. Treasury securities to fund the ongoing operations of the U.S. federal government. There are three types of securities in the category of treasuries that you can expect to be covered on the SIE Exam:

1. Treasury Bills   2. Treasury Notes   3. Treasury Bonds

MEMORY TIP! Here is an easy way to remember the order of treasury maturities from longest to shortest. BoNoBill

Bo = Bonds   No = Notes   Bill = Bills

The U.S. Treasury issues each of these types of securities. Although each of these debt obligations has different names, they are still backed by the full faith and credit of the U.S. federal government, viewed by investors as very safe, almost risk free investments. U.S. Treasuries are also known as government bonds. Due to their risk free status (no credit risk), the market for U.S. Treasury securities are extremely liquid. When either on the SIE exam or in real life scenarios, you may be asked about the "risk free" rate. U.S. Treasury securities are used as a proxy for the risk free rate.

The U.S. Treasury issues securities in varying maturities depending on the U.S. Treasury's funding needs and investor demand.

Figure 20: Treasury Bond, Note, and Bill Maturities

Treasury Bills mature in one year or less and *are considered zero-coupon bonds* because they do not pay any type of coupon payment during the life of the bond. Treasury bills are issued at a discount to face value and at maturity are worth full face value. For T-Bills, remember that they are mature in one year or less AND that they are issued as zero-coupon securities.

Treasury Notes are the second type of debt instrument issued by the U.S. Treasury and mature between 1-10 years.

Treasury Bonds are the final type of debt instrument issued by the U.S. Treasury, are the longest maturing bond issued by the U.S. Treasury, and can be issued between 20 – 30+ years. Treasury Notes and Bonds pay interest on a semi-annual basis.

U.S. Agency Securities

The U.S. Department of Treasury[26] defines agency securities as follows:

> The term "agency securities" is sometimes used by brokers, dealers and investment advisors to refer to securities issued or guaranteed by a variety of entities other than the U.S. Treasury. Agency securities are not the same as U.S. Treasury securities. An agency security represents a loan by the security purchaser (the investor) to the issuing entity and an investor should consider the different characteristics and different guarantees of agency securities. The term "agency securities" refers to securities issued by or guaranteed by:

- Government corporations -- Examples of these include the Government National Mortgage Association (Ginnie Mae) and the Tennessee Valley Authority (TVA)

- Government sponsored enterprises (GSEs) -- GSEs are privately owned, but were chartered by Congress to perform certain public functions in particular sectors of the economy.

Figure 21: U.S. Treasury Yields, 1990-2016[27]

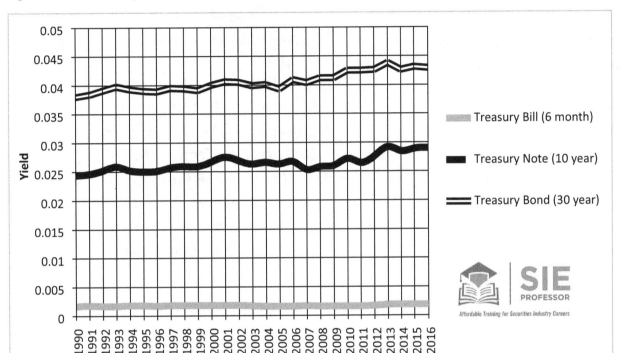

An example of a common GSE is the Federal Home Loan Mortgage Corporation, otherwise known as Freddie Mac. There are many agency bond issuers or guarantors operating within the market. Bonds issued by U.S. federal agencies are called agency bonds. These bonds are issued to finance agency operations. Most of these bonds are not technically backed by the full faith and credit of the U.S. government, so there is typically a risk premium associated with these bonds when compared to treasury securities. U.S. Agency bonds are said to have the implicit backing of the U.S. government. Trading at a premium to treasury securities means that a purchaser of an agency bond would typically require a higher yield when comparing that agency bond to an equivalent treasury bond (all things being equity like maturity, size, etc...).

Securitized Products (Asset and Mortgage Backed Securities)

U.S. Agencies also issue another category of fixed income securities called securitized products. A few of the more familiar securitized products include Asset Backed

Securities (ABS) and Mortgage Backed Securities (MBS). The type of securitized product will typically depend on the assets, or cash flows, that fund the security itself.

Figure 22: Entity Types That Issue or Guarantee U.S. Agency Securities

Government Corporations	Government Sponsored Enterprises (GSE's)
Government National Mortgage Corporation or Ginnie Mae (GNMA) Tennessee Valley Authority (TVA)	Federal Home Loan Banks (FHLB) Federal National Mortgage Association (Fannie Mae) Federal Home Loan Mortgage Corporation (Freddie Mac) Farm Credit Bank Funding Corporation Federal Agricultural Mortgage Corporation (Farmer Mac)

Asset backed securities are supported by one of many different types of assets. Mortgage Backed Securities are funded by mortgages. Some common asset backed securities are supported, or backed by items such as student loans, credit cards, or even music royalties. At first glance, these do not look like fixed income securities or perhaps even assets! Let's take student loans as an example. There are two sides to this transaction – the borrower and the lender. As the borrower, you borrow funds from the lender in order to pay for school. This transaction takes place through a student loan contract. At some point in the future, you must begin repaying the lender according to a determined frequency and payment amount. The repayment process is a series of negative cash flows from the borrower's perspective, but a series of positive cash flows from the lender's perspective. If the lender chooses to hold the loan on its balance sheet, then the lender will able to recoup the cash flow payments.

What often happens, however, is that the lender sells the loan to a third party, and all future cash flows to this third party. In exchange for selling the loan, the lender will, of course, receive cash up front, recouping the cost of the loan plus a profit. Lenders do this many, many times as they are writing new loans.

The process by which the loans are resold, packaged together, and then turned into securities is called the securitization process. Once the loans have been securitized, they are sold to investors who are interested in receiving a stream of cash flows. Securitized products do not pay out a predetermined coupon payment like a corporate bond. The payouts to the investor, or owner of the securitized product, depend entirely on the performance of the underlying cash flows. As such, asset backed or mortgage backed securities trade based on their average life, not their stated maturity. A traditional bond will have more predictable payments to bondholders as a set amount each period. If an individual MBS or ABS receives cash flows earlier than expected, the ABS or MBS will mature sooner than the maturity date, which is why ABS and MBS trade off of their average life remaining instead of the maturity date like a typical bond.

Municipal Securities

Municipal securities are typically issued by a municipal entity, such as a state, city, school district, or township. In exchange for purchasing the municipal securities, the investor receives the promise to receive their principal back when the bonds have matured. In addition, the investor receives periodic coupon payments. These are characteristics similar to corporate bonds. A big difference is tax deductibility. Municipal securities, or "munis" as they are sometimes called, pay interest that is typically exempt from federal taxes. If the coupon paid from municipal securities is only exempt from federal taxes, the munis are said to be (federal) *tax-exempt*. This coupon may also be tax exempt at the state level as well, as long as the investor is a resident of the same state of the municipal entity issuing the bonds. These bonds are referred to as *double tax exempt* because the investor does not have to pay federal or state taxes on the coupon. This tax treatment makes many munis very attractive to investors in high marginal tax brackets. Typically for a municipal bond, an investor living in the same state that issues the municipal bond has a tax advantage over those who do not live in the same state. Being a resident of the state that issued the municipal bond will give an investor the opportunity to take advantage of the state tax exemption, and avoid paying both federal and state income taxes on their interest/coupon income. For instance, if George lives in State of Wisconsin and wants to buy a municipal bond issued by the State of Wisconsin, George has a much better chance of the interest on his Wisconsin municipal bond being state tax exempt than if George purchased a State of Iowa municipal bond.

You should note however that not every municipal security is tax exempt. Some municipal securities are indeed taxable, due to the type of entity involved with the security and those entities' activities. For purposes of the SIE Exam, assume that a municipal security is tax-exempt unless it is clearly stated to the contrary.

General obligation ("GO" or "G-O") Bonds are a specific type of municipal bonds. GO bonds are bonds that are backed by the full taxing power of the municipality issuing the bonds For instance, if the state of Nevada issues a GO bond, the bondholders are relying in part on the State of Nevada's ability to levy taxes on sales, property, etc. to repay bondholders. This provides a layer of security to bondholders and reduces the amount of risk taken by the investor in the GO bonds.

Revenue bonds are another type of municipal security. Revenue bonds are backed by a specific revenue project. Let's say that the state of Missouri wants to build a new toll plaza along one of their highways. To build it, Missouri would need to come up with the funds out of their current tax revenues to pay for the construction. This might be a problem, when weighed against other projects requiring those same funds. To alleviate this problem, revenue bonds were created. Instead of Missouri having to fund the construction of the toll plaza, Missouri issued bonds that are backed from the expected revenue of the toll plaza. The next time you pay your toll, understand that some of the money goes to the state, but some of your toll payment is sent to repay bond revenue bond investors that funded the construction of the toll plaza itself!
As discussed above, the two primary types of municipal bonds are general obligation and revenue bonds. There are also a few special bonds types that you should have a rudimentary understanding of for purposes of the SIE Exam.

Short term funding obligations of municipalities can be met a few different ways, namely by the issuance of BANs and TANs. BANs, or Bond Anticipation Notes are typically issued ahead of a formal bond issuance. TANs, or Tax Anticipation Notes are typically issued ahead of the receipt of taxes paid by businesses and individuals. BANs and TANs are both a form of bridge or short term financing that gives the municipality access to funds ahead of getting future funds from tax receipts or a bond issuance. Once the taxes are received or the bonds are issued, the municipality pays back the BANs or TANs with some or all of the tax receipts or bond proceeds. Another way municipalities can meet short term funding needs is simply to go to the bank and get a loan. Bank loans are not technically securities under the securities laws, but bank loans are often a real source of funding for municipalities.

A quick note about Municipal Fund Securities for this chapter. There are three types of Municipal Fund Securities that you will need to be aware of for the SIE Exam – LGIPs, 529 Plans, and ABLE accounts. 529 Plans and ABLE accounts are covered in detail in Chapter 8. LGIPs will be covered here, as they the fit best within the activities of municipalities and how those municipalities fund their operations. LGIP stands for Local Government Investment Pool. The Government Finance Officers Association[28] describes LGIPs as follows:

> "In many states, the state treasurer or the authorized governing board of another governmental entity (such as a county) oversees a pooled investment fund that operates like a money market mutual fund for the exclusive benefit of governments within the entity's jurisdiction.

Unlike mutual funds, however, local government investment pools (LGIPs) are not registered with the Securities and Exchange Commission (SEC) and are exempt from SEC regulatory requirements because they fall under a governmental exclusion clause. While this exemption allows pools greater flexibility, it also reduces investor protection. Investments in these pools are not insured or guaranteed and substantial losses have occurred in the past.

These pools typically combine the cash of participating jurisdictions and invest the cash in securities allowed under the state's laws regarding government investments. By pooling funds, participating governments benefit from economies of scale, full-time portfolio management, diversification, and liquidity (especially in the case of pools that seek a constant net asset value of $1.00). Interest is normally allocated to the participants on a daily basis, proportionate to the size of the investment. Most pools offer a check writing or wire transfer feature that adds value as a cash management tool."

Corporate Bonds

Corporate bonds are another type of fixed income product that is covered on the SIE Exam. Corporate bonds are very similar to municipal bonds in many respects – they are both issued by an entity, share common bond characteristics, and pay out coupons and principal. Corporate bonds are issued by non-municipal entities, mostly by corporations. Otherwise, they are issued and trade in functionally the exact same ways. So what are some of the differences and things you should be aware of?

Let's say your friend Angela is considering making an investment in bonds but isn't sure if municipal bonds or corporate bonds are better for her. Angela does not mind taking a little risk, but does not want to take too much risk, so she decides to purchase a bond rate 'A' or better. An 'A' rated corporate bond has a yield to maturity of 5.75%, and an 'A' rated municipal bond has a yield to maturity of 4.25%. Given that the corporate bond has a much higher yield for the same amount of risk (as measured by the bond's credit rating), this is an easy decision, right?

Not so fast.

If she purchased the corporate bond, she would have to pay taxes on her coupon payments. If she purchased a municipal bond, she would not have to pay income taxes on her coupon payments. So how do you compare the yields on a municipal bond, which are typically income tax exempt, with a corporate (taxable) bond? An investor will need to understand the concept of tax equivalent yield.

Tax equivalent yield is the yield at which a municipal bond would need to trade given an investor's marginal tax rate. Since different investors have different marginal tax rates, the tax equivalent yield will be different as well for each investor.
If Angela, who is not married, makes $50,000 per year, she would be in the 3rd tax bracket, with her marginal tax rate being 22% (see U.S. Federal Tax Brackets). To find the tax equivalent yield, use the following formula:

Tax equivalent yield = Municipal Yield / (1 – marginal tax rate)

So in our example, the inputs look like this:
4.25% / (1 - .22) = 5.45%. Given this information, which bond should Angela choose?
The corporate bond that pays 5.75%, or the municipal bond that pays 4.25%, but has a
tax equivalent yield of 5.45%?

2019 U.S. Federal Tax Brackets

Rate	For Unmarried Individuals, Taxable Income Over	For Married Individuals Filing Joint Returns, Taxable Income Over	For Heads of Households, Taxable Income Over
10%	$0	$0	$0
12%	$9,700	$19,400	$13,850
22%	$39,475	$78,950	$52,850
24%	$84,200	$168,400	$84,200
32%	$160,725	$321,450	$160,700
35%	$204,100	$408,200	$204,100
37%	$510,300	$612,350	$510,300

Source: Tax Foundation

Even with the tax-exempt nature of the municipal bonds, it makes financial sense for
Angela to choose the corporate bonds given that the corporate bond has a slightly
higher tax equivalent yield. The Tax Equivalent Yield calculation allows you to
compare bonds that have exactly the same characteristics, except for the overall
yield to the investor.

When using tax equivalent yields to compare bonds, be sure to make an 'apples to
apples comparison'. The bonds you are comparing should for instance have the
same credit rating. Otherwise, one bond is inherently riskier than the other. An investor
taking on additional risk should be compensated for that risk by expecting a higher
return (yield). All other bonds features should also be the same – call and put features,
maturity date, etc....

Let's change the parameters of our problem a bit now. All of the other information is
the same, with the exception of Angela's income. Instead of making $50,000 per year,
she now makes $200,000 per year. This puts Angela in a new tax bracket, where her

marginal tax rate is much higher, at 32%. What is Angela's tax equivalent yield on the municipal securities?

Tax equivalent yield = Municipal Yield / (1 – marginal tax rate)
4.25% / (1 - .32) = 6.25%.

With Angela's new, higher income purchasing the municipal with a yield of 4.25, but a tax equivalent yield of 6.25% makes more sense than purchasing the corporate bond yielding 5.75%. Municipal securities typically make more sense for someone in a higher tax bracket, and typically less sense for those in a lower tax bracket.

Other Bond Terminology
There are a few other types of bonds in which you should be familiar – Yankee, and Eurodollar bonds. Yankee Bonds are foreign bonds that are issued in the United States after registering with the SEC. Yankee bonds pay interest and principal in U.S. Dollars and trade immediately upon registration being approved by the SEC. Eurodollar bonds are similar to Yankee bonds but with some distinguishing features. Like Yankee bonds, Eurodollar bonds pay interest and principal in U.S. Dollars. However, Eurodollar bonds are foreign bonds issued outside of the U.S. and are exempt from SEC registration.

Variable Rate Demand Obligations and Notes
Most types of fixed income securities we have discussed so far have been fixed rate securities – a set coupon payment made over the life of the bond. Variable Rate Demand Obligations ("VRDOs")[29] are a very different but important type of variable, or floating rate fixed income securities. Issuers use VRDO's to help raise capital or address their own cash flow needs, just like with a fixed rate security. Investors use VRDO's for many reasons, the most important of which are safety of principal, ability to collect interest income, and high level of liquidity allowing investors to sell out of their position quickly if necessary. Some characteristics of VRDO's include:
- Term to maturity of between 20-30 years
- Interest rate reset periodically
- Interest rate can be reset daily, weekly, monthly, semi-annually, or as needed
- Includes a put feature that allows the investor to sell the VRDO back to the issuer on demand
- Put feature requires the remarketing agent to sell the investor the VRDO's back at full face value plus interest
- Investor must notify remarketing agent a certain period of time in advance in order to put the bonds
- Nothing is guaranteed however – a Remarketing Agent may not be able to buy back the VRDO under all circumstances

If VRDO's are a useful investment product for investors, what are some of the risks? There are three that you should be most familiar with:

- **Interest Rate Risk** – Since VRDOs are short term focused, any large movement in short term interest rates would be felt by both the issuer and investor. For the issuer, an increase in short term rates means that the issuer must pay out more interest to the investor. For the investor, an increase in interest rates means that they collect more interest from the issuer. For a drop in short term interest rates, the opposite would be true, of course.
- **Liquidity Risk** – If an investor has put the VRDO back to the issuer, the Remarketing Agent must find another buyer or access the bank line of credit supporting the VRDO. If the bank backs out, the VRDO's liquidity may not work as intended.
- **Default Risk** – Repayment of an investor's principal is protected in many ways with VRDOs. However, there are no guarantees. If the issuer is not able to make principal and interest repayments due to the issuer's own financial issues, the investor may not receive the promised full interest and principal amounts. This risk exists with VRDOs just like it does with other fixed income securities.

Money Market Instruments

The money markets are used by typically large institutions and the federal government in an effort to fund and supply other market participants with needed liquidity. Although there are several types of money market instruments, each different instrument is not so different as to cause widely dissimilar market yields. Money market instruments are short term instruments that mature in less than one year and are highly liquid.

Three of the most common examples of money market instruments are:
1. Certificates of Deposit
2. Banker's Acceptance
3. Commercial Paper

Although already discussed, Treasury Bills are also considered part of the money markets due to their short term maturity (less than one year) and high credit backing from the full faith and credit of the U.S. Government.

Certificates of Deposit

CD's, or Certificates of Deposit, have been around for a long time. There are two primary types of CD's – negotiable and non-negotiable. Both types of CD's have a few things in common – they are both considered time deposits, meaning that money used to purchase a CD is unavailable until the CD matures in the future. Another thing in common of all CD's is that they pay a fixed rate of interest from the issuing bank to the CD holder/owner on an agreed upon schedule – monthly, annually, etc.... Most

CD's that consumers buy at their bank are non-negotiable, meaning they cannot be traded with someone else in exchange for cash. Said another way, there is no secondary trading market for non-negotiable CD's. In order to get your money back prior to maturity, you must work through the bank that sold you the CD and most likely pay an early termination penalty. For negotiable, or jumbo CD's, these can be traded with other market participants, but beware: negotiable CD's typically trade in the $1-10 million range. These are not typically for retail investors! CD's are NOT zero-coupon financial instruments because they pay interest during the life of the CD.

Banker's Acceptance

A banker's acceptance is a document created by a company drawn on and accepted by that company's bank. The bank must agree to the banker's acceptance and promises to pay a specific amount at a specific date. Given the bank's written promise to pay, the bank's credit is substituted for the company's credit. Banker's acceptances are typically used in short term financing (30 to 180 days) and are considered time drafts because they promise payment in the future. Banker's acceptance are considered discount financial products, in that they do not pay a coupon but are sold at less than face value, and then pay the full face amount on the future agreed upon date.

Commercial Paper

Commercial paper is typically issued by large corporations to help those corporations finance a short-term money/capital need. When issued, commercial paper matures between 1 and 270 days. Almost 100% of the commercial paper market matures prior to 270 days. Why? If commercial paper issued were to mature greater than 270 days, the issuing corporation would be required to comply with SEC registration and prospectus requirements. In order to avoid this requirement, most commercial paper therefore matures in less than 270 days (and often in less than 90 days). Although any corporation can issue corporate paper, only those with high credit quality and therefore the lowest default risk typically do so, as the issued commercial paper is unsecured (i.e., no corporate assets are pledged against it). Similar to bankers' acceptance and Treasury Bills, commercial paper is issued on a discount basis to par value.

Day-Count Conventions

How do we calculate the amount of accrued interest and present value of bonds? We use a convention showing the number of days in any given month divided by the number of days in the year. The calculation shows the fraction of the year remaining that is used to calculate the amount of future interest owed.

Figure 23: Day Count Conventions by Security

Type of Security	Day Count Convention
Corporate, Agency, Municipal Bonds, Mortgaged-Backed Securities	30 days/360
Commercial Paper, T-bills	Actual number of days in the month/360
Treasury Bonds	Actual number of days in the month/365

End of Chapter Quiz

Complete these end of chapter questions to assess your understanding of the subject matter discussed in this chapter. The answers follow on the next page. For those questions you have answered incorrectly, review the appropriate section of the chapter again to make sure you understand the concepts.

1. Which of the following is NOT a form of temporary or bridge financing?
   a. BAN
   b. TAN
   c. LGIP
   d. Bank loan

2. Which of the following features is common between a Yankee bond and a Eurodollar bond?
   a. Pay interest and principal in U.S. dollars
   b. Require a put option to be included
   c. Issued outside of the U.S.
   d. Registered in the U.S. after SEC approval

3. As a bond's price goes _____, the bond's yield goes _____.
   a. Down, up
   b. Down, flat
   c. Flat, up
   d. Up, flat

4. Which of the following shows the order of maturity in treasury securities, from longest to shortest?
   a. Bills, Bonds, Notes
   b. Bills, Notes, Bonds
   c. Bonds, Bills, Notes
   d. Bonds, Notes, Bills

5. Which of the following securities are typically sold on a discount basis?
   a. Bankers' acceptance and Treasury bills
   b. Certificate of deposit and Treasury bills
   c. Commercial paper and certificate of deposit
   d. Treasury bonds and commercial paper

6. For a Nevada Municipal General Obligation Bond, the bond is backed by which of the following?
    a. Revenue from a newly constructed toll plaza in Nevada
    b. Federal government tax receipts paid by residents of Nevada
    c. Nevada taxing authority on state residents and activities in the state
    d. Las Vegas, Nevada property taxes

7. When an issuer's bonds reach maturity, the issuer must:
    a. Make a principal payment to the bondholders
    b. Provide notice of exercise of the call feature
    c. Provide notice of exercise of the put feature
    d. Do nothing

8. Treasury bills typically make coupon payments:
    a. Monthly
    b. Quarterly
    c. Semi-Annually
    d. Never

9. Which of the following is TRUE regarding a non-negotiable jumbo CD?
    a. The CD can only be purchased on the last calendar day of the month
    b. The rate of interest on the CD is variable
    c. The CD is sold on a discount basis
    d. The purchaser can resell the CD

10. Which of the following is true regarding Local Government Investment Pools (LGIPs)?
    a. Investments in the pools are insured
    b. Investments in the pools are guaranteed not to lose value
    c. The pools are exempt from SEC registration requirements
    d. The pools are issued on a discount basis

End of Chapter Quiz Answers

1. C

BANs, or Bond Anticipation Notes are a type of bridge or temporary financing that allows the borrower to access funds before a longer term bond financing is completed. TANs, or Tax Anticipation Notes are a type of bridge or temporary financing that allows the borrower to access funds before receipt of annual tax revenues. LGIP, or Local Government Investment Pools are a type of funds that municipalities can use for cash management. They are typically state specific and subject to various criteria and usage restrictions. Although bank loans can be used for short or long term borrowing needs, the can be used as a bridge or temporary financing.

2. A

Both of these types of bonds pay interest and principal in U.S. dollars. Although there may be put options with either bond type, put options are not required. Eurodollar bonds are issued outside the U.S. Yankee bonds are issued in the U.S. Eurodollar bonds are exempt from SEC registration. Yankee bonds are subject to SEC registration.

3. A

Bond prices and yields are inversely correlated, meaning they move in opposite directions. As bond prices go down, bond yields go up.

4. D

Bonds, Notes, Bills is the correct order. Treasury Bonds have maturities up to 30 years. Treasury Notes have maturities from 1 to 10 years. Treasury Bills mature in less than one year.

5. A

Banker's acceptance and Treasury Bills are the only two choices that trade on a discount basis. Discount means trading below par value of final maturity amount. CD's and commercial paper pay interest and the holder receives the same principal amount invested back at maturity.

6. C

Revenue received from a toll plaza is likely pledged to revenue bonds used to build the toll plaza. Taxes paid to the Federal government by the residents of Nevada would not be used to back a Nevada GO bond offering. Nevada has the power to tax state residents and activities occurring within the state. These would be sources of revenue that a GO bond would like be supported by. Property taxes paid with a city would like not be used to support a Statewide GO bond.

7. A

The issuer returns the agreed upon principal amount to the investor at maturity. The call feature is activated prior to maturity of the bonds. The put feature is activated prior to maturity of the bonds. The issuer must return the agreed upon principal amount to the investor at maturity.

8. D

Treasury Bills are zero coupon securities or in other words, do not make coupon payments. Bills are zero coupon securities or in other words, do not make coupon payments.

9. D

CD purchases are not typically limited to a particular time of the month. The purchaser can typically resell a jumbo CD prior to maturity. CD rates are typically fixed. CD's are not sold on a discount basis.

10. C

LGIP's are exempt from SEC registration but are not typically insured. LGIPs are not typically issued on a discount basis nor are they guaranteed against loss.

Chapter 6: Options

Options are one of the primary types of derivative securities, or securities that derive their value from an underlying asset. Options can be written on many different types of assets, including equity securities, currencies, commodities, or indexes. Since this material only covers securities, we will only discuss options with securities as the underlying assets. If you remember nothing else about options, remember this – an option grants the RIGHT, but NOT the OBLIGATION to buy or sell an asset at a specified price on a specified date. Let's fill in the details.

Option Basics

Options can be one of the most confusing topics for students new to the securities industry. Let's go through a few basics to hopefully make this a bit clearer. First up – basic definitions of the following:

- Option buyer
- Option writer/seller
- Strike/Exercise Price
- Expiration Date
- Premium
- Underlying Security
- Option Classifications

There are two primary options roles – the option buyer and the option writer/seller. The option writer creates the option and first sells it to a buyer. Buyers can then hold the option or resell it in the secondary market to another buyer.

The *option writer/option seller* is a person or entity who writes/creates the option and earns the premium for selling it to another party. An option contract can be sold many times before expiration date. Each time the option is resold, the seller earns the market premium for that particular option.

The *option buyer* is the person or entity that purchases the option from the option writer/seller. In exchange for the option's right, but not the obligation, to purchase the underlying security at a specified price by a specific date, the option buyer gives the option writer/seller the agreed upon premium.

Options contracts always have these two sides to them – the buyer and the seller. The buyer of the option contract is considered long the option, while the option seller is considered short the option. Being long the option though is not the same as wanting the value of the underlying security to increase. Being long the option simply means that you own the option and can control whether or not to exercise it.

The writer of an option sells that option to another party in exchange for a specific dollar amount, or *premium*. The premium is different for each option. The dollar amount of the premium is influenced by:
- the value of the underlying security;

- the number of days left on the option until expiration date;
- how far the option is from being out of the money or in the money;
- whether the option is in the money, out of the money, or at the money; and
- how volatile the underlying security is in comparison to other securities.

By selling an options contract and collecting a premium from the purchaser, the individual or entity selling the options contract assumes the risk that the option will pay off, or be in the money for the option holder. This means that the option seller takes the risk that, in the event the underlying security in call option they sold goes up in price, they are on the hook for the increase in price!

One option contract is equivalent to 100 shares of the underlying security. The underlying security is what the option is based on – in the securities world these underlying securities are typically equities or indexes made up of equities. The predetermined price that the option will be executed at is also known as the *strike or exercise price*. All options expire on a specific date, known as the *expiration date*.

For the option writer or seller to take the risk that they may have to buy or sell stock at a later unfavorable price, the option writer demands compensation in the form of the premium. This premium compensates the option writer that on expiration date, the option holder will exercise the option, or force the option writer to buy or sell the underlying security at the strike price. The right to exercise, or use the option ends once the option reaches its expiration date.

Figure 24: Options Order Components

Option Classifications
There are four types of option classifications that you should be familiar with for the SIE Exam:

1. Option Type
2. Option Style
3. Option Class
4. Option Series

As you further and further classify an option, you get to a specific option that an investor can actually purchase or sell.

Option Type – Two choices here – *put or call*.
A call option grants the right, but not the obligation to purchase a specific number of shares of the underlying security by a predetermined price and date. A call option becomes more valuable as the price of the underlying security increases. Investors purchase call options if they want to participate in an increase in price of the underlying security, hedge short stock positions, or to lock in the purchase price of the underlying equity security.

A put option grants the right, but not the obligation, to sell a specific number of shares of the underlying security by a predetermined price and date. A put option becomes more valuable as the price of the underlying security decreases. Investors purchase put options if they want to participate in a decrease in price of the underlying security or hedge long stock positions.

Option Style – Two choices here - *American or European*.
An American call option gives the option holder the right to purchase the security at a fixed price on or before the expiration date. A European call option grants the right to purchase the security at a fixed price, just like an American option. But unlike an American call option, a European call option can only be exercised on expiration date. If the option style is not specified, assume it is an American style option. The right to exercise the option earlier than the expiration date has some value to option investors. This increased market value means that all else being equal, an American style option will have a slightly higher premium than a European style option.

Option Class – Four choices here. All of the
- American style call options or
- American style put options or
- European style put options or
- European style call options

for a particular underlying security or index denotes the option class.

Option Series – All options with the same *option class, strike price, and expiration date* are all part of the same option series.

Options Strategies
Exercise and Assignment
Since the option gives the holder the right, but not the obligation to exercise the option, the option holder can let the option expire on expiration date with no specific action required. The option writer/seller cannot force the option holder to exercise the option. This makes the exercise of an option contract a one-sided decision up to expiration date. *Options that expire without being exercised because they have no economic value occur quite often*, with only the premium paid for the option being lost in the process. Only those options contracts that are favorable to the option holder then are likely to be exercised – those options

considered to be "in the money". *For single security based options, settlement is met by delivering the equivalent number of shares and underlying security written into the option.* **For index-based options, these are settled via cash, as it would be impractical to settle the entire index upon which the option is based!**

Practically speaking, many options positions are exited by simply buying another options contract opposite to the investor's current position. Many options market participants do just this instead of waiting until the options contract reaches expiration day, especially if the options position is moving against them. The value of an option contract changes throughout its life – from the day it is created until expiration date. We have already talked about the factors that cause an options contract's value or premium to change.

Short term options expire within one year from their creation. Options that expire greater than one year are called LEAPS (long-term equity anticipation securities). How are LEAPs and short term options different?
*   Length of time until expiration
*   LEAPs are less liquid
*   LEAPs are available on fewer underlying securities

Listed options typically expire on the third Friday of every month, although there are some contracts that expire weekly instead of monthly.

Options Positions
Once you own an options contract, there are three different monetary positions you can be in – in the money, at the money, or out of the money. Let's say you own the 10 JPM August 75 calls at $7 we discussed earlier in Figure 24. The options owner or holder makes money on call options when the price of the underlying security goes up. Remember that when you own a call option, you have the right, but not the obligation, to purchase the underlying security or index at the strike price. An owner or holder of call options makes money when the price of the underlying security goes **up** in price. For CALL OPTIONS to be considered:
*   *in the money*, the market price of the underlying security needs to be more than the strike price;
*   *at the money*, the market price of the underlying security needs to be equal to the strike price;
*   *away from/out of the money*, the market price of the underlying security needs to be less than the strike price.

Figure 25: Determining an Option Owner's Monetary Position

At what price would the underlying equity security, JPM, need to be trading at to fit into each of three different monetary positions? In our JPM options example – anytime the equity security JPM trades above $75, the option is in the money. Note thought that when JPM trades between $75 and $82, the option owner does not actually make any money. Why? Remember that option cost $7, so $75 + $7 = $82. Above $82, the option owner actually makes a profit, which is different than being in the money. At the money is easy – the strike price of $75 is equal the underlying stock price of $75. Away from/out of the money means that the underlying stock in this case trades below $75.

Put options work in exactly the opposite way. Why? Remember that when you own a put option, you have the right, but not the obligation to purchase the underlying security or index at the strike price. An owner or holder of put options makes money when the price of the underlying security goes **down** in price. For PUT OPTIONS to be considered:
- *in the money*, the market price of the underlying security needs to be less than the strike price;
- *at the money*, the market price of the underlying security needs to be equal to the strike price;
- *out of/away from the money*, the market price of the underlying security needs to be more than the strike price.

At what price would the underlying equity security, JPM, need to be trading at to fit into each of three different monetary positions? In our JPM options example (for puts this time) – anytime the equity security JPM trades below $75, the option is in the money. Note thought that when JPM trades between $68 - 75, the option owner does not actually make any money. Why? Remember that option cost $7, so $75 - $7 = $68. Below $68, the option owner actually makes a profit, which is different than being in the money.

Figure 26: Long and Short Option Positions

At the money is easy – the strike price of $75 is equal the underlying stock price of $75. Away from/out of the money means that the underlying stock in this case trades above $75.

Hedging or Speculation
Individuals or entities enter into options contracts for one of two reasons – hedging or speculation. In hedging transactions, an individual or entity will enter into an options contract to reduce risk from an already existing securities position. For instance, say you own 100 shares of XYZ equity security. You are concerned that the price of XYZ may decrease in the near future, but you do not want to actually sell the security. So what do you do? You purchase a put option.

For the owner of the call option, the strike price is the price at which the owner of the option can purchase the underlying security.

Covered – Vs- Uncovered

As we have already discussed, options contracts are written on some type of underlying security. This underlying security can be a single equity security, like Coca-Cola (symbol KO) or an index, like S&P 500 (symbol SPDR). An option position is considered covered if the individual who owns the option contract also owns the underlying security on which the options contract is written. Because 1 options contract equals 100 shares of the underlying security, it is also important to point out that an options contract holder can be fully covered or partially covered. If you hold 100 shares of the underlying security and 1 call options contract, you would be considered fully covered. If, though, you only held only 50 shares of the underlying security and 1 call options contract, you would be considered only partially covered. To be considered uncovered, you would simply NOT have a position in the underlying security. This is also referred to as a 'naked' position.

Now that you understand covered and uncovered options positions, let's go through the first options strategy that you might see on the SIE Exam – the buy-write strategy. In a buy-write strategy, you must enter into two separate securities transactions. First, buy the equity security or index in the secondary market. Second, sell or write a call option contract in the secondary market on the underlying equity security that was just purchased. You have just executed the buy-write options strategy! The goal of this strategy is to both own the underlying security and make some income through the premium you receive from selling or writing the option. Using this strategy, you are essentially giving up future gains in the underlying security in exchange for the premium. Selling calls where you own the underlying security is also called a covered calls strategy. The profit and loss are both limited in this scenario.

A few other transaction types or strategies include:
- **Opening purchase** – This one is easy. If you do not already own the option, your option purchase is considered your opening purchase. This establishes your position as you are buying the option.
- **Opening sale** – The counter side of the opening purchase is the opening sale. Instead of buying the option, you are writing the option.
- **Closing sale** - You execute this strategy to flatten, or eliminate your earlier opening purchase position. The closing sale is executed by selling your option back to the market. The price of the option may have increased, decreased or stayed the same since your opening purchase.
- **Closing purchase** – You execute this strategy to flatten, or eliminate your earlier opening sale position. The closing purchase is executed by buying your option back in the market. The price of the option may have increased, decreased or stayed the same since your opening sale.

Let's go through an easy way to figure out when an investor makes money. An investor makes money in one of these two basic scenarios:

1. When the underlying security price goes up by owning calls and/or long the underlying security.
2. When the underlying security price goes down by being short the underlying security and/or owning puts.

Figure 27: Options Position Breakdown

	Action	Strategy	Maximum Loss	Maximum Gain	Breakeven Point
Calls					
Buy (long)	Right to Buy	Bullish	Premium	Unlimited	Strike Price + Premium
Write (short)	Obligation to Sell	N/A	Unlimited	Premium	Strike Price + Premium
Uncovered/Naked	Do Not Own Underlying Security	Bearish	Unlimited	Premium	Strike Price + Premium
Covered	Long Underlying and Short Call	Bearish	Underlying Price - Premium	Strike Price + Premium - Underlying Price	Underlying Price - Premium
Puts					
Buy (long)	Right to Sell	Bearish	Premium	Strike Price - Premium	Strike Price - Premium
Write (short)	Obligation to Buy	N/A	Strike Price - Premium	Premium	Strike Price - Premium
Uncovered/Naked	Do Not Own Underlying Security	Bullish	Strike Price - Premium	Premium	Strike Price - Premium
Covered	Short Underlying and Short Put	Bullish	Unlimited	Short Underlying Proceeds + Premium - Strike Price	Short Underlying Proceeds + Premium

Listed -vs- OTC Options

Options that trade on exchanges are called listed options. Options that are not traded on exchanges are considered OTC (Over the Counter) options. The fundamental concepts of options work equally for listed and OTC options alike, with a few major differences, namely settlement and terms. All listed options settle through the OCC, or Options Clearing Corporation. Both the buyer and seller of the option do not settle with each other, but instead with the OCC. Having the OCC in the middle of the trade helps to reduce counterparty risk as options are often a risky type of securities transaction. Listed options are inherently less risky because of the reduced counterparty risk, given the exact same option otherwise.

The other major difference between OTC and listed options are the terms of the options itself. Listed options trade under standard terms. This means that when you buy or sell a listed options contract, you know that 1 contract equals 100 underlying shares of an equity security. In addition, there are standard expiration dates for listed options, allowing an investor to compare various options quickly and easily. Price comparison for listed options is very easy to do, as these prices are disseminated quickly within the securities market.

Risks, Approvals and Disclosures

All options accounts, upon opening, are required to be sent the Characteristics and Risks of Standardized Options, otherwise known as the Options Disclosure Document ("ODD"). As the ODD is updated, customers must also be sent any updates to the ODD.

The ODD is not updated very frequently. It is available at: http://optionsclearing.com/about/publications/character-risks.jsp.

The broker dealer holding your account must send the ODD to their options customers. Options accounts must also be pre-approved by a registered options principal.
Quick options summary:
- owning/holding/being long the option gives you the *right, but not the obligation* to buy or sell an asset at a specific price
- most options *expire worthless* and are never exercised
- selling calls means that *you give up the opportunity* to participate an increase in the price of the stock
- covered options mean that you own the underlying security on which the option is written
- *1 options equals 100 shares* of the underlying security, so 2 option contracts equates to 200 shares in the underlying security (generally speaking)

End of Chapter Quiz

Complete these end of chapter questions to assess your understanding of the subject matter discussed in this chapter. The answers follow on the next page. For those questions you have answered incorrectly, review the appropriate section of the chapter again to make sure you understand the concepts.

1. You currently hold 10 ABC April 80 calls. Of the following, at what price does the underlying security needs to trade at to be considered at the money?
    a. $8
    b. $75
    c. $80
    d. $85

2. You currently hold 10 ABC August 85 puts. Of the following, at what price does the underlying security needs to trade at to be considered away from the money?
    a. $10.00
    b. $80.00
    c. $85.00
    d. $88.00

3. The amount of money paid to purchase an option is called the:
    a. Strike price
    b. Premium
    c. Exercise price
    d. Underlying price

4. The type of call option that can only be exercised on expiration date is a
    a. Short settlement option
    b. American option
    c. Market maker option
    d. European option

5. Which of the following is a unique benefit of OTC options in comparison to listed options?
    a. Uniform trade terms
    b. Allows for a unique contract between buyer and seller
    c. Uniform settlement terms
    d. Settle through OCC

6. A _____ option becomes more valuable if the price of the underlying security _____.
    a. Put, increases
    b. Call, decreases
    c. Put, stays the same
    d. Call, increases

7. The dollar amount of the premium is most influenced by which of the following?
    a. Name of the exchange the underlying security is listed on
    b. Volatility of the underlying security
    c. Price at which the option was originally sold
    d. The number of option market makers

8. You currently hold 10 ABC April 80 calls. Of the following, at what price does the underlying security needs to trade at to be considered in the money?
    a. $8
    b. $75
    c. $80
    d. $85

9. Which of the following positions does the option holder make money if the price of the underlying stock increases?
    a. Short call options
    b. Sell call options
    c. Long call options
    d. Long put options

10. You currently hold 10 ABC April 90 puts. Of the following, at what price does the underlying security needs to trade at to be considered at the money?
    a. $10
    b. $85
    c. $90
    d. $95

End of Chapter Quiz Answers

1. C
At the money means the underlying security trades at an equivalent price to the strike price of the option which in this case is $80. This is true for call and put options. A call option is in the money when the underlying security trades above the strike price. A call option is out of the money when the underlying security trades below the strike price.

2. D
Holding a put option means that you want the price of the underlying security to go down. To be away from the strike price of the put option needs to be lower than the price of the underlying security. If the price of the underlying security is below the strike price, the put option is in the money. When the strike price and underlying security price are the same, the put option is at the money.

3. B
The strike price is the price at which an option can be exercised. A premium is paid to acquire an options position. Exercise price has the same meaning as strike price. The underlying price is the price of the security on which the option is based. It can be a single security, ETF, or index.

4. D
Short settlement option refers to settling a securities transaction prior to settlement date. European options can only be exercised on expiration date. American options can be exercised any time prior to expiration.   Market makers can and do trade options. Options traded by market makers settle according to the type of option.

5. B
Each OTC option is unique and tailored between the buyer and seller. They do not have uniform settlement terms. Listed options have standard terms and do not allow the buyer and seller to change those terms. OTC options do not settle through the OCC. Listed options do settle through the OCC.

6. D

A call option becomes more valuable if the price of the underlying security increases for the holder of the call option. A call option is right, but not the obligation to purchase the underlying security at the strike price prior to or on expiration date.

7. B

The volatility of the underlying security has the most impact on the premium of the option. Recall that an option premium is exchanged for the purchase of an option. The more volatile the underlying security is, the more likely that option will be in the money at some point prior to expiration. The other factors have little to no impact on the dollar amount of the premium.

8. D

When holding call options, the price of the underlying security needs to be higher than the option strike price. In this case, the strike price is $80, so the underlying security must trade above $80 for the option to be in the money. When the underlying is $75, the option is out of the money and at $80, the option is at the money.

9. C

When an investor is long call options, they are hoping for the price of the underlying security to increase. The higher the underlying security rises above the strike price, the more money the option holder makes. An investor who is long put options is hoping for the underlying price to decrease. Being short or selling call options means that this position will lose money if the price of the underlying security increases.

10. C

At the money options are the easiest to understand. An option that is at the money means that the strike price of the option is equal to the market price of the underlying security. For put options, an investor is in the money if the price of the underlying security decreases below the strike price, and out of the money if the price of the underlying security increases above the strike price.

Chapter 7: Investment Companies

There are four basic types of investment or management companies[30]:
1. Closed end fund (otherwise known as a closed end company)
2. Open end fund
3. Unit Investment Trusts (UITs)   4. Variable contracts/annuities

The Investment Company Act of 1940 defines open-end and closed end companies as follows:

*   *Open-end company* means a management company which is offering for sale or has outstanding any redeemable security of which it is the issuer
*   *Closed-end company* means any management company other than an open-end company

The term Mutual Fund most often refers to shares of open-end companies and is one of the most popular types of investments made by investors. Mutual Funds are found in all types of accounts – individual, joint, trust, education, and retirement accounts. Since mutual funds are used in so many accounts and are better known in comparison to closed end funds, let's review them first.

Mutual Funds

The term mutual fund might be self-explanatory to understand. The word mutual in this case means 'shared'. Perhaps then the translation from mutual funds to shared funds makes things a bit simpler. When investors buy mutual funds, the investors are pooling their shared resources to purchase more securities than they ever would be able to purchase individually. By sharing resources, the mutual fund investors essentially have lower transactions costs than they would if invested in the same manner individually; the mutual fund investors also hire a mutual fund manager who will help them execute the desired strategy of the mutual fund. In exchange for an investment amount, the mutual fund takes the investment funds and purchases securities for the mutual fund consistent with the mutual fund's strategy.

Individuals who make investment decisions for mutual funds are called *Mutual Fund Managers*. These managers determine what to buy or sell, and when to buy or sell it. The manager must typically follow the Mutual Fund's investment policy as to what securities can be purchased or sold and the amount of the purchases or sales, but the manager may have some manner of discretion.

A *mutual fund distributor* is typically a broker-dealer that sells, or distributes the mutual fund to customers or other broker-dealers. The purpose of the distributor is to get others to invest in the mutual fund, thereby increasing the level of assets in the mutual fund and the overall number of investors. This helps to spread the cost out over a larger group of people and assets, thereby lowering the costs for everyone. Distributors do not make investment decisions for the mutual fund itself.

A *mutual fund prospectus* lays out all of the important facts and details about the mutual fund for the customer. A mutual fund prospectus can be in electronic or in hard copy form. The SEC requires mutual funds to contain the following categories within the prospectus[31]:

- the fund's investment objectives or goals;
- its strategies for reaching those goals;
- the principal risks of investing in the fund;
- the fund's fees and expenses; and
- its past performance.

In addition to the above items, mutual fund prospectuses also typically include disclosures made by the mutual fund company themselves. These disclosures may describe potential conflicts of interest, indicate how and where orders are executed in the underlying securities, and when the mutual fund company may restrict fund inflows and outflows. Let's go through a few basics on mutual funds that you will be expected to know:

- Mutual Fund Share Classes
- Types of Mutual Funds
- Net Asset Value (NAV)

Mutual Fund Share Classes

Mutual funds are a popular way to invest in the securities markets. When investing in mutual funds, many investors choose to invest in various mutual funds within the same fund family, or branded mutual fund. Mutual funds have several different types of shares classes, each intended for a different customer focus. Class A shares charge an upfront sales charge or a load, thereby reducing the amount invested, as some of the potential investment is used to pay the sales charge instead of being invested in the mutual fund. Class A shares make sense for customers intending to hold their position for a long period of time, thereby spreading the initial cost out over several years. In exchange for paying a higher upfront charge, there is typically no (or very little) ongoing fees charged in subsequent years. In addition to the upfront sales charge, Class A shares also typically charge a 12b-1 fee, which is paid to the registered representative selling the mutual fund to the customer. FINRA limits the amount of 12b-1 fees that can be assessed on Class A shares to 8.5%. In reality, most mutual funds charge significantly less than the 8.5% amount.

Class B shares also have an upfront load, just like Class A shares. However, this upfront sales charge is not paid immediately like in Class A shares. Class B shares have a contingent deferred sales charge ("CDSC") attached to them. A contingent deferred sales charge applies to shares sold within a specific time period from initial purchase, thereby encouraging longer term holdings. The longer the shares are held when subsequently sold, the lower the CDSC. Class B shares are typically used by customers who have long investment horizon and are unable to meet breakpoint thresholds. CDSC can also be referred to as a surrender charge. 12b-1 fees are also assessed on Class B shares and are typically higher than the fees assessed on Class A shares.

Class C shares have no upfront sales charge at all. Instead, Class C shares have higher annual fees when compared to Class A or B shares. To deter customers from immediately selling after purchase, Class C shares may have a CDSC feature attached to them, thereby charging a fee if Class C shares are sold 'too soon'. Class C shares are typically best used when a customer has a short investment horizon.

When recommending mutual funds to clients, registered representatives have an obligation to put clients into the lowest cost mutual fund share class.

Breakpoints are offered by Mutual Fund Families as a way to reward investors who choose to invest more and more money within the Mutual Fund Family. Think of breakpoints as a 'bulk buying' discount – the more you buy, the more you save in mutual fund fees. The line where the customer saves money on fees is the breakpoint. A prohibited breakpoint sale would occur if the broker sold a customer a mutual fund in a different Mutual Fund Family for the purpose of avoiding the breakpoint savings to the customer.

Review Figure 28. The breakpoints occur at $5,000, $10,000 and $20,000. As you invest money beyond those breakpoints, you notice that the fees charged to the customer decrease. There is no difference in the investment, only in the fees paid by the customer. If a customer invested $3,000, they would pay .57% per year to the mutual fund company for holding the investment. If the investor purchased $5,500 of mutual funds in the same mutual fund family, their mutual fund fee would be .50%.

Industry rules[32] allow firms to accept a Letter of Intent from a customer, indicating that they intend to purchase additional mutual fund shares within the next 13 months. This Letter of Intent allows the customer to benefit from the lower costs at a higher breakpoint. In our example above, an investor purchased $3,000 worth of mutual funds. If that same investor signed a Letter of Intent to purchase another $2,000 worth of mutual funds in the same family during the next quarter, that investor would only be charged .50% instead of the .57% mutual fund fee. The breakpoints will vary between mutual fund families, but will add up over time – every dollar not paid in fees goes into the investor's pocket as part of their total return.

Customers may choose to sign a Letter of Intent (LOI) in order to take advantage of mutual fund breakpoints. A LOI indicates that the customer intends to purchase additional shares in the mutual fund over the next 13 months. By having an LOI in place, the customer is entitled to receive the (lower) sales charge at the level which assumes are purchases are made as intended.

With LOIs and Rights of Accumulation (ROA), it is important to have a thorough understanding of mutual fund breakpoints. LOI's deal with potential future purchases. ROAs deal with purchases occurring in real time. For instance, if a customer wants to purchase additional shares of a mutual fund within the same fund family, that customer is allowed to add their existing holdings to their current purchases, and if the total accumulation exceeds a breakpoint, that customer is entitled to receive the lower charge on the entire purchase, not just the amount of purchase above the breakpoint.

Figure 28: Example Mutual Fund Breakpoints

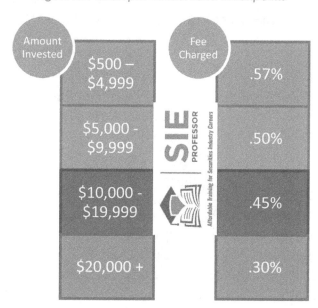

A mutual fund with a load means that there is a fee attached to the purchase or sale of that mutual fund. A no-load mutual fund means that there is no fee attached to the purchase or sale of the mutual fund. Loads can be front-loaded (at purchase) or back loaded (at sale). Just because a mutual fund is no-load does not mean that there are zero expenses charged. Other expenses can be charged, such as maintenance fees or 12b-1 fees (which are capped at no more than 25 basis points for no-load funds). All fees must be disclosed in the mutual fund's prospectus. No-fee mutual funds do exist, primarily in an account structure that does not charge commissions.

NAV

NAV, or Net Asset Value refers to the calculated value of all assets held within the mutual fund, divided by the number of shares. Purchases and sales of mutual funds are typically made at NAV. NAV is set for the day once the market closes at 4pm ET. Market timing is a prohibited activity pertaining to mutual funds. All orders for mutual funds must typically be placed prior to the market close or 4pm Eastern Time. Orders placed before this cutoff time are typically filled at the price available after the market close. Market timing refers to placing orders in mutual funds after the market close, then receiving the price calculated at the market close. Why is this a problem? Well, if you know how the market did that day, you can make an educated guess as to whether the mutual fund you are interested in purchasing or selling has an increased or decreased NAV. Market timing is illegal because it provides an unfair advantage to the individual wanting to buy tomorrow's mutual fund at today's prices! Therefore, once an order is placed to purchase an open-end investment company's shares, the purchase price is based on the next calculated NAV.

Types of Mutual Funds

There are three types of mutual funds that should be familiar. These include:
1. Target Date Funds
2. Index Funds
3. Actively Managed Funds

Mutual funds can have a variety of securities contained in them, or even just one type. In the securities industry, mutual funds are typically organized into three categories – equity, fixed income, and blended. An equity-focused mutual fund can be an index fund, a REIT-focused fund, or any other type of fund that solely focuses on equity securities. A fixed income fund follows a similar path. Fixed income mutual funds contain only fixed income securities – municipal bonds, government bonds, or corporate bonds are common, as are 'short term' and 'long term' bond mutual funds that buy bonds with shorter or longer maturities. A blended fund contains both equity and fixed income securities. A good example of a blended fund is a target date fund, described below. Some mutual funds may also hold non-U.S. securities. Like their U.S. counterparts, non-U.S. securities can be equities or fixed income as well. Their country of origin – where their listing exchange is located or where the company issuing the debt is located will be outside of the U.S. If the mutual fund invests in non-U.S. securities, this will be listed in the Prospectus.

Target Date Funds

Target date funds are created for *people who need money at specific ages*. They are common in retirement account plans. For instance, a Target Date Fund for 2050 would be intended for an individual who wants to retire in 2050 when they reach the age of 65. If the current year is 2020, that means someone around the age of 35 might be interested in purchasing this target date fund. The closer the current date is to the Target date, the more conservative the blended fund becomes – shifting from primarily equities to primarily fixed income securities (but still containing both). Target date funds are appealing because they alter their investment mix over time, gradually becoming more and more conservative as time progresses toward the year 2050. At the onset the target date fund would invest primarily in equity securities.

Index Funds

Mutual funds that attempt to track the performance of a specific index, by purchasing the same group of underlying securities, are referred to as index funds. In many cases, investing in index funds is a form of passive investment. The mutual fund manager does not add new securities to the mutual fund or remove other securities from the mutual fund on a regular basis because the list of what the mutual fund holds is really determined by the index the mutual fund follows. For instance, if a mutual fund's purpose is to track a REIT index, the manager is not deciding to add a non-REIT security like Apple, nor would the mutual fund manager add a REIT not listed in the specific REIT index.   An index fund is typically a low-turnover fund, meaning the underlying securities in the fund are not bought and sold, or turned over, on a frequent basis. A common index fund is one that tracks the S&P 500 or other popular index. As a result of this type of passive management, an index fund will often have lower management fees when compared to an actively managed fund.

Actively Managed Funds

While index funds are often considered to be passively managed, actively managed mutual funds take a different approach. Instead of being mandated to closely follow the makeup of an index, an actively managed fund has more freedom to invest in securities that the mutual fund manager thinks offer an appropriate return.   This freedom allows the active fund manager to change strategies or take large positions inside the fund that would normally not be permitted in a passive fund. Actively managed funds invest in the same types of securities that passively managed funds do.   In most cases, actively managed funds have higher costs than do passively managed funds.

Closed End Funds

Open end funds and closed end funds have many similarities, including the pooling or sharing of investor resources to hire an investment manager and the ability to invest in a wide range of securities. Closed end funds have several important characteristics that distinguish them from other types of investment companies:

- Owning a closed end fund means that you own shares of the closed end fund, *not the underlying assets* (those inside the closed end fund).

- There is a *fixed amount of shares of closed end funds* that does not typically change over time.
- *Shares in the closed end fund are typically sold through the IPO process* to public investors.
- *The price of the closed end fund shares post-IPO is determined by the secondary market.* The price of the shares can go up or down just like any other type of investment.
- Although the closed end fund has a net asset value (NAV), *the price of the closed end fund shares trading in the secondary market are often higher or lower than the NAV.*
- *Closed end funds do not constantly sell shares to investors* who want to buy more shares in the closed end fund. Investors wanting to purchase new shares of the closed end fund must purchase those shares in the secondary market.
- *Closed end funds are subject to SEC registration* and regulation under the Investment Company Act of 1940, but also the Securities Act of 1933 and the Securities Exchange Act of 1934.
- *Shares in closed end funds may be listed on U.S. Stock Exchanges* such as NYSE or Nasdaq, or in over the counter markets. Shares in open end funds are not listed on U.S. Stock Exchanges or over the counter markets and are only traded after the NAV is set post market close – 4pm ET. Orders to buy or sell open end funds use the next calculated NAV as the redemption price.
- *Redemption value is the next NAV after the order is received.* Customers do not get the old NAV when buying or selling, they get the next NAV.

Figure 29: Closed and Open End Funds

Category	Closed End	Open End
Share Count	Fixed number of shares	Continuously offer shares
Prospectus	Prospectus for IPO only	Always sold by prospectus
Market Type	Secondary market only	No secondary trading
When to Buy or Sell	Typically during market hours	Order placed before market close
Price to Buy or Sell	Market price (not NAV)	Typically NAV
Assets Invested	All security types	All security types
Fees	Commission	Various fees depending on share class

Unit Investments Trusts

In a mutual fund, the securities held by the mutual fund can be changed over time, either because the index that the mutual fund seeks to mimic changes in the case on an index fund, or in the case of an active fund, the mutual fund manager decides to buy or sell specific securities. A UIT is most similar then to a closed end fund, in that both a UIT and a closed end fund have a fixed investment portfolio that does not change. Unlike a closed end fund however, a UIT has a finite life. At the onset of the UIT, the investor knows exactly how long the UIT will exist. When the UIT reaches maturity or the end of its life, the underlying assets within the UIT are sold and the principal is returned to the owners/investors.

Annuities

A variable annuity is a tax-deferred product that is often used by retired individuals or those seeking a steady stream of income. An upfront sum or series of payments is invested and used to purchase the annuity. An annuity begins paying to the annuitant (annuity holder) immediately, or at some future date. The assets inside the annuity generate an investment return, which is then passed along to the annuity holder at the agreed upon date. The annuity itself is a contract between the annuitant and an insurance company. An annuity may last a set period of years or until the death of one individual, or an individual and their spouse/partner.

Generally speaking, there are three types of annuities:
1. **Fixed annuities** earn a fixed rate of interest initially, and then pay out a prescribed amount to the annuitant once a specific date in the annuity contract has been reached.
2. **Variable annuities** have a range of potential returns, depending on the performance of the underlying investments. *Any product with a variable interest rate component is going to have an inherent interest rate risk, as the interest rate is designed to move!* A variable annuity will typically invest in mutual funds, which of course have a wide range of returns. Given the annuity returns are driven in part by how the underlying investments perform, market risk is the greatest risk facing a variable annuity. Because an investor is taking risk (the variable part of the annuity as opposed to a fixed annuity), the returns but also the risk are typically higher for these types of products. The returns earned on a variable annuity vary greatly, as well as the periodic dollars paid out to the annuitant. However, the securities inside the variable annuity are exactly the same as those you may find in mutual funds, closed end companies, or UITs. Many variable annuities have both floor and ceiling returns, meaning that the company selling the variable annuity will pay a return to the investor no lower than the minimum (or floor), and no higher than the maximum (or ceiling). An investor often seeks out this type of annuity to remove some of the risk of unpredictability from the returns instead of investing in the market directly.

3. **Index annuities** are similar to variable annuities, but instead of a wider range of mutual fund investments inside the annuity, the annuity only invests in index funds. Given the annuity returns are driven in part by how the underlying index performs, market risk is the greatest risk facing an index annuity.

What determines the price of an annuity?

The type of annuity purchased determines, in part, the payment amount made the annuitant. An immediate annuity, or an annuity that begins to pay the annuitant right away, will typically be more expensive and or offer smaller payouts, because the investments have not had any time to grow.

The age and sex of the annuitant have an impact on the payment amounts due to life and health expectancy differences (i.e. women live longer than men on average). The longer someone is expected to live, the greater the amount the insurance company will need to pay out.

Common Characteristics of Annuities
- **Periodic payments** – Annuities make periodic payments to the annuitant once the annuity reaches the agreed upon date in the annuity contract.
- **Death benefit** – Many annuities offer a death benefit if the annuitant dies while the annuity is still active.
- **Tax deferred** - Any gains are not taxed until they are withdrawn from the account, as long as withdrawals are not made until after 59 1/2. Like many retirement vehicles, a variable annuity holder is assessed a 10% penalty if they withdrawals money from the variable annuity prior to the age of 59 1/2. Payouts of an investment in a nonqualified annuity are not typically income tax free.

For all of the benefits of annuities, they often have much higher fees in comparison to other investment products, such as index mutual funds. In addition, capital gains for variable annuities are taxed as ordinary income, which can be materially higher for some investors, depending upon their income.

End of Chapter Quiz

Complete these end of chapter questions to assess your understanding of the subject matter discussed in this chapter. The answers follow on the next page. For those questions you have answered incorrectly, review the appropriate section of the chapter again to make sure you understand the concepts.

1. A no-load mutual fund means there is no:
    a. fee paid by the investor
    b. upfront fee paid by the investor
    c. Dividends paid by the mutual fund
    d. Annual fee paid by the investor

2. Which of the following is TRUE about open-end funds?
    a. Open end funds have a fixed number of shares
    b. Open end funds only invest in one type of security
    c. Open end funds are also known as mutual funds
    d. Open end funds are bought and sold 2.5% above NAV

3. Which of the following best describes Letter of Intent:
    a. A written acknowledgement signed by an investor, with the investor promising to follow all industry rules.
    b. A document informing an investor about how NAV works.
    c. A written indication provided by the investor to purchase a set number of mutual fund shares in the future.
    d. A signed authorization by the investor promising to repay borrowed funds.

4. A target date fund may be useful for an investor who:
    a. has a short term investing time horizon
    b. is looking to increase their risk over time
    c. only wants to maintain exposure to the equity markets
    d. wants to decrease risk exposure over time

5. Which of the following is true regarding a closed-end company?
    a. Must redeem shares with the closed end company upon sale
    b. Price determined by supply and demand
    c. A prospectus is always required to be sent to new purchasers
    d. There is a continuous offering of shares

6. Which of the following is true regarding Class C Mutual Fund shares?
    a. They have no upfront sales charge.
    b. They may have a deferred sales charge.
    c. They have no fees charged at all.
    d. They always have 12b-1 fees assessed.

7. A term used to describe the decrease in mutual fund expenses as you invest more money within the same mutual fund family over certain thresholds.
    a. NAV
    b. Letter of Intent
    c. Breakpoint
    d. Net Transactions

8. Which of the following typically trades at NAV?
    a. Open end fund
    b. Closed end fund
    c. UIT
    d. Variable annuity

9. Which of the following statements is true regarding an open-end company?
    a. There is a fixed number of shares
    b. Traded on the secondary market
    c. No prospectus after the IPO
    d. Issue common shares only

10. Which type of investment company has a finite life established at creation?
    a. Open end fund
    b. Closed end fund
    c. UIT
    d. Variable annuity

End of Chapter Quiz Answers

1. B

Dividends paid by the mutual fund have nothing to do with whether a mutual fund is a no-load fund. No-load funds have no upfront sales or commission charges, or fees paid by the investor. Investor pay be charged annual fees, but those are not considered loads.

2. C

Open end funds are bought and sold at NAV. Open end funds are also known as mutual funds. Open end funds do not have a fixed number of shares and invest in many types of securities.

3. C

A Letter of Intent is used to signal that the investor intends to purchase additional mutual fund shares in the next 13 months, thereby receiving potential lower fees (breakpoints). NAV is covered in the prospectus. A Letter of Intent does not deal with borrowing funds.

4. D

Target date funds typically decrease their equity exposure over time, while also increasing their fixed income exposure. This decreases overall market risk. Target date funds would not be appropriate for short term investors - they are intended for long term investors.

5. B

Closed end fund shares can be sold to other investors. Open end funds can only be sold back to the open end fund company. Closed end companies do not trade at NAV, but instead trade at the market price of the shares. A prospectus is only required to be sent in the closed end fund company's IPO. A closed end company only offers shares on a specific date, not continuously.

6. B
Class C Mutual Fund shares may have a deferred sales charged attached to them. The fee structures of mutual funds are laid out in the mutual fund prospectus. Class C mutual fund shares will typically have some type of fee charged, but this fee does not always include 12b-1 fees.

7. C
A breakpoint is a series of thresholds that once exceeded, lowers the expenses on the mutual fund. This is an incentive structure to investors that encourages them to invest more and spreads the cost out over larger and larger positions. NAV is Net Asset Value, or the on paper worth of the collection of assets inside the mutual fund. Letter of intent is the written indication by the customer that the customer will purchase additional shares of the mutual fund over the next 13 months.

8. A
Of the choices, only open end funds trade at NAV, or Net Asset Value. Closed end funds typically trade above or below NAV. Variable annuities by themselves are traded in the secondary market and therefore NAV is irrelevant from this perspective.

9. D
An open end company only issues common equity shares, with no preferred share options offered. The remaining choices are all characteristics of closed-end companies.

10. C
A UIT often has a finite life attached to it at creation, meaning at some point determined when created, the UIT will cease to exist. Open end and closed end funds exist for so long as the companies that create the funds want them to remain open.

Chapter 8: College Savings Accounts

Saving money for college is not exactly a new concept. Parents, grandparents, aunts, uncles, and even the students themselves have saved for college for decades. There are three main types of college savings accounts addressed on the SIE Exam:
1. Coverdell Education Savings Accounts
2. 529 Plans   3. ABLE accounts

Each of these types of college savings plans has unique benefits and features. It is important that you understand the differences between each of the college savings account types. These primary vehicles by which people can save for college have not changed much over the last 20+ years. Coverdell Education Savings Accounts ("Coverdell ESA") have been around in some form since being established by the Taxpayer Relief Act in 1997. 529 Plans were established by Congress in 1996 and refer to the section of the IRS code where the legal description resides. Both 529 Plans and the Coverdell ESAs were established to help families pay for the rising costs of college by using the tax code to their advantage[33]. Both 529 Plans and Coverdell ESAs allow funds invested for college in either of the college savings plans to grow on a tax advantaged basis. The specific rules and regulations that apply individually to each type of college savings account determine the amount and level of the tax advantaged savings.

Coverdell Education Savings Accounts

These accounts were originally referred to as Education IRAs, but were renamed Coverdell Education Savings Accounts after their primary champion, Senator Paul Coverdell who pushed legislation to expand their usefulness.

Like a 529 Plan, a Coverdell ESA is an account that can help save for future college expenses. An ESA can be opened up with any broker-dealer firm in the securities industry, just like opening up an individual, joint, IRA, or other account type. One of the big differences with a Coverdell ESA is it can also be used to pay for qualified elementary, middle school, and high school educational expenses. The account is established for the sole benefit of the child, with a responsible adult making investment decisions for the child's Coverdell ESA account. The responsible adult is not considered the custodian of the Coverdell ESA account. The Coverdell ESA custodian is most typically the bank or brokerage firm that opened up the account, or in the case of the brokerage firm, that brokerage firm's clearing firm.

The contributions to a Coverdell ESA are limited to $2,000 per beneficiary in a calendar year and can be made by anyone, not just the beneficiary's parent or guardian. The beneficiary can even make the contributions to their own account. Contributions made into the Coverdell ESA grow income tax free. When the funds are withdrawn and used for a qualified educational expense, they are exempt from federal and likely state taxes. There is no upfront tax deduction on contributions. However, there are income limits on who can contribute to the account – no one is permitted to contribute to a Coverdell ESA if their income exceeds certain thresholds.

Coverdell ESA contributions are not revocable and must also be for the sole benefit of the child. Should a beneficiary choose to not use their Coverdell ESA funds for qualified educational expenses, or if they still have funds in the ESA when they turn 30 years old, the IRS (as well potentially the states) impose a 10% penalty plus income tax on the growth in the account. This is an incentive to use the assets in the account for qualified educational expenses. To avoid the tax and penalty that would come due for a beneficiary once they reach the age of 30, that beneficiary may transfer some or all of the account assets to a younger sibling. This would allow the beneficiary to avoid paying taxes and penalties on the assets and help out their younger sibling in the process. The downside of course is that the original beneficiary loses the assets – once transferred, they become the property of the new beneficiary.

One of the key differences that a Coverdell ESA account has with a 529 account is that the investments are self-directed and not sold by an advisor or predetermined by a fund manager. This means that the responsible adult can choose the investments made in the account – mutual funds, bonds, stocks, options, etc... The self-directed nature of the investment selection is one of the primary distinctions between 529's and ESA's. In a 529 account, the responsible adult making investment selections chooses between one or a few investment funds. The 529 plan does not allow for investment in individual securities (stocks, bonds, options, etc...). Assets remaining in the Coverdell ESA must be used by the beneficiary by the time that beneficiary reaches the age of 30. The IRS has published a good resource on Coverdell ESA accounts that students should read through for additional information[34].

529 Plans

There are two primary types of 529 plans: prepaid tuition plans and savings plans[35]. The term 529 Plan was named after the IRS code that created the plans[36].

Prepaid tuition plans operate as you might suspect based upon their name. The investor pre-pays all or a portion of tuition at a point in time prior to the student using the funds. This prepayment locks in the student tuition rates as of the date that the prepayment is made. If tuition prices go up between the time the prepayment is made and the time that the student enrolls in the college, the student does not pay any additional funds. Either of these plans can be purchased through an advisor or can be purchased directly by the investor through the various state 529 Plan websites. Each state typically has their own plan, which is third party administered.

Figure 30: 529 Plan Characteristics

Prepaid Tuition Plan	Savings Plans
Locks in tuition rate	No impact on future tuition rates
No specific investment choices made	Investments made into choices pre-selected by investment manager
Account owner is not typically the student/minor	Account owner is not typically the student/minor
potential state tax deductibility of contributions	Potential state tax deductibility of contributions
Use of funds are limited to specific expenses	Use of funds are limited to specific expenses
Penalty applied to funds used for improper expenses, plus the funds are subject to income taxes	Penalty applied to funds used for improper expenses, plus the funds are subject to income taxes

The account owner is usually the parent or guardian of the beneficiary, or prospective future student who will use the funds. In this way, the parent as a legal adult can make investment decisions on behalf of the prospective future student, who is typically a minor when the 529 Plan is established. The beneficiary will get to use those funds for higher education purposes. Some 529 plan accounts are established by an account owner individual who is not the beneficiary's guardian, like a grandparent, aunt or uncle.

529 Plans have several tax advantages that make them attractive to both parents and future post high school students. First, contributions made to a 529 Plan account may be tax deductible on the contributor's state tax return for the year in which the contribution is made. Not all states allow the contribution to be deducted from state taxes, and the states that do allow the deduction have different dollar limits per state per year. Second, contributions made to a 529 Plan account grow tax free while in the account. There is no federal tax deductibility for 529 Plan contributions of any kind. However, each state does set their own annual contribution limits, so different 529 Plans will have different contribution limits.   529 plans are subject to gift tax limits,

meaning potential contributors are limited to the IRS gift limit of $15,000 in 2020. Contributions made above this amount are subject to IRS gift taxes, generally keeping borrowing below this threshold. The IRS does allow a contributor to a 529 plan to bunch up to 5 years of contributions in a single year, meaning someone could contribute $75,000 in one year ($15,000 x 5 years), and then make no additional contributions for the remaining 4 years and not be subject to the gift tax.

If 529 plan assets are withdrawn from the account and used for non-eligible expenses, the amount withdrawn is taxed as ordinary income plus a 10% penalty. A firm's registered representative who works with their customers on college funding options should be careful when making recommendations about specific state 529 plans. Given that 529 Plan contributions are not federally tax deductible; there is no federal income tax component here in the year the contribution is made. However, a registered representative should note that a contribution made to a customer's resident state 529 Plan may come with the added benefit of state income tax deductibility up to a point for the customer making the contribution. Other factors, such as the rights of an account beneficiary to control the 529 Plan assets at the age of majority would play no role in the recommendation of a specific 529 Plan. This would only matter if the question was whether to contribute to any 529 Plan at all!

Both Coverdell ESA and 529 Plan assets may only be used for higher education purposes at eligible educations institutions. Some examples of legitimate uses of Coverdell ESA and 529 Plan funds include:

- Tuition
- Books
- Fees
- Supplies and equipment necessary for school
- Room and board (with limitations for off campus housing)
- Computers for educational purposes

ABLE Accounts

Achieving a Better Life Experience ("ABLE") accounts are tax-advantaged savings accounts created for the benefit of individuals with disabilities. Established under Section 529A of the IRS codes, these accounts work exactly like other 529 accounts do. ABLE accounts can only be funded up to a maximum of $15,000 per year from all contributors. ABLE accounts can be established for anyone with a qualifying disability, if that qualifying disability has established prior to the beneficiary's 26th birthday. Only one ABLE account can be established per beneficiary. If the proceeds from the account are used for qualifying disability expenses, such as medical treatment, special needs transportation, assistive technology, transportation, or other qualifying disability expenses, there are no adverse tax implications or penalties. However, if ABLE account funds are used for non-qualified purchases, the beneficiary will have to pay income taxes and a 10% penalty on the funds.

Figure 31: Comparison of Education Accounts

Coverdell ESA's

Can be used to pay for qualified elementary + secondary education + college expenses

Contributions are prohibited above modified adjusted gross income of $110k individual/$220k joint

Investments are self-directed within the account, grow tax free and are not taxable when withdrawn if used for qualified education expenses or before age 30

No federal or state tax deduction on the contributions to the account

Contributions are limited to $2000 per year

529 Plans

Can be used to pay for qualified elementary + secondary education + college expenses

There are no income based limits , but gifts above the IRS gift tax of $15k/year is subjec to gift tax

Investments within the account grow tax free and are not taxable when withdrawn if used for qualified education expenses

Although no federal tax deductions exist, many states offer a residents a tax deduction on contributions to the state 529

Investment choices are not self-directed and instead but be selected from the list of options in the fund

Contribution limits are set by each state.

A quick note about municipal fund securities. Under industry definitions, 529 plans, Local Government Investment Pools, and ABLE accounts are considered municipal fund securities. LGIPs were covered in Chapter 5 and should not be forgotten in this context. It is important to know what types of investments are under the heading of municipal fund securities.

End of Chapter Quiz

Complete these end of chapter questions to assess your understanding of the subject matter discussed in this chapter. The answers follow on the next page. For those questions you have answered incorrectly, review the appropriate section of the chapter again to make sure you understand the concepts.

1. Which type of savings plan typically does not allow the purchase and sale of individual equity securities?
    a. Coverdell ESA
    b. 529 Plan
    c. UGMA/UTMA
    d. ABLE Accounts

2. Which of the following statement is true about 529 Plans?
    a. 529 Plans do not limit the ability to contribute based on income.
    b. 529 Plans offer a wider array of investment choices when compared to Coverdell ESA's.
    c. There are no restrictions on what proceeds from a 529 Plan can be used to pay for.
    d. Only direct sales of 520 Plans are permitted; sales through a financial advisor are not permitted.

3. Qualified expenses reimbursable from a 529 plan include:
    a. Transportation expenses
    b. Student loan repayment
    c. Insurance
    d. Computer

4. The individual who makes investment decisions on behalf of a minor's 529 Plan is known as:
    a. Custodian
    b. Beneficiary
    c. Contributor
    d. Owner

5. The maximum amount that can be contributed to a Coverdell ESA in a given calendar year is:
    a. $1,000
    b. $2,000
    c. $3,000
    d. $4,000

6. Proceeds from Education Savings Accounts, if used for qualified educational expenses are considered:
    a. Tax deferred
    b. Tax free
    c. Tax deductible
    d. Tax credit

7. Your rich uncle started a 529 Plan for you when you were born, investing $50,000 in the plan. The 529 Plan balance has now grown to $100,000 as you plan to enter college in the fall. If you use the $100,000 balance for qualified education expenses, what are the tax implications of withdrawing the money from the 529 Plan?
    a. You will be taxed only on the gain of $50,000 in the account
    b. You will be taxed on the entire $100,000 balance in the account
    c. No tax because you did not make the contribution
    d. No tax because you are using the proceeds for qualified expenses

8. Withdrawing funds from an Education Savings Account for non-qualified education expense causes which of the following:
    a. 10% penalty + proceeds taxed as earned income
    b. 10% penalty + proceeds taxed as capital gains
    c. 20% penalty + proceeds taxed as earned income
    d. 20% penalty + proceeds taxed as capital gains

9. Assets held inside a Coverdell ESA must be used by the beneficiary's:
    a. 18th birthday
    b. 25th birthday
    c. 29th birthday
    d. 30th birthday

10. A Coverdell ESA must be opened prior to the beneficiary's:
    a. 18th birthday
    b. 25th birthday
    c. 29th birthday
    d. 30th birthday

End of Chapter Quiz Answers

1. B
Some 529 Plans are invested in equity securities, but account holders cannot buy and sell individual equity securities. Investors can purchase individual equity securities through Coverdell ESAs, UGMA/UTMAs, and ABLE Accounts.

2. A
There is no income limit on 529 Plan contributions. There is an income limit on ESA contributions. Coverdell ESA's provide a wider choice of investments when compared to 529 Plans. 529 Plan proceeds can only be used to pay for qualified education expenses, as defined by the IRS. Both direct and indirect sales of 529 Plans are permitted to investors.

3. D
Of the available choices, only a computer would be a qualified education expense. The other options are not considered qualified education expenses.

4. D
A contributor could be the individual who makes investment decisions, but these roles may be filled by different individuals. The account owner makes the investment decisions. An account owner could also be a contributor or beneficiary, but technically these roles and their level of authority are separate. The beneficiary may be a minor, or even if not a minor, is not typically the account owner. The custodian does not typically make investment decisions. Their responsibility is to hold the assets/account.

5. B
The maximum amount that can be contributed to a Coverdell ESA is $2,000.

6. B

Proceeds from an ESA when used for qualified educational expenses are considered tax free. Tax deferral means that you may taxes later. ESAs do not have a tax deductible feature associated with them, although 529 Account contributions may be tax deductible for some states.

7. D

Similar to an ESA, a 529 plan's proceeds, if used for qualified educational expenses, are free of taxes. If the 529 plans proceeds were used for non-qualified education expenses, taxes would need to be paid on the gains in the account, plus any fees.

8. A

Using proceeds from an ESA or a 529 plan for non-qualified education expenses will result in a 10% penalty plus having the proceeds taxed as earned income. This is meant to discourage anyone from using education accounts for non-qualified expenses.

9. D

Assets held inside a Coverdell ESA must be used by the beneficiary's 30th birthday. A Coverdell ESA must be opened prior to the beneficiary's 18th birthday.

10. A

Assets held inside a Coverdell ESA must be used by the beneficiary's 30th birthday. A Coverdell ESA must be opened prior to the beneficiary's 18th birthday.

Chapter 9: Other Products

By now, you should be familiar with the core securities products available to investors in the securities industry.   Equities, fixed income, options, and mutual funds are certainly the four main types of investments that can be made and are certainly the most popular and well known for retail investors.   There are however, several other types of products available to securities industry investors, depending on their specific needs.   Note however, that some of these other products function in very similar fashion to products like mutual funds that we have already discussed.   For the SIE Exam, you should be familiar enough with these other products that you can recognize their characteristics and contrast them with other securities products.

Direct Participation Programs (DPPs)

DPPs, or direct participation programs are one type of alternative investments available primarily to retail investors. In a DPP structure, the DPP itself is not publicly traded. The DPP entity instead invests in a wide range of investments, most typically in sectors such as real estate and energy. The DPP offers investors exposure to non-correlated assets with steady returns. The DPP owner does not get to determine the specific investments made by the DPP however – those decisions are made by the DPP manager. Similar to hedge funds, DPPs are considered illiquid investments, as the DPP owner is not permitted to buy and sell whenever they would like as you would with owning 100 shares of a publicly traded stock, such as Apple. In fact, this is often a big factor that makes DPPs attractive to investors; DPP returns do not often follow the broader equity markets, meaning DPPs and the equity market are considered non-correlated. DPPs also often have a finite life to them of 5-15 years and aim for steady returns, which are additional distinguishing characteristics from other types of securities like equities.   DPPs include non-publicly traded REITs, non-publicly traded Business Development Corporations (BDCs), oil and gas royalty/tax deduction programs, and equipment leasing programs. To invest in a DPP, an investor must typically have a net worth above a certain threshold as established by the DPP and state requirements. Like a hedge fund, a DPP is often structured using an LLC. The LLC's tax benefits refer to 'pass through' tax treatment, meaning gains and losses incurred by the hedge fund are passed through to owners. Why is this important?   In other corporate structure, profits can be taxed twice – once at the corporate level, and another time at the ownership level. This pass through tax treatment minimizes taxes paid by the owners.
Another DPP structure includes Tenants in Common (TIC). In a TIC DPP structure, each DPP owner is consider a TIC with all other owners. This means that they own a proportion share of the DPP commensurate with their original purchase.

Partnership structures can also be used with DPPs. In many cases, a partnership structure is used for oil and gas investments. The DPP partnership may own either the entire real estate where the oil and gas is located, or they may just own the royalty rights to the oil and gas extracted from the real estate itself.   Given the royalty payments, oil and gas investments can be creative ways to generate income for investors.

Real Estate Investment Trusts

Real Estate Investment Trusts or REITs (pronounced 'Reets') are closed end investment companies that must invest in some form of real estate. The REIT does not need to be directly invested in physical real estate. REITs are a way for investors to invest indirectly into the real estate sector. In a REIT, investors purchase direct ownership in the REIT itself. The REIT then uses those funds to purchase income-producing real estate – apartment complexes, single family homes, commercial properties, mortgages, data centers, and storage facilities – anything and everything that deals with real estate and produces income. There are generally three types of REITs – equity, mortgage, and hybrid. An equity REIT invests in actual real estate. Mortgage REITs invest in mortgages on real estate. A hybrid REIT invests in both equity and mortgages.

Unlike other corporate structures, REITs are required to pay out at least 90% of profits to shareholders. The structure provides tax advantaged income without double taxation. In other types of corporate structures, the company pays taxes to the government, and the shareholder pays taxes to the government on any investment proceeds received, either through dividends and capital appreciations when the investment is sold. Since REITs are required to pay out 90% of their profits, the REIT receives favorable tax treatment in exchange for this provision. The REIT itself does not pay taxes, only the REIT owners do.

The REIT collects rent from those entities or individuals using the real estate pursuant to a leasing agreement. The REIT passes along all profits back to the REIT owners after all expensed have been taken care of – paying off loans taken out to acquire the real estate, management fees, marketing expenses, etc. REITs are not typically permitted to purchase real estate for the primary purpose of capital appreciation. All REITs operate basically the same way. However, there are a few nuances that you should be aware of when studying REITs.

REITs can be either publicly traded or privately held. When publicly traded, REITs can be listed and traded on exchanges just like Apple (symbol APPL) or Coca Cola (symbol KO) or in the OTC market. This often classifies them alongside equity securities. Equities represent an ownership in a company. REITs are just a different company ownership structure. Private REITs present a bigger hurdle for retail investors, as information about how the REIT operates and its past financial performance is not available to the general public. Further, a REIT can be registered with the SEC, but not publically traded. These types of REITs are called a non-traded REIT.

Figure 32: REIT Types

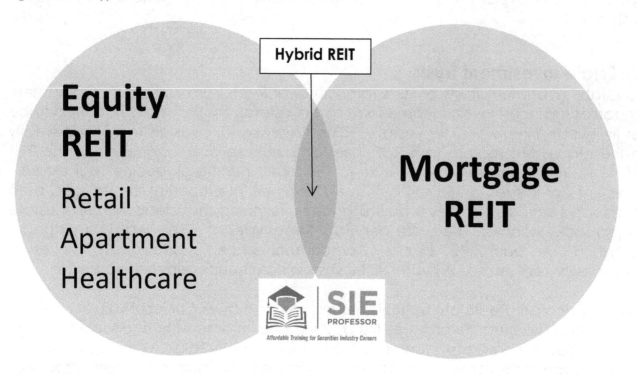

According to the SEC[37], a REIT must also:

1. Be an entity that would be taxable as a corporation but for its REIT status;
2. Be managed by a board of directors or trustees;
3. Have shares that are fully transferable;
4. Have a minimum of 100 shareholders after its first year as a REIT;
5. Have no more than 50 percent of its shares held by five or fewer individuals during the last half of the taxable year;
6. Invest at least 75 percent of its total assets in real estate assets and cash;
7. Derive at least 75 percent of its gross income from real estate related sources, including rents from real property and interest on mortgages financing real property;
8. Derive at least 95 percent of its gross income from such real estate sources and dividends or interest from any source; and
9. Have no more than 25 percent of its assets consist of non-qualifying securities or stock in taxable REIT subsidiaries.

Now that you have a thorough understanding of REITs, let's move on to another type of product you may have heard about – hedge funds.

Hedge Funds

Hedge funds are simply a different type of investment vehicle that are typically used by very wealthy individuals. Most hedge funds will have some minimum investment amount to participate in the hedge fund. Hedge funds typically require their investors to attest to many things to invest, including their high level of financial sophistication, minimum levels and assets and/or income, and that the potential investor/customer understands that they are not permitted to withdrawal funds outside of predefined time periods.

Hedge funds typically have some type of lock-up provision in their agreements with the hedge fund owners. The lock-up provisions typically restrict the fund owner's ability to sell out of their ownership stake in the hedge fund during certain periods of time, both at the initial investment and thereafter. Due to these limitations, hedge funds are considered illiquid investments. Think of hedge funds as very similar in structure and purpose to non-passive mutual funds. Like a mutual fund, a hedge fund pools cash together to purchase a basket of underlying assets – equities, fixed income, commodities (gold, silver), real estate, etc.

Although there can be varying types of hedge fund structures, a common structure has the hedge fund set up as a general partnership. In a general partnership, there are two primary entities – the general partner, and the limited partners. The general partner makes decisions on how the partnership, in this case a hedge fund, is run. The limited partners do not run the hedge fund day to day, but put up the capital to fund the hedge fund. For domestic individuals (U.S. citizens and investors) a limited liability company can be established as the fund's general partner. The LLC structure provides tax benefits and legal protections to the funds owners and managers. The LLC's tax benefits refer to 'pass through' tax treatment, meaning gains and losses incurred by the hedge fund are passed through to owners. Why is this important? In other corporate structure, profits can be taxed twice – once at the corporate level, and another time at the ownership level. This pass through tax treatment minimizes taxes paid by the owners.

Hedge funds typically charge different types of fees, including management fees and performance fees. Management fees are charged regardless of performance and go to support the ongoing expenses of running the fund – salaries, equipment, offices, etc. Performance fees are only charged if the hedge fund makes money. In a typical arrangement, the hedge fund manager keeps 20% of the gains that the hedge fund makes, with the remaining 80% of the gains being split proportionally between the hedge fund owners.

One note about hedge funds and private equity funds, terms that sometimes used interchangeably, but are in fact very different. Both are considered illiquid investments that are only available to high net worth income individuals. Hedge funds are viewed as more short term, immediate return investments. Private equity instead takes a longer view and invests in companies with a view towards playing a role in their management and oversight. Private equity looks out over the time horizon and expects to own the companies in which they invest for a significant period of time.

Hedge funds are more likely to move in and out of securities positions quickly to capture gains or avoid losses.

Exchange Traded Products (ETPs)[38]

There are two types of Exchange Traded Products, or ETPs - ETFs and ETNs. ETPs are most similar to mutual funds, in that the ETP is made up of many different underlying securities. ETPs can contain a group of equity securities meant to track an index, track a section of the equity market, hold both equity and fixed income securities, etc.

An Exchange Traded Fund, or ETF, is an investment company that, through their shares, is traded on exchanges like Nasdaq or NYSE. The prices of ETF's fluctuate throughout the day. Although similar to a closed end fund (Mutual Fund), an ETF has unique features that keep the price close to the ETF's net asset value. How is an ETF different from a mutual fund? Any investor can buy or sell an ETF any time the markets are open. A mutual fund can typically only be bought or sold after the close of traditional equity market exchanges, usually post 4pm Eastern Time. A mutual fund order can be placed at any point during the day, but it only filled after 4pm. Why is this the case? Since the mutual fund is itself made up of individual securities, the mutual fund uses the composite value of all of the individual securities closing prices to determine the aggregate value of the mutual fund. ETFs are also SEC registered investment companies just like mutual funds. Since ETFs are bought and sold on exchanges, the ETF entity itself does not buy and sell directly with investors.

An ETN, or Exchange Traded Note, is another type of ETP. Unlike an ETF, an ETN typically includes fixed income securities and are sold as a structured product. The ETN itself is a debt security. ETNs are put together by the sponsoring underwriter. Since ETNs are made up of fixed income securities, they have a finite life to them. The sponsoring underwriter/issuer makes the promise to pay the ETN security holders their dividends and interest on a regular basis. Therefore, the ETN's creditworthiness is tied to the creditworthiness of the underwriter/issuer.

Both ETFs and mutual funds can be passively managed or actively managed. ETFs are often viewed as alternative to mutual funds because although they can invest in the same underlying securities, ETFs can have lower fees and ability to trade in and out of the ETF during normal market hours. Mutual funds can only be bought and sold once per day, normally after the close of the trading day. Both mutual funds and ETFs offer investors diversification, professional management, a prospectus to review investment strategies & disclosures, and low investment minimums in similar ways. What investors gain in these areas, they give up control over investment decisions inside the mutual fund or ETF.

End of Chapter Quiz

Complete these end of chapter questions to assess your understanding of the subject matter discussed in this chapter. The answers follow on the next page. For those questions you have answered incorrectly, review the appropriate section of the chapter again to make sure you understand the concepts.

1. Which of the following is true regarding a Real Estate Investment Trust (REIT)?
    a. REITs are required to be listed on an exchange.
    b. REITs can invest in debt or equity real estate, but not both.
    c. REITs provide tax-advantaged income without double taxation.
    d. REITs are not allowed to be held by mutual funds.

2. Which of the following best describes a difference between ETFs and open-end (mutual) funds?
    a. ETFs invest in a many securities, but mutual funds invest in only a few securities.
    b. ETFs can be bought or sold throughout the day, while mutual funds can only be bought and sold after 4pm EST.
    c. ETFs may charge fees to investors, while mutual funds may not charge fees.
    d. Mutual funds are traded on an exchange, while ETFs are only redeemable to the fund company.

3. Which of the following is generally considered to be an illiquid investment?
    a. Hedge fund
    b. REIT
    c. ETF
    d. Closed-end fund

4. Which of the following may be traded publicly?
    a. DPP
    b. Open-end fund
    c. Hedge fund
    d. REIT

5. Which of the following is TRUE regarding REITs?
    a. Be managed by a board of directors or trustees
    b. Be an entity that would be non-taxable as a corporation but for its REIT status
    c. Have a minimum of 10 shareholders after its first year as a REIT
    d. Pay out at least 75% of its profits to shareholders as dividends.

6. A hybrid REIT combines which of the following two types of REITs?
   a. Retail and Apartment
   b. Mortgage and Healthcare
   c. Commercial and Healthcare
   d. Retail and Healthcare

7. Which of the following is TRUE regarding Hedge Funds?
   a. Hedge funds are the same as private equity funds
   b. Hedge funds are type of Exchange Traded Product (ETP)
   c. The Hedge Fund manager typically keeps 20% of the gains
   d. Fees are only charged by Hedge Funds if they are profitable

8. Which of the following is TRUE regarding DPPs?
   a. Often have a defined life
   b. Can be bought or sold on the secondary market similar to listed equities
   c. DPPs do not typically include REITs or BDCs
   d. DPPs often invest in the technology and healthcare sectors

9. In a hedge fund investment, what are management fees?
   a. Pay the broker dealer who sold the hedge fund
   b. Pay the management teams of the underlying owned companies
   c. Pay the ongoing expenses of running the fund
   d. Pay hedge fund for making money

10. Hedge fund investments are generally available to:
    a. Qualified institutional buyers only
    b. All retail investors
    c. Retail investors who meet minimum net worth or income thresholds
    d. Only U.S. registered broker dealers

End of Chapter Quiz Answers

1. C

Some REITs are exchange traded, some are OTC, some are private. REITs can invest in debit, equity or both debt and equity. REIT income is not taxed at the corporate level as long as the company complies with specific requirements. REITs can be held as single securities or within a mutual fund, just like an equity security.

2. B

Both ETFs and open-end funds invest in various securities. These products could be narrowly focused to one sector, or broadly focused across the market (or anywhere in between). ETFs are traded in the secondary market, while open end funds are only traded after the market close. Both ETFs and mutual funds typically have some type of fee charged to purchasers.

3. A

Hedge funds cannot usually be sold by the owner whenever the owner wants. There are specific time period where owners can sell in some cases, in other cases they most hold the investment until the underlying assets are liquidated. REITs, ETFs and closed end funds are all generally considered to be liquid investments, meaning the owner of that investment can resell their interest relatively easily and quickly. Each of these types of investments may be publicly traded, but not always.

4. D

Of the choices, only REITs can be publicly traded. Open end funds, or mutual funds can be bought by the public but are not listed or traded on an exchanged. Closed end funds can be publicly traded however.

5. A

A REIT structure requires that the REIT be managed by a board of directors or a trustee. A REIT must also have a minimum of 100 shareholder after its first year, and pay out 90% of profits to the REIT owners. A REIT must also be an entity that would be taxable, if not for its REIT status.

6. B
A hybrid REIT combines Mortgage REITs with another type of REIT, such as a Healthcare REIT. If the REIT only contains mortgage or healthcare real estate assets, it would not be considered a hybrid REIT. Retail, Apartment, and Commercial are all types or REIT, that when combined with a Mortgage REIT, would be considered a hybrid REIT.

7. C
Hedge funds can be similar in structure and investment philosophy to a private equity fund, but they are different. Hedge Funds are not a type of ETP as they are not typically exchange traded. Hedge fund managers do get to keep approximately 20% of the gains in the hedge fund, but also collect a management fee for their management of the portfolio assets.

8. A
DPPs are types of securities that have a defined life to them. They are not typically bought and sold on the secondary market like equities would be, but do typically contain REITs and BDCs. Although not absolute, DPPs often invest in the real estate and energy sectors.

9. C
Management fees are fees used to cover the costs of running the fund. A broker dealer may receive a finder's fee, or commission for their role in the investor's purchase of the hedge fund investment. Performance fees are paid to the hedge fund if/when the hedge fun makes money.

10. C
Both hedge funds and mutual funds can hold equity securities. Hedge funds charge higher fees than mutual funds. Mutual fund holder can typically sell their ownership stake daily, whereas hedge fund owners can only sell it during predetermined time periods. Lastly, retail investors may be able to invest in hedge funds, but may not depending on the income and net worth thresholds.

Chapter 10:   Investment Risks

All securities carry some risk. If you recall, U.S. Government securities (Treasury Bills, Bonds, and Notes) are considered riskless because the U.S. Government has extended an explicit guarantee against default. But this riskless concept only extends to default risk, not against all other potential risks. So what risks are inherent when investing in securities? What can be done to mitigate these risks? Let's begin with the types of risks that you should be familiar with for the SIE Exam.

Types of Risks

1. **Interest rate risk** - The risk when a change in interest rates will result in a change in the price or yield of a financial product. When a change in interest rates have a greater impact on the price or yields of the financial product, the greater the interest rate risk. Changes in interest rates have the most obvious impact on fixed income securities--when interest rates rise for fixed income securities, prices go down.

2. **Reinvestment risk** - An investor takes this risk when investing in a bond that pays a coupon or in a stock that pays a dividend. When receiving the promised coupon payment from the issuer, the prevailing market interest rate may be higher, or lower than the current interest rate on the bonds. If the prevailing market interest rate is lower, the investor will be forced to reinvest the coupon payment at that lower market interest rate.

3. **Inflation risk** - Inflation occurs when general prices within the economy rise. Inflation risk occurs when the rise in prices (inflation) is greater than expected. Higher expected inflation tends to push up the general level of interest rates across the economy. Inflation risk is greatest for issuers of fixed income securities as the issuer locks in bond interest payments (coupons), which do not change during the life of the bond. The bondholder, however, is also concerned about inflation, as the value of the bond drops as the interest rate increases.

4. **Call risk** - The risk that an investor takes when purchasing a bond with a call feature. Bonds can be called away (or bought back) by the issuer on a certain date, or schedule of dates, for a certain price.

5. **Default risk** – Also known as credit risk. The risk that the issuer of the security will not make promised interest or principal payments as required. Failure to make the required payments is considered a default by the issuer. Default risk includes when the issuer makes partial or late payments to bondholders. Equity securities holders do not technically have default risk, even if the company pays dividends. Dividend payments are almost always not contractually or legally required, meaning that the issuer's Board of Directors has to authorize the payments each month or quarter.   Since dividends are not contractually required like bond coupon payments and principal repayments, no default risk exists for equity security holders. Bankruptcy risk, however, is a risk worth discussing for both equity and bondholders.

6. **Bankruptcy risk** – This type of risk often works in conjunction with, or drives default risk. If you are a bondholder, and the issuer declares bankruptcy, there is a good chance that the issuer will then default on the bonds (not pay the bondholders required principal or interest payments). Likewise for equity security holders, if an issuer declares bankruptcy, your equity shares are likely to be worth zero, or near zero. In the event of bankruptcy, you should remember that equity security holders sit behind bondholders when determining who gets what assets are left of the bankrupt company.

7. **Currency risk** - The risk that results from any change in currency exchange rates which impact the returns of foreign currency denominated financial products.

8. **Liquidity risk** – If an investment is liquid, it can be bought and sold easily and quickly because there is an active and regular marketplace for that investment. The risk comes into play if it would be harder to buy or sell an investment due to there being a lack of an active and regular marketplace for that particular investment. Treasury bills, bonds and notes are considered very liquid markets. A small capitalization equity security would be considered an illiquid security.

9. **Capital risk –** The risk that an investor takes when that investor puts their own money in an investment or the risk that a fixed income security might decrease in value prior to being sold. Absent a default from the issuer, this risk only comes up if an investor sells the bond prior to maturity.

10. **Political risk** - This type of risk is mostly focused on government entities that have the power to change tax, trade, commerce, or other similar laws.

11. **Market/systematic risk** - The risk accepted by an investor that the market will increase or decrease in the absence of any security specific or any other specific or quantifiable risk. For instance, an increase in the unemployment rate means that more people are not working. If people are not working, they cannot typically afford to spend as much money on goods and services. If you are a company, and consumers are broadly not spending as much money because more of them are unemployed, they will buy less of your product. Most companies will be impacted by the negative employment outlook, which depresses the entire economy. Another example that helps illustrate market or systematic risk is a war. If large scale war were to occur, the market would surely reactive negatively. These are factors outside the company's control. These are also factors outside the security holder's control.

12. **Nonsystematic risk** - This type of risk can be described as the uncertainty that exists in an investment in a specific company or industry. Some examples of nonsystematic risk are: a new competitor which results in decreased sales, a change in the company's finances or management, or a product recall. Negative news about the company can also affect nonsystematic risk. Nonsystematic, a/k/a unsystematic, risk can be reduced using a diversified portfolio with securities in different sectors or industries.

13. **Prepayment risk** – This type of risk primarily exists with mortgage or asset backed securities. A mortgage backed security is made up of a pool or collection of

individual mortgages. As individual borrowers make their monthly mortgage payments each month, some borrowers pay a little bit extra or in some cases, pay off the mortgage entirely (due to a sale of a home for instance). The 'paying back someone early' part is the prepayment risk. When you have loaned money to someone else, and they pay you back early, you no longer earn a return on that investment. As an investor, you now need to find another investment to make.

Risk Mitigation Strategies

With investors facing so many risks, why would anyone decide to invest? What can investors do to reduce the chances of losing money on their investment? Some risks must be accepted when making an investment decision. As noted above, if you were to purchase a mortgage backed security, an investor should assume that there may be prepayments made by homeowners on the underlying mortgages that make up the mortgage backed security. This risk should be priced into the mortgage backed security, and investor should probably not be surprised if the prepayments are faster or slower than anticipated.

Any time an investor holds a security, that investor is taking on a degree of risk. How much risk that investor takes depends entirely on the security itself and how long the investor holds that security. For other risks that an investor can do something about, the concept of risk mitigation exists. Risk mitigation is any action an investor takes to reduce, manage, or eliminate the applicable risk, such as

- Diversification
- Portfolio rebalancing
- Hedging

Diversification

The easiest risk mitigation strategy to understand is diversification. An investor who applies diversification, or diversifies their investments, spreads their investing dollars across multiple different investments. For instance, an investor who only holds 100 shares of Microsoft equity stock may have made a smart investment, but would not be considered diversified because they only hold one security. Diversification, though, is a relative term. It means different things to different people. Some might consider themselves diversified because they hold 50 equity securities in their investment portfolio. Others might look at this investment portfolio and note that the investor is surely not diversified, because they only hold equity securities, but no fixed income securities! The basic concept of diversification does not require a specific number of securities or types of securities to be considered 'diversified'. Diversification exists on a continuum, meaning that the more securities an investor holds in their investment portfolio and/or the more types of securities an investor holds, the more diversified their portfolio would be considered.

What risks that were discussed in the Types of Risks Section above would diversification help to mitigate? Some are more obvious than others. Default risk would be mitigated very easily by a well-diversified portfolio. If an investor holds a portfolio of 100 fixed income securities and one of the issuers out of the 100 securities is unable to pay the required coupon payments to bondholders, it is considered a default. This risk exists for every fixed income, equity, or option security that an investor holds. The way to mitigate the risk is to hold a variety of security types and a larger number of securities, which minimizes or mitigates the impact to your overall portfolio of a single security defaulting.

The diversification strategy can be used to mitigate risk for almost all securities because, as an investor, you are not just holding one security. The chances of something drastic like default risk having a material impact on your portfolio are significantly reduced as the number and type of securities increase within an investor's portfolio. Any risk that can impact different securities in different ways can be mitigated (to a degree) by diversification.

Some risks can have a much wider impact than others, such as political risk, or market/systematic risk. With political risk, the U.S. government could decide to tax rates on capital gains or dividends and interest, or some other significant policy or law change that would negatively impact all securities investments. There is little an investor can do to blunt the impact of this type of risk. An investor could be well diversified and still subject to market or systematic risk with their equity or fixed income holdings. Although the primary purpose of diversification is to mitigate non-systematic risk, an investor cannot diversify away market or systematic risk.

Portfolio Rebalancing

Portfolio rebalancing is a concept used by many financial advisors. Portfolio rebalancing is a risk mitigation method periodically used to adjust the percentage of each type of asset held within a portfolio. For example, on January 1, an investor's portfolio has the following components:

- Equities: 70%
- Municipal Bonds: 15%
- Corporate Bonds: 10%
- Cash/Money Markets: 5%

Due to changes in the market and the growth of the overall portfolio (note that individual portfolio components will grow at different rates over time) over the course of the year, the investor's portfolio now looks like this on December 31 of the same year:

- Equities: 80%
- Municipal Bonds: 12%
- Corporate Bonds: 5%
- Cash/Money Markets: 3%

If the investor wants to maintain the portfolio composition that they had on January 1, the investor must now rebalance the portfolio. This can be accomplished in a few ways - investment of new dollars or the purchase and sale of individual portfolio components. If the investor was investing new funds, they would simply invest all of the new funds into municipal bonds, corporate bonds, and cash, with enough new money invested to increase the portfolio percentages to 15% for municipal bonds, 10% for corporate bonds, and 5% for cash. If the investor was not investing new money into the portfolio, the investor in this case would sell off enough equities to lower the equity component of the portfolio back down to 70%. As the cash is received within the portfolio from the sale of equities, enough of the proceeds are invested into municipal bonds, corporate bonds, and cash to get those portfolio components back up to 15%, 10%, and 5% respectively.

Portfolio rebalancing helps to address almost all risks. As the portfolio is rebalanced, securities that have grown too large in comparison to the target holding percentage are sold. This helps keep any single security or sector of the economy from growing too large in the portfolio. If part of the portfolio grows too large without being rebalanced and that part of the portfolio crashes due to some of the risks we outlined above (e.g., interest rate, inflation, political risk) the portfolio's risk exposure is higher. If the holdings in the portfolio are kept in check at a reasonable percentage of the portfolio, the risk would be somewhat mitigated.

Hedging

Hedging is a risk mitigation strategy used by some investors and market participants. Like diversification and portfolio rebalancing, hedging is a useful way to reduce risk. In hedging, an investor purchases another security that is expected to act in an opposite direction from the security currently owned. From a statistics perspective, two things that move in opposite direction from one another are negatively correlated. Two things that move in the same direction are positively correlated. For hedging to work effectively, you will need to have two securities that move in opposite directions. How about an example to illustrate this concept?

Let's say you own 100 shares of YUP equity stock. After doing research, you really like the company's business model and long term prospects. However, you are concerned that your estimates may not prove out to be correct in the near term. Hedging the risk of YUM decreasing in price short term has an easy solution – options. Remember that when you buy call options, you are hoping the price of the underlying security increases. When you buy put options, you are hoping the price of the underlying security decreases. Since we own 100 shares of YUP (long the stock), we want the stock to increase. However, remember that we are trying to protect the downside – the possibility that the stock might fall in price. What kind of option makes money when the price of the underlying security falls? Put options!

Since 1 option contract equals 100 shares of the underlying YUP equity stock, we only need to buy one contract. Here is the situation:

- Long 100 shares of YUP
- Current price of YUP equity stock is $100
- Long 1 YUP August 100 put

If the price of the YUM equity stock increases, you make money because you are long the stock. The put option expires worthless. If the price of the YUM equity stock decreases below $100, you lose money on your YUM equity stock position, but you make money on the put option position. For every dollar you lose on the YUM equity stock, you gain it back on the put option. You must however account for the option premium.

If you were willing to risk a bit more, you could buy the put option at a lower strike price and a smaller premium. If the roles are reversed, and you were short the stock (hoping YUM equity decreased in price), you would buy call options. Remember this about hedging – you want two financial instruments that move in opposite direction of another. Also, recall one thing about listed options – they have an expiration date. Therefore, if you want to stay hedged, you will need to purchase another put option contract when your first option contract expires!

Compared to diversification and portfolio rebalancing, hedging is a more complex way to mitigate investment risk. Hedging is also not limited to securities. Many investors hedge with non-securities products, such as commodities – oil and currency, depending on which risks they are trying to mitigate.

End of Chapter Quiz

Complete these end of chapter questions to assess your understanding of the subject matter discussed in this chapter. The answers follow on the next page. For those questions you have answered incorrectly, review the appropriate section of the chapter again to make sure you understand the concepts.

1. Which of the following best describes credit risk?
   a. borrower of funds may not pay back the principal or interest of a loan
   b. the government may change tax, trade or other laws/regulations
   c. a credit card company raises the interest rate charged to customers
   d. the borrower of funds pays back a mortgage earlier than expected

2. Which risk mitigation strategy involves spreading out the risk of loss amongst many different types of securities?
   a. Portfolio rebalancing   c. Diversification
   b. Hedging   d. Model portfolio

3. An investor purchases two securities, Security 1 and Security 2. If Security 2 is purchased because it is expected to move in an opposite direction from Security 1, Security 2 is considered:
   a. A hedge   c. A bad investment
   b. Proper diversification   d. Portfolio rebalancing

4. A rise in prices greater than expected is what type of risk?
   a. Default risk   c. Interest rate risk
   b. Political risk   d. Inflation risk

5. Which of the following investments has the most liquidity risk?
   a. S&P 500 Index Fund   c. Hedge fund
   b. AA rated corporate bond   d. Listed REIT

6. Which of the following investments likely has currency risk?
   a. Treasury bond
   b. STRIP
   c. ADR
   d. US corporate bond

7. An investor has the following preferred portfolio at the beginning of the calendar year:

Equities: 50%
Municipal Bonds: 20%
Corporate Bonds: 10%
Cash/Money Markets: 10%

At the end of the year, the portfolio looks like this:

Equities: 40%
Municipal Bonds: 30%
Corporate Bonds: 20%
Cash/Money Markets: 10%

If the investor wants to return to the asset mix in the portfolio at the beginning of the year, what should the investor do?

   a. Buy equities, sell municipal bonds, sell corporate bonds
   b. Sell equities, buy municipal bonds, buy corporate bonds
   c. Buy equities, sell municipal bonds, buy corporate bonds
   d. Sell equities, buy municipal bonds, sell corporate bonds

8. Which security below has the most reinvestment risk?
   a. Treasury Bill   c. Equity dividend stock
   b. Equity growth stock   d. US savings bond

9. The risk that the issuer will require the bond owner to sell the bond back to the issuer at a specific date and price is referred to as:
   a. Default risk   c. Price risk
   b. Call risk   d. Bond risk

10. In the event of falling interest rates, which of the following risk might a mortgage loan company be more concerned with?
   a. Prepayment risk   c. Political risk
   b. Capital risk   d. Interest rate risk

End of Chapter Quiz Answers

1. A
The risk that an individual or entity will not pay back a loan or make a required principal/interest payment, is considered credit risk. Paying back a loan or bond early is called prepayment risk. When the government changes laws or regulations that may impact a business or a loan/bond, that is considered political risk.

2. C
Portfolio rebalancing helps to diversify your investments in the percentages you want to target. It involves selling some investments, and buying others on a regular, but not frequent basis. Hedging involves taking a position in another security that is negatively correlated, or moves in the opposite direction, of the first security you own. Diversification occurs when you spread out your investment amongst several securities and different types of securities.

3. A
Diversification, although not specifically defined by a number of securities, would certainly require more than 2 securities to be considered diversified. If an investor is expecting two securities to move in opposite direction from one another, this would be considered hedging. On its own, an investment that decreases in value and loses money for the investor may indeed be considered a bad investment, but that is not the case here. Rebalancing requires buying and selling securities within the portfolio to achieve the desired asset allocation.

4. D
Default risk is the risk an issuer or borrower will not pay back their loan or funds borrowed. Political risks occur when a government or regulator changes the laws or rules impacting business conditions. Interest rate risk exists because interest rates change up or down as a result of numerous factors. Inflation risk is the risk that prices on goods or services may rise more/less quickly than expected.

5. C
Liquidity risk measure how quickly an investment can be turned into cash. Listed REITs, AA rated corporate bonds, and S&P 500 Index Fund are all considered relatively liquid. A hedge fund is not, as the hedge fund investor cannot immediately sell their investment.

6. C
An ADR may have currency risk, as the underlying security associated with an ADR is a foreign security. Foreign securities are much more likely to be denominated in a currency other than US dollars. The remained choices are all denominated in US dollars and do not have currency risk associated with the investment.

7. A

This question is asking whether or not you understand portfolio rebalancing. Based upon your target allocation, sell more of what you own too much of, and buy more of what you have too little of.

8. C

The equity dividend stock has the most reinvestment risk, because that is the only security of the four options that pay a dividend or coupon to the investor on a regular basis prior to maturity. A security cannot have reinvestment risk if it does not pay a coupon or dividend, unless there is the possibility of the security being called (investor being given their money back) prior to maturity.

9. B

An issuer may have right to force the investor to sell the bond back to the issuer at a predetermined price and date. This right is called a call provision, and is known to the investor at the time of purchase. This gives the investor call risk, as the bond could be 'called away' by the issuer prior to maturity.

10. A

Falling interest rates means that the mortgage company should be concerned with homeowners refinancing their mortgages, resulting in a prepayment of the existing loan. Since mortgages are often securitized (made into securities), securities investors should be aware of this prepayment risk as it will affect the returns on their investment. The other risks may indeed be present, but are not something the mortgage company would be more concerned with in a falling interest rate environment.

SIE Exam Study Guide 2020

Section 3: Understanding Trading, Customer Accounts, and Prohibited Activities

Chapter 11:   Orders, Trading, and Strategies

Types of Orders[39]
There are numerous order types used by various market participants. The exam will not require you to know every single order type. Let's review the significant order types used in the securities market, including:

market	limit	stop
stop limit	day	good til cancelled
other good til orders	fill or kill	all or none
immediate or cancel	discretionary	non-discretionary
solicited/non-solicited		

If you were to go out to a restaurant with your friends, each of you would consider what was on the menu, talk to your waiter or waitress, and then decide what you were going to eat for that meal. Just like a customer orders food in a restaurant, a customer in a securities transaction places an order for the securities that they are looking to buy or sell.   There are many different types of orders that a customer can place, depending on how quickly they want to buy or sell, at what price they would like to buy or sell, how the long the order is open, and many other types. Next, let's review a few types of orders.

Here is the basic structure of an order:

[Buy/Sell] [Number of Shares/Contracts/Bonds] of [Security Name or Symbol] at [market or limit order price] +any terms or conditions on the order

Now, let's break down the components of an order and introduce several of the common order types.

Market Order
The easiest order to get started with is the market order.   With a market order, a customer knows exactly what security they would like to buy or sell, and how much of that security they would like to buy or sell.   For instance, a customer order would typically look something like this:

Buy 100 shares of XYZ at the market

The 100 shares indicate how much of the security wants to buy. XYZ is the stock symbol for the security. Every equity security has a symbol the represents that security in the public market, on a customer's brokerage statement, or the books and records of the broker-dealer. By noting 'at the market', the customer is willing to buy 100 shares of the security at wherever the market is trading when the order is executed by the broker-dealer executing the order.

Limit Order

A limit order is a priced order, or an order that has a price condition attached to it. If the order is to purchase a security, the order would look something like this:

Buy 150 WZY at $72

150 shares indicate how much of the security the customer wants to buy. The customer wants to buy shares of WZY, the equity security symbol that the equity issuer trades under in the public equity markets. The price of $72 means that the customer placing the order wants to buy the equity security, or WZY stock at $72 *or less.* For this order, $72 is known as the limit price, or the maximum price at which the customer is willing to buy. If you were looking to spend $72 on something, would you be willing to purchase that item for less than $72 if the item was on sale? Of course you would. That is an easy way to keep track of the fact that buy limit orders can be executed at the limit price or less. If the order is to sell a security, the order would look something like this:

Sell 200 XYZ at $25

200 indicates how many shares of the security the customer wants to sell. The customer wants to sell shares of XYZ, the equity security symbol that the issuer trades under in the public equity markets. The price of $25 means that the customer wants to sell the equity security, or XYZ stock at $25 *or more.* For this order, $25 is known as the limit price, or the minimum price at which the customer is willing to sell. Consider instead something you were interested in selling for $25. Would you take more than $25 if someone offered you more? Of course you would! That is an easy way to keep track of the fact that sell limit orders can be executed at the limit price or greater.

A quick review – limit orders are priced orders and will always have a dollar amount attached to the order information. Market orders are unpriced orders and will have no dollar amount attached to the order information. Some market orders may actually indicate 'at the market' or 'at market'. The presence of a price or lack thereof is what drives the distinction between limit and market orders.

Stop Order

Entering a stop order is a more elaborate order strategy than just using market or limit orders to buy and sell securities. A stop order allows the person or entity entering the order to enter the order away from the current market. Since most customers do not track the minute by minute, hour by hour, day by day movements of the overall market, let alone individual securities, it makes sense that those customers have a mechanism to buy or sell at a predetermined price should a severe price change happen in an individual security.

Why use a stop order though? Also called a stop loss order, a stop order is most often used to protect profits, therefore, most stop loss orders are sell orders. Let's say you buy 100 shares of equity security GHN at $50. The price per share rises in the market from the $50 per share that you paid for it, to $100. Nice profit! This profit though is an unrealized gain at the moment – a gain that is only on paper since you have not yet sold all of your GHN shares. To actually make the profit a realized gain, you would need to sell your 100 shares of GHN. But what if the price of the stock goes up even higher? What if the price of the stock goes lower? A stop loss order can certainly help for situations where a customer owns a security, does not want to sell the security at the moment, but wants to protect some or all of their unrealized profits.

A stop order is triggered when the price of the security trades at the price of the stop order. Once the stop order is triggered, the stop order becomes a market order to buy or sell. After the order becomes a market order, the order has all of the characteristics of any other market order that were noted in the earlier market order discussion.

Sell Stop 100 XYZ at $25
Buy Stop 100 WZY at $72

The XYZ stop order would be triggered when XYZ trades at $25 or lower. The WZY stop order would be triggered when WZY trades at $72 or higher. Why though would the XYZ stop order be triggered lower than $25, and not just at $25? Securities do not trade in a predictable fashion most of the time. Securities can move up or move down in price rather quickly – often skipping over our nicely rounded pricing increments, like $25.

Stop Limit Order

A stop limit order is almost exactly the same as a stop order, with one key difference. Once a stop order is triggered, the stop order becomes a market order. Once a stop limit order is triggered, the stop limit order becomes a limit order. Why not just use a stop order instead of a stop limit? The reason for why you would use a stop order or a stop limit order goes back to the basic difference between the two order types. If you choose to use stop order, once triggered, this order becomes a market order – meaning – the order is executed at the market as soon as possible. If a stop limit order is used, the triggered limit order does not execute right away, instead acting like a limit order in every sense. This lack of immediate execution is exactly what the customer is looking for when they use the stop limit order instead of the stop order. Stop limit orders trigger a limit order; stop orders trigger a market order. This difference can be important in an extremely volatile market, where the prices of a particular security, a specific sector, or the entire market are moving hard in one direction or the other (up or down).

Sell 100 XYZ at $25, stop limit $22
Buy Stop 100 WZY at $72

Day Order

When a customer places an order, the order is often defaulted to a day order. This means that the order is only good for that particular trading day. After the trading day is over, the part of the order (if partially executed) that has not been executed expires. If the order is not executed at all, the entire order expires. A day order may be a priced, or limit order, but may also be an unpriced, or market order. A couple examples of day orders would look like:

Sell 100 XYZ at $25 day = Sell 100 XYZ at $25
Buy 100 WZY at $72 day = Buy 100 WZY at $72

An order is assumed to be a day order absent any other specific terms, conditions, or instructions. One of the common instructions is GTC.

Good til Cancelled (GTC)

If an order is considered good til cancelled, or GTC, it remains an order until it is cancelled by the person placing the order. This order type is useful if you would like to buy shares of XYZ equity security if the securities fall to a certain price at some point in the future. A good til cancel order does not expire, but is usually a priced, or limit order. A typical GTC order would look like something like this:

Buy 100 shares of XYZ at $25 GTC

Of course, the reverse is also true. If you wanted to sell shares of XYZ equity security if the securities increase to a certain price at some point in the future allowing you to convert an unrealized gain to a realized gain – the order would look like this:

Sell 100 shares of XYZ at $125 GTC

When reviewing GTC orders for the SIE Exam, remember that the orders do not expire until they are cancelled by the individual who placed the order. An order cannot be both a Day order and a GTC order.

Other Good til Order Types

There are several other types of "Good til" orders that work in a very similar manner to the Good til Cancel (GTC) order type. These similar good til orders include both Good til Day (GTD) and Good til Month (GTM).

A few other order types to be aware of include:

- **AON** – All or None – An All or None order works exactly as you might think – either the order gets filled 100% of the way, or does not get filled at all. An AON order stays active until it is cancelled.
- **FOK** – Fill or Kill – A Fill or Kill order is 100% filled, or killed (cancelled) almost instantly. The order does not stay live for more than a second or two after it is entered.
- **IOC** - Immediate or Cancel – An IOC order is executed immediately or cancelled. An IOC is exactly like a FOK order, except for one important difference. An IOC order can be partially filled (i.e., the order is for 500 shares, and 250 shares were executed), where a FOK order must be 100 % filled.

Discretionary and Non-Discretionary Orders

The root word of discretionary is **discretion, or choice**. In this case, the discretion, or choice is given the customer to the broker-dealer taking the order. More specifically, the discretion is given to customer's financial advisor. Therefore, a discretionary order is one where the security is determined by the customer, but the financial advisor decides when to buy/sell the security and how to buy/sell the security, by placing a limit order, market order or some other order. *This differs from a discretionary account where the broker-dealer has the ability to pick and choose what, when and how to buy or sell securities within the account, and at which price.* For a discretionary order, the financial advisor only has the ability to pick and choose when and how the order is placed, but not the actual security to be bought or sold.

Solicited vs Unsolicited Orders

Orders are always considered either solicited or unsolicited. Whether an order is solicited or unsolicited has absolutely nothing to do with whether any other order terms and conditions apply to that order. A solicited order simply means that the registered representative responsible for your brokerage account had the idea to place the order to purchase or sell a security. An unsolicited trade means that the account owner or person authorized to place trades in the account had the idea to buy or sell the security. Regardless of whether the order is marked solicited or unsolicited, the order still can have other order terms and conditions, such as a market, limit, or stop limit order, etc... It should be noted however that all orders and trades that are made in a discretionary account are solicited by definition, as the account owner has given the responsibility in the account to their registered representative. The account holder does not make investment decision in this type of account and therefore cannot possibly place unsolicited orders and trades.

Now that you have a reasonable understanding of the different types of orders, how, when, and why would you place those orders? That all depends on your understanding and use of various simple trading strategies.

Market Maker Quotations

Market makers post their quotes a little differently, using the following format to indicate what actions they are willing to take:

Purchase price, then Sales price [purchase size x100 **x** sales size x100]

For example, if the market maker quote reads as follows:

25.00 - 25.05 [10x20]

This quote means that the market maker is willing to buy 1,000 shares at $25 and sell 2,000 shares at $25.05.

Trading Strategies

Here are the trading strategies that we will go through in this section:
- Buying and Selling
- Bearish and Bullish
- Bid-Ask
- Long and Short
- Naked and Covered
- Trade Capacity

Buying and Selling

As we have covered in previous chapters, the securities market is a diverse universe of market participants, security types, and regulations. The universe of market participants, security types, and regulations come together very neatly when customers want to buy or sell securities in the marketplace. Let's first begin by understanding what the look of the market and how it works.

To buy a security means to purchase it. Buying means ownership - someone who buys a security owns that security. Based on the type of security, that can mean vastly different things.
- **Equity** - Own shares in the company. As a (part) owner in the company, you are entitled to receive dividends (if paid), vote in the Board of Director elections or proxies, and other items covered in Chapter 12 and 13.

- **Debt** - Own part of the debt of the company. As an owner of the company's debt, you are entitled to future interest payments, and other items covered in Chapter 5.
- **Options** - Own the right, but not the obligation, to exercise the option to purchase or sell the equity in the company.

Bearish and Bullish

If you have followed the markets at all, you have probably heard the terms bull and bear market. A bull market is a market that is increasing in market value, expanding, or growing. A bear market is a market that is decreasing in market value, contracting, or declining. Derivatives of bear and bull are used when noting indicators, or predictors of future movement. A jump in U.S. unemployment is generally considered a bearish indicator, since more people are out of work, less able to buy goods and services, and thereby decreasing demand for those companies' products and services. As fewer goods and services are purchased, companies reduce production, lay off workers, and the bearish cycle continues.

There are of course bullish indicators as well. We can use the same measurement (U.S. unemployment rate) as an example for simplicity's sake. Whereas a jump in unemployment may be a bearish indicator, a drop in unemployment may be considered a bullish indicator. This is because more people will be employed and therefore more able to buy goods and services. This in turn increases demand for those companies' products and services, causing them to expand their operations.

In the past, FINRA has provided market participants with guidance on which indicators are the most cited and used on a regular basis. Many of these indicators are common sense both on what is measured and the implications in expansion or contraction of the measured data – does the data show an increase or decrease relative to prior measuring periods? One quick note about indicators in general. Although indicators are reported as increases or decreases when compared to prior periods, it is also important to take into consideration the expectations that accompany the indicator. If the unemployed rate was expected to drop by .1%, but it instead drops by .3%, not only is unemployment decreasing, it is decreasing faster than what was expected. This would be a 'positive surprise'. The same effect is true in the other direction. If the unemployed rate was expected to drop by .1%, but it instead it stays the same, this would be a 'negative surprise'. Unemployment in this case is not getting worse, but since it was expected to drop, unemployment is worse than expected. One last point – anything that expands the economy or puts more money into people's pockets is generally bullish. Higher prices and putting fewer dollars into people's pockets is generally bearish.

Here are a few indicators that FINRA thinks are important (and therefore you should as well) to determine bearish or bullish sentiment[40]:

1. **Real GDP** – You should already be familiar with GDP (Gross Domestic Product) from Chapter 2. Real GDP is simply GDP, but adjusted for changes in prices. Real GDP helps to determine if the economy is actually expanding, or simply appearing to expand due to higher prices. As GDP takes into account the price of goods in the economy, any higher prices in those goods would increase GDP. Real GDP therefore will be more sensitive to more goods being sold at the same price, not just selling the same number of goods at a higher price. An increase in Real GDP is bullish for the economy and a decrease in Real GDP is bearish for the economy.

2. **Non-Farm Payrolls and Unemployment Rate** – Although we reviewed unemployment examples earlier in this section, the importance of the unemployment data bears repeating – when fewer people are looking for jobs, both companies and individuals have more money. When companies and individuals have more money, they tend to spend some or all of that money. A decrease in the unemployment rate is therefore bullish for the economy. An increase in the unemployment rate is bearish for the economy.

3. **Price Indexes – CPI and PPI** – We can simply refresh what we learned back in Chapter 2. Recall that inflation is defined as the increase in the price of a good or service. Most commonly, inflation is measured through two indicators – CPI and PPI. CPI is the Consumer Price Index. PPI is the Producer Price Index. The CPI measures the increase in the prices that consumers pay for goods – everything from bananas to milk, bread, and cars (and lots of other goods in between!). The CPI does exclude more volatile goods like energy prices (i.e., gasoline and oil) to help ensure a more consistent and fair representation of typical prices of everyday goods. It is assumed that generally speaking, prices for most goods and services will rise over time. However, prices rising too quickly will often cause the Fed to adjust their interest rate policy. For this reason, mild increases in the CPI and PPI are considered normal – material rises in the CPI and PPI indicate inflation is higher than normal and will likely cause the Fed to slow the economy down by increasing interest rates.

4. **Consumer Confidence and Consumer Sentiment** – Consumer sentiment is measured by several different indicators, the most widely known is the University of Michigan Consumer Sentiment Index ®. Consumer sentiment indicators try to capture how optimistic or pessimistic consumers are about the economy today and where things are headed in the economy tomorrow. Increases in consumer sentiment are therefore bullish – when consumers are more optimistic today and expect to be so in the future, they tend to spend more money which helps grow the economy. Decreases in consumer sentiment are bearish, as consumers are more pessimistic today than they were during the last consumer sentiment index reading. Pessimistic consumers are less likely to spend the same and may even spend less money, thereby decreasing the economic growth or even contracting the economy.

5. **Retail Sales** – When retail stores sell more goods, the economy is likely headed in a bullish direction. When retail sales sell fewer goods, the economy is likely headed in a bearish direction. Retail sales data helps to determine how much customers are

spending in retail stores, and the potential positive impact to those businesses manufacturing retail goods. An increase in retail sales is bullish for the economy. A decrease in retail sales will be bearish for the economy.

6. **Durable Goods Orders** – These types of orders are representative of U.S. manufacturing activity. Retail sales measure how many goods consumers are buying; durable goods order represent how many goods manufacturers are making. Durable goods are not notebooks, lamps, or picture frames; instead durable goods orders represent cars, washing machines, refrigerators, etc... Anything large and more expensive that is expected to last at least several years. An increase in durable goods orders is bullish for the economy and a decrease in durable goods orders is bearish for the economy.

Figure 33: Bearish and Bullish Indicators

7. **Federal Reserve Interest Rate Announcements and Meeting Minutes** – Many years ago, it was not common practice for the Fed to publish publicly the minutes of their regular policy setting meetings. As a matter of practice these days however, the Fed does publish their meeting minutes. In the meeting minutes, market observers look for clues on how the Fed thinks the economy is doing, potential trouble spots or areas of strength. In the end though, these observers are looking to guess whether or not the Fed will implement any aspect of their monetary policy tools – most specifically changes to interest rates. Any anticipated raise in interest rates will be bearish for the economy. Why? Interest rates as you will recall are also the cost of money. When money gets more expensive (a rise in interest rates), fewer will use it to create new goods and services. Therefore, higher interest rates are

bearish for the economy, and lower interest rates are bullish for the economy – all due to interest rates representing the relative cost of money. Figure 33 shows a simplified representation of the bearish and bullish indicators. You will note that the Fed actions and the CPI/PPI indicators are not represented there. These have a bit more detail attached to them and are not as easily distilled into a graphic.

Bid and Ask (or Offer)

The bid is the price at which a market participant (broker-dealer, exchange, ECN, etc...) is willing to buy a security from another market participant, including a customer of a broker dealer. The ask, or offer, is the price at which a market participant (broker-dealer, exchange, ECN, etc...) is willing to sell a security from another market participant, including a customer of a broker-dealer. There are always two parties to any transaction, including a securities transaction.

An example will help illustrate the roles and definitions more clearly.

XYZ Security			
Name	Bid	Name	Ask
MMA	25.01 x 1	MMB	25.03 x 1

MMA is bidding, or willing to buy 100 shares of XYZ at a price of $25.01. MMB is willing to sell 100 shares of XYZ at a price of $25.03. Note that in the marketplace, the market maker is willing to buy at the bid and sell at the ask, or buying low and selling high. The *difference between the bid and ask is the spread*. The spread is what the dealer is able to make for being willing to buy and sell that security from customers. So, if MMA is to buy at the bid that means that a customer wanting to sell must sell at the bid. The reverse is of course true as well on the ask side. If MMB is willing to sell at ask, then the customer wanting to buy the security must buy at the ask. The highest bid and the lowest offer combine to make up the National Best Bid and Offer, or NBBO.

Long and Short

A customer, broker-dealer, or market maker is said to be *long a security if they own that security*. When you are long a security, you are hoping that the price of the security increases. A customer is said to be *short a security if they sell a security they do not own*. The party who owns the security is officially the owner as of the settlement date of the transaction. Each type of security settles on a certain number of days after trade date. This is typically represented as T+?, where T = Trade Date, and ? = the number of days until settlement. For instance, equity securities normally settle on a T+2 settlement cycle. Two days after the securities have been traded, the trade settles and the ownership record is updated to reflect removal of the prior owner and addition of the new owner.

Naked and Covered

The terms naked and covered can refer to both an equity or option transaction. In an equity transaction, naked (or uncovered) typically refers to a customer or other party who sells a security without owning, borrowing or locating the security first. The short seller is naked because they do not own the security, nor have they located or borrowed the security first before selling short. A short seller is considered covered if they own, locate, or borrow the security prior to sale.

In an options transaction, being naked indicates that the seller of the option does not own the underlying security. If the option were to be exercised, the seller of the option would need to go into the market and purchase the security for delivery.

Trade Capacity

There are three different trade capacities that exist in the world of trading – agency, principal, and riskless principal. A broker always executes in **an agency capacity**. As agent, the broker never buys or sells securities from their own proprietary account. Just like a real estate agent does not buy the house you are interested in before selling it to you, your securities broker never buys the securities for their own account before selling those securities to you.

In a **principal trade capacity**, the dealer buys or sells the security to the customer out of their own inventory account. The dealer may have already owned those securities, or may have sold short the securities (because the dealer did not own them).

In a **riskless principal trade capacity**, the dealer first buys or sells the security from another counterparty, then turns around and buys or sells the same security to you, the customer. Riskless principal capacities are considered to be 'agency like', because the dealer only typically holds the securities in their own inventory account for a very short amount of time, almost not even really owning them at all!

Brokers = Agency   Dealers = Principal or Riskless Principal

For firms that are registered as brokers and dealers, they may trade with clients in one, two or all three capacities. A trade executed in more than one capacity can be expressed as agency and principal, riskless principal and agency, etc... In addition to any combination of the three capacities, a trade capacity could simply be noted as mixed capacity, or more than one of the three trading capacities.

The trade capacity has nothing to do with terms and conditions, solicited or unsolicited, discretionary or non-discretionary orders or account types.

End of Chapter Quiz

Complete these end of chapter questions to assess your understanding of the subject matter discussed in this chapter. The answers follow on the next page. For those questions you have answered incorrectly, review the appropriate section of the chapter again to make sure you understand the concepts.

1. A customer has decided to let her financial advisor make purchase and sale decisions in her individual brokerage account, but does not allow the financial advisor to wire money out of the account. What type of account is this?
   - a. Discretionary
   - b. Non-discretionary
   - c. Unsolicited
   - d. Agency

2. ABC equity security recently traded as follows:

   100 shares @ **$50.00**
   100 shares @ **$50.04**
   200 shares @ **$50.10**

   The current NBBO is **$50.09 - $50.12**. What is the bid-ask spread?
   - a. $.03
   - b. $.04
   - c. $.06
   - d. $.12

3. Which type of order is expected to be executed immediately?
   - a. Limit
   - b. Day
   - c. Stop
   - d. Market

4. You have decided to enter a stop limit order in XYZ security. Once triggered, the stop limit order becomes a(n):
   - a. market order
   - b. limit order
   - c. fill or kill order
   - d. all or nothing order

5. You have entered a stop order in XYZ security that looks like this:

   Sell Stop 100 XYZ at $23.80

   What happens to this order if the market price moves from $23.81 to $25.71?
   - a. The sell stop becomes a market order
   - b. Nothing happens
   - c. The sell stop becomes a limit order
   - d. The sell stop order is cancelled

6. In your investments class, you have been researching ABC equity security and think it would make a good investment. However, the price is too high for your liking right now. What type of order would you enter to ensure you could purchase ABC equity security without having to monitor the market minute by minute, in the event the price of ABC drops?
    a. Unsolicited order
    b. Discretionary order
    c. Market order
    d. Limit order

7. Which of the following would indicate an increase in bullish market sentiment?
    a. Lower rate of employment
    b. An increase in Real GDP
    c. Rapid increases in the CPI
    d. A fall in durable goods orders

8. Please review the following.

XYZ Security

Name	Bid	Name	Ask
MMA	$5.15 x 1	MMA	$5.24 x 2

Last five transactions occurred at $5.16, $5.17, $5.18, $5.18, $5.21 (most recent).

Given the above information, at which price is Market Maker A ("MMA") willing to buy XYZ?
    a. $5.16
    b. $5.21
    c. $5.15
    d. $5.24

9. Your financial advisor calls you up and tells you that he has found a stock that makes sense for you to purchase. After thinking about it some, you agree and tell him to buy the stock in your individual account. What type of order is this?
    a. Solicited order
    b. Unsolicited order
    c. Discretionary order
    d. Stop limit order

10. A trader at TGIF broker dealer wants to make some money trading stocks. If she sells the stock without owning it first, the trader is hoping what happens to the stock?
    a. Stock drops in price
    b. Stock increases in price
    c. Stock prices stays the same
    d. Stock price is volatile

End of Chapter Quiz Answers

1. A

The customer has given her financial advisor discretionary authority over her brokerage account. Non-discretionary would mean that the customer is making individual purchase and sale decisions for the account. Unsolicited means that the registered representative on the brokerage account did not bring the purchase or sale idea to the customer, instead the customer came up with the idea to purchase or sell the specific security on their own. Agency is a type of trading capacity, one where the firm executing the trade does not have the security pass through a firm proprietary account.

2. A

The bid ask spread is the difference between the highest bid and lowest offer. The bid ask spread does not take into consideration recent trades in the security. In this case, the bid ask spread is $.03.

3. D

Market orders should be executed immediately. A limit order is only executed once the market price reaches the limit order price. A day order is only good for that trading day. A stop order only becomes active once the market price of the security reaches the stop order price, otherwise it remains unexecuted.

4. B

Once triggered, the stop limit order becomes a normal limit order. A stop order, once triggered, becomes a market order. Fill or kill and all or nothing orders are other types of orders that can be entered, but are not triggered by a stop limit order.

5. B

Nothing happens in this case, because the sell stop order did not trade below the market price of $23.80. Sell stops are triggered when the market price falls below the sell stop order price. If the price were to move in the opposite direction below $23.80, the sell stop order would be triggered. Sell stop orders are not cancelled by movements in the security price. When stop orders are triggered, they become market orders. When stop limit orders are triggered, they become limit orders.

6. A

Of the choices provided, a limit order is the only type of order that makes sense.   A limit order is a priced order, meaning the order only executes once the market price equals or passes through the limit price on the order.   A market order executes immediately, regardless of where the stock is currently trading.   An unsolicited order does not have anything to do with price.   Instead, it only indicates that the order in that security was not solicited by the financial advisor   to the customer.   A discretionary order is a type of order that indicates that the customer provided the financial advisor and trader with flexibility on when and at what price an order was to be executed.

7. B

Recall that bullish means expansion or an increase in economic growth, and bearish means contraction or a decrease in economic growth. Of the choices, an increase in Real GDP would be bullish. Lower unemployment and a fall in durable goods orders would be obviously bearish, as these indicate economic growth could be shrinking. A rapid increase in the CPI would cause the Federal Reserve to increase interest rates, which would also be bearish for the economy.

8. C

MMA's published bid is at $5.15. This is the price at which MMA is willing to purchase XYZ security. $5.24 is MMA's ask, or the price at which MMA is willing to sell. The prices of $5.16 and $5.21 are recent trade prices for XYZ, which have no direct bearing on MMA's bid.

9. A

Given your financial advisor came up with the idea to purchase that specific security, this would be a solicited order. An unsolicited order would only fit if the customer, not the financial advisor, came up with the idea to purchase or sell a security. A discretionary order is a type of order that indicates that the customer provided the financial advisor and trader with flexibility on when and at what price an order was to be executed.

10. A

This describes short selling. A short seller makes money when the price of the stock goes down. A volatile stock moves substantially in price over a given period of time. If the price of the stock went up, the short seller would lose money. The short seller neither loses nor makes money if the stock price stays the same.

Chapter 12:   Investment Returns

Investors put their hard earned money into the securities markets for a lot of specific reasons. In the big picture however, investors are typically looking to make money (i.e., earn a return on their investment) or at least preserve what they already have (i.e., not lose money). With that in mind, let's go through the different types of investment returns.

Types of Investment Returns

Investors can earn a return on their investment in several different ways. There are seven primary ways to earn a return on investment:

1. Interest
2. Dividends
3. Realized gains
4. Unrealized gains
5. Return of capital
6. Ordinary income
7. Return on capital

Return on investment can also be called a return on capital or return on equity.

Interest

Most people are familiar with the concept of interest if they have ever had a bank savings account. The account owner deposits cash into his or her account. In exchange for the cash deposited in the bank and therefore available for the bank to loan out, the account owner receives compensation in the form of interest. In the securities industry, customers deposit funds in their brokerage account. Those funds not used immediately to purchase investments, begin to accrue interest. Likewise, if an investor sold a security, they would receive cash in their brokerage account pursuant to the sale of the investment. These funds as well would begin to accrue interest, up until the time they were used for another investment purchase.

Dividends

As noted in Chapter 4, equity securities often pay out dividends to investors. The general idea is that the company makes a profit, and shares a part of that profit with the owners/investors in the company on a regular or one-off basis. Many companies pay dividends on a quarterly basis in the U.S. Although any company can decide to pay dividends, many investors often think of mature companies that have been around a long time, like Coca-Cola, General Electric, Proctor and Gamble, etc... However, many companies that have been around for a lot less time also pay dividends, like Microsoft, Apple, and Intel. A company does not need to be profitable to pay a dividend. Dividends are paid out in one of two ways - in cash or in stock. In both cases, the company, through the Board of Directors, decides to pay out a total amount to shareholders. The difference of course comes in the form of that payout.

In the case of a cash dividend, the company typically pays the dividend in dollars and cents per share on a quarterly basis. For a stock dividend, the dividend payout can follow a similar quarterly cadence but in lieu of cash, the stockholder receives shares in the company. The company's Board of Directors has approved an amount that will be paid out in dividends, but the method of those dividends getting into the investors hands can be in cash or stock. The company typically has a press release announcing the dividend. As an example, please read the below excerpt of a press release from the Coca Cola Company[41] which looks something like Figure 34.

There are four key dates to be aware of when learning about dividends:

- Declaration date
- Record date
- Ex-date (or ex-dividend date)
- Payable date

The declaration date is the first date in time sequence and an easy concept to grasp. The declaration date is the date that board of directors announces, or declares a new dividend. The record date is the date by which you must own the stock in order to receive the dividends. In the press release above, the declaration date was October 15 (date of the press release) and the record date was noted as December 1. For a stockholder (owner of the stock) that has been an owner for a long time and anticipates owning for the foreseeable future, the record date has little real meaning. You are currently an owner and plan on continuing to be an owner of Coca Cola (symbol KO). It does have significant meaning however for a potential new stockholder. Here is why: In order to capture the dividend payment from the company, you must be considered a stockholder as of the record date.

Trade date is represented by the letter "T". Following the letter is a number, indicating the number of days after trade date. Therefore, T+2 means that this trade will settle 2 days after trade date. *T+1 means that the trade will settle 1 day after trade date*, and so on.

Figure 34: Dividend Announcement Press Release

Press Release: <u>The Board of Directors of The Coca-Cola Company Declares Regular Quarterly Dividend</u>

By: The Coca Cola Company | October 15, 2015

SIE PROFESSOR
Affordable Training for Securities Industry Careers

ATLANTA, Oct. 15, 2015 – The Board of Directors of The Coca-Cola Company today declared a regular quarterly dividend of 33 cents per common share. The dividend is payable Dec. 15, 2015 to share owners of record as of Dec. 1, 2015. The Board earlier this year approved the Company's 53rd consecutive annual dividend increase, raising the quarterly dividend 8 percent from 30.5 cents to 33 cents per common share. This is equivalent to an annual dividend of $1.32 per share, up from $1.22 per share in 2014. The increase reflects the Board's confidence in the Company's long-term cash flow.

Dividends are paid out to equity owners of common or preferred stock and must be declared by the issuer company's Board of Directors. In 2017, the settlement period for many securities was changed from T+3 to T+2. For the foreseeable future, equity securities will settle on a trade date + 2 days basis, or T+2. When purchasing a security, you are considered a shareholder or owner of the security on settlement date, not on trade date. To receive the dividend, you must be an owner of the security. Therefore, the ex-dividend date is typically one business day prior to the record date.

Let's recall the four key dates with dividends, and layer in the dates applicable to the Coca-Cola Press Release that we know so far:
- Declaration date: October 15
- Ex-date (or ex-dividend date): ?
- Record date: December 1
- Payable date: December 15

How do we figure out the ex-dividend date?

In order to figure out the ex-dividend date, you need to focus on the *record date*, or the date on which you are considered an owner of the security. If you want to receive the dividend payment, you must already own the security on the record date. You are considered the owner of the security on settlement date. Since equity securities settle on a Trade Date + 2 (T+2) basis, to calculate the day you need to purchase the security, simply purchase the security 2 settlement days prior to the record date. A settlement day is typically any day the market is opened - weekdays except for market holidays like Christmas, Good Friday, Labor Day, Memorial Day, Independence Day, etc...

If we assume December 1 (settlement day) is a Friday, that would be T+2. Counting backwards:
- T+1 would be Thursday, November 30
- T+0 (or simply T, trade date) would be Wednesday, November 29

So if you want to be an owner of Coca Cola on December 1, assuming a normal settlement, you would need to purchase Coca Cola stock on November 29. This allows 2 days to pass until settlement of the purchase.

So is November 29 the ex-dividend date? No!

Recall that the ex-dividend date is the first day the stock trades without the dividend included. That means that the ex-dividend date is T+1, or November 30. This is a question that you can expect to have to answer on the SIE Exam. A variation of this question might expect you to figure out the ex-dividend date over a weekend. Remember, weekends (Saturday and Sunday) are not considered settlement days, so they DO NOT COUNT when trying to figure out answers to stock ownership and dividend questions.

For instance, if Apple decides to pay a dividend this quarter, and notes that the record date is Tuesday, May 1, when is the ex-dividend date and the date you would have buy the stock (remember – this is the record date) to be considered the owner, and thus receive the dividend payment?

Counting backwards for Tuesday, May 1, which is T+2:
- T+1 – Monday, April 30
- Sunday, April 29 – Not a settlement date, do not count
- Saturday, April 28 - Not a settlement date, do not count
- T (Trade date) – Friday, April 27

So if you want to be an owner of Apple on May 1, assuming a normal settlement, you would need to purchase Apple stock on Friday, April 27. This allows 2 business days to pass until settlement of the purchase. The first day the stock trades without the dividend (i.e., the ex-dividend date) is Monday, April 30.

Realized and Unrealized Gains
Realized gains are the gains an investor has physically obtained through the purchase or sale of a security. Unrealized gains are the gains an investor has obtained on paper only, but not as a result of the purchase or sale of a security.

Do not let the differences between short and long positions confuse you. The key to understanding how these different positions impact your understanding is to stay focused on what the investor holding the position wants the stock to do. How does that investor make money? If you keep that in mind, you can work your way through any questions that test your understanding of the differences between long and short, unrealized and realized gains and losses.

Realized gains can be further classified as long term gains or short term gains. The method by which gains and losses are calculated is the same in both cases. The only difference is in the tax rate paid on the gains is higher when the period the securities were held for is shorter, currently one year or less. For securities held over one year then sold, any capital gains paid are taxed at the lower long-term capital gains rate.

Long Position with Unrealized Gain and Loss
Joe buys 100 shares of Apple (symbol AAPL) for $50 per share. Joe's position in AAPL increases in value when the stock price increases in value. Ninety days later, the price of AAPL is now $55 per share. Although Joe is thrilled to see the price of his APPL stock go up, he decides to hold the stock for now. Joe has an unrealized gain of $5 per share, or $500 in total. The gain or loss would become realized the moment Joe sells his shares. Up until that time, the gain or loss is unrealized (in this case, of course, it is a

gain). The realized gain or loss is calculated by subtracting the sale price from the purchase price, just like the calculation for an unrealized gain or loss.

If the price had instead dropped from $50 per share to $45 per share with Joe still deciding to hold the stock, Joe instead would have a loss of $5 per share, or a $500 total unrealized loss. The gain or the loss is considered unrealized because the gain or loss is only on paper. The investor is still willing hold the position and absorb future losses or gains.

Short Position with Unrealized Gain and Loss

Instead of buying this time, Joe instead sells short 100 shares of AAPL for $50 per share. By selling short the shares, Joe's position in AAPL increases in value when the stock price decreases. Ninety days later, the price of AAPL is now $55 per share. Although Joe is disappointed to see the price of his AAPL stock go up, he decides to hold the stock for now. Joe has an unrealized loss of $5 per share, or $500 in total. The gain or loss would become realized the moment Joe decides to buy back shares, thereby covering his short position. Up until that time, the gain or loss is unrealized. The realized gain or loss is calculated by subtracting the sale price from the purchase price, just like the calculation for an unrealized gain or loss. If the price had instead dropped from $50 per share to $45 per share with Joe still deciding to hold the stock, Joe instead would have a gain of $5 per share or $500 total unrealized gain. The gain or the loss is considered unrealized because said gain or loss is only on paper. The investor is still willing hold the position and absorb future losses or gains.

Return of Capital

Part of an investor's investment return may include a return of capital. When an investor's return includes a return of capital, part or all of that total return is, as the name alludes, returning part of the original capital investment to the investor. The return of capital as part of the investor's total return cannot include other examples of total return like dividends or interest. Return of capital is actually specified by the issuer when the return is provided to the investor. Return of capital is most common with specific types of securities, like Master Limited Partnerships ("MLPs").

Ordinary Income

Ordinary income is another type of investment return that you should be familiar with for the SIE Exam. For individual investors, ordinary income is most commonly comprised of sources such as wages, salaries, tips, commissions, and bonuses. For individual investors, ordinary income also includes interest, dividends, rental income, and short-term capital gains. Short term capital gains refer to an investment purchased and then sold in less than one year. These short term capital gains are considered, and therefore taxed as, ordinary income. One important point to note – dividends are considered ordinary income, but can be taxed at different rates in comparison to other types of ordinary income. For businesses, ordinary income is generally considered pre-tax income.

Figure 35: Components of Investment Return

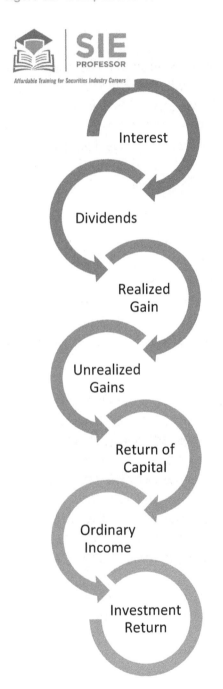

Return on Capital

An investor's return on capital (ROC"), sometimes known as return on equity is another important return measurement. Not to be confused with return OF capital, return ON capital is a measure of profitability. When an investor invests his or her money, they will rightfully want to know how much money they will make on their investment. From an investor's perspective, how effective is the company at turning an investor's capital into actual profits? There are several different types of mathematical formulas that get to return on capital, but a common formula used is as follows:

**Net Income/(Debt Capital + Equity Capital) =
Return on Capital**

The higher a company's ROC, the better it is doing for its investors at transforming the capital invested into profits. A high consistent ROC likely indicates a growth company, while a low ROC would indicate a slower growing, yet stable company. A negative ROC would indicate the company is headed in the wrong financial direction!

Return Measurements

So now we know what types of returns there are for your securities investments. How do we measure those returns so investment returns can be compared on an even and fair basis? Well, there are five primary ways to measure an investor's return:

1. Yield
2. Yield to Maturity

3. Yield to Call
4. Tax Equivalent Yield   5. Total Return

We will go through each of these return measurements now so you have an understanding of what each one means, but also the similarities and differences between them. The foundation for many measurements is yield, so let's start there.

Yield

The first concept to understand is simply yield. An investor's yield is the expected return on their investment. Simple yield is often used to describe what is expected to happen to the investment over the next year, in cash flow terms. For instance, if a bond trader states, 'this bond yields 4.5%', what they mean is that when you take the anticipated coupon payments over the next year and divide them by the price you would pay for the bond today, you would get the bond's yield. This version of yield does not attempt to determine how long you would hold the bond or what changes in interest rates might do to the price of the bond.

Let's say a bond is expected to pay an 8% coupon. Remember though that this coupon is expressed as a percentage of coupon payments to the bond's par value – NOT the price of the bond in the secondary market. If you are an investor looking to purchase a bond in the secondary market today, you do not really care what the bond pays as a percentage of the par value. You care what the bond pays as a percentage of the bond's current market price. Now that we have that out of the way, let's look at some hard numbers.

Using our 8% coupon bond and assuming the bond's par value is $1,000, we can then determine that the bondholder receives $80/year in coupon payments ($1,000 x .08 = $80). The coupons might be paid semi-annually in some cases, so you just need to be careful that you calculate the bond's annual coupon payments when determining yield. If interest rates have increased a bit recently, the price of our 8% coupon bond has dropped a bit in the secondary market – it was recently trading for $958. To determine the bond's yield, we take the anticipated coupon payments divided by the price the investor pays for the bond. Since we are buying this bond in the secondary market and not at issuance, we calculate yield as $80/$958 or approximately 8.35%.

A bond yields the coupon payment; an equity security that pays a dividend is noted as the dividend yield. The same calculation would apply to both types of securities.

Yield to Maturity

With Yield to Maturity, an investor's beginning measurement period begins on the date of purchase. It is assumed the investor will hold the investment until the investment (typically a bond) matures. Traditional equity securities do not mature – they are held until either sold, the company is acquired, or the company goes bankrupt. Equity securities will not typically be valued on a Yield to Maturity basis. Any type of security that has a maturity date though can be valued on a YTM basis.

Yield to Call

The concept of Yield to Call is measured in almost the exact same way as YTM, except the measurement period is different. The measurement period begins when the security is purchased, but ends on the first call date listed in the bond indenture. This allows the investor to determine the yield that they would receive if they were forced to sell it back to the issuer due to the call provision. Combined with the yield to maturity measurement, an investor is able to determine their yield to worst, meaning what is the least amount of investment return an investor would receive if the security was either called (yield to call) or matured without the investor doing anything at all (yield to maturity).

Tax-Equivalent Yield

This was already covered in Chapter 5, so we will not go into extra detail here. The tax-equivalent yield is used to compare the yield on a taxable investment with the yield on a non-taxable investment. Consider the following investment dilemma – Susan is trying to decide between two investments she is considering that mature on nearly the same date. The first is an AA-rated corporate bond with a yield to maturity of 3.50%. The second investment is an AA-rated municipal security with a yield to maturity of 2.75%. Note that as an investor, you are comparing two different securities, but each security is rated the same (AA) and mature on nearly the same date. This allows for an apples to apples comparison of the securities. Determining tax exempt/tax equivalent yields on securities that do not have the same rating introduces other variables into an investor's analysis, such as credit risk (the risk an issuer will default on their bonds). At first glance (all else being equal), an investor would clearly select the higher yielding corporate bond since both bonds are AA-rated, right?

Examples of various securities and their yields
- State of Alabama Municipal Bond, AA rated: 3.25%
- State of Wisconsin Municipal Bond, AA- rated: 3.40%
- IBM Corporate Bond, AA rated: 4.01%
- Waste Management Corporate Bond, AA- rated: 4.22%

What do you notice about these securities and their yields?

First, there are two types of bonds shown – corporate bonds and municipal bonds. Since we know that municipal bonds pay coupons exempt from federal taxes (unless specifically noted as taxable municipal bonds), we would expect to have municipal bonds pay a lower pre-tax rate when compared to a similarly rated corporate bond. The corporate bond is not a tax exempt bond.

Second, note the slight differences in rating. Two bonds are rated as AA; two bonds are rated as AA-. AA- rated bonds are slightly more risky than AA rated bonds. For this increased level of risk, the issuer and market forces typically require a slightly higher yield. Always make sure you look at these types of details, as it matters when trying to determine specific answers to the question! Go back to Chapter 5 to review the tax exempt yield calculations.

Total Return

The total return encompasses all types of returns that an investor has received. Total return can either be unrealized or realized gains or losses. Both dividends/interest/coupons paid to an investor and the any capital appreciation in the price of the asset are added together to come up with the total return. Let's go through a few examples.

On May 1, 2020, you purchased 100 shares of Apple stock for a price of $200 per share, making your total purchase amount equal to $20,000. This example ignores fees for simplicity's sake. Apple pays a quarterly dividend of $.10 per share. If you sell all 100 shares of your Apple stock for $225 per share one year later and have not reinvested dividends, what is your total return?

The return on the sale of the Apple stock would be calculated as the difference in purchase price and sale price. In this case, $225 - $200 = $25 per share gain. $25 per share x 100 shares = $2,500 capital gain on the sale of the stock. But over the course of the last year, you as the investor have also collected dividends. If you collected 4 dividends payments totaling $.40 per share and you owned 100 shares, you would have also collected $40 in dividend payments. These dividend payments must also be added with the capital gains to calculate total return. Recall that our capital gain on the sale of Apple stock was $2,500, so adding our $40 dividend payments to this amount gives a grand total return of $2,540 over the last year. To calculate the Total Return as a percentage of invested capital (recall that this was $20,000), simply take the $2,540 / $20,000, which equals 12.7%.

Note that there can be variations of this calculation depending on the types of investment you are talking about, and whether or not the coupons or dividends are reinvested during the invested period. For these scenarios, just make sure you understand how often the various coupons or dividends are being paid and whether or not these payments are being reinvested. If, for instance, dividends are being reinvested, you will likely be given how many additional shares have been purchased through the dividend reinvestment. If this is the case, you will simply sell a higher number of shares than when you first purchased the stock, because the dividends went to buying more shares each quarter instead of receiving the dividends as cash.

Basis Points

Basis points refer to the absolute changes in a percentage. In the securities world, this means changes in things like interest rates, yield, or return. The best way to understand the concept is through an example. On Monday, the yield on a 10 Year Treasury Bond is 1.56%. On Wednesday of the same week, the yield on the 10 Year Treasury Bond increases to 1.62%. In basis points, the yield on the Treasury Bond increased 6 basis points, or 1.62% - 1.56% = .06%. The same of course is true if the percentage unit of measurement decreases over time. Let's say on Tuesday, the yield on AA rated corporate bond is 3.56%. On Friday, the yield on the AA rates corporate bond is 3.39%. How many basis points did AA rated corporate bonds change over those few days? The answer? A decrease by 17 basis points, or 3.56% - 3.39% = .17%, where .17% can be expressed as a single number 17. In industry parlance, basis points are abbreviated as *bps*, which is pronounced as *bips*. When observing the move in interest rates, an observer might note something like, "the 30 Year T-Bill moved up 7 bps this week." This means that the yield on the 30 Year Treasury Bill increased by 7 basis points.

Cost Basis

An investor's cost basis is most typically the price at which the investor paid for the security. This is straightforward when an investor purchase the security all on the same day, at the exact time, at the exact price. Cost basis can get more complex though when a single security has been purchased on multiple days at multiple prices. An investor's cost basis is important to determine, as the amount of taxes an investor has pay on investment gains is calculated by subtracting the cost basis from the sale price of the security. Let's review a few examples.

Suppose you have purchased some Disney stock (equity symbol DIS).

On 3/1 you purchase 100 shares at $105.98.
On 3/15 you purchase 75 shares at $103.76.

What would your cost basis in the stock be?

Your total cost would be $10,598 (100 x $105.98) + $7,782 (75 x $103.76) = $18,380. The average cost basis would then take $18,380 divided by the total number of shares purchased of 175, to get $105.03. This is the average cost method of determining an investors' cost basis.
What other cost basis methods are available to investors when selling securities?

- **FIFO** – First In, First Out – This is the default method for many investors and firms.
- **Specific Share Identification** – An investor identifies at the time of the sale the specific shares that they are selling.
- **Minimum Tax** – An investor identifies the shares to be sold through the lens of which shares, when sold, incur the least amount of income taxes.
- **Maximum Gain** – In this method, the investor identifies which shares, when sold, offer the maximum gain on the sale. In other words, which shares have the biggest difference between the purchase and sale price?
- **Average Cost** – As discussed in the above example, this method blends the cost of all share purchases together and comes up with an aggregate or average cost of the shares. When selling, the investor uses the average cost it took to purchase the shares and uses that as their cost basis.
- **Inherited securities** - The cost basis of securities that an investor inherits would be the value of the securities on the date of death of the prior owner. For mutual funds, the cost basis to the new owner is the NAV at death.

The cost basis method by which an investor is selling shares (Average cost, FIFO, etc.) must be determined at the time of sale by the investor. The varying strategies can be used for different security sales, in different years, in different accounts, depending on the investor's strategies around taxes and cash flow needs[42].

Benchmarks and Indices

We have spent a lot of time so far reviewing single securities like Apple equity stock, Walmart corporate bonds, or the State of Alabama municipal bonds. Many investors prefer to buy, sell, and hold these and other types of single securities. How might an investor compare how his or her investments are performing? Are the investments doing well, or not so well? Even if the investor's investments are going 'up' in value, a particular investment may not be performing as well as it should. This is where benchmarks and indices come into play.

In its August 2017 release titled, "UNDERSTANDING MUNICIPAL MARKET INDICES, YIELD CURVES AND BENCHMARKS", the MSRB provided clear definitions of both indices and benchmarks[43]:

"An index is a statistical composite that can be used to measure changes in a market. An index measures market movement reflecting changes in prices or yields. A benchmark is the basis of measurement for an interest rate, an index or peer group of bond prices or other values that is used as a reference point."

Suppose you were trying to figure out which of two trees, which were not next to each other, was taller. The way to determine which tree is taller is to measure the height of each tree. The tree with the greatest height is the tallest, of course. Figuring out the answer to this question is impossible without a uniform system of measurement to use against the tree. This is the same concept used in the financial industry. Instead of saying 'I have the tallest tree', the security investment is measured against the securities version of the tape measure – the benchmark. Only when measuring a security against the benchmark can we determine how well or how poorly an investment is performing. Note that an index can be used as a benchmark. A benchmark is used as a reference point to compare other securities.

Examples of well-known indices include:

- **S&P 500 Index™** – the top 500 largest listed equity securities in the U.S., by market capitalization. This index is weighted by market capitalization instead of price, meaning each stock in the index make up 1/500th of the indexes' value. The index represents somewhere between 80-85% of the U.S. stock market's value.

- **Wilshire 5000 Index™** – this index encompasses virtually the entire U.S. equity securities market. It includes large capitalization, medium capitalization, and small capitalization companies.

- **Russell 3000 Index™** – this index is made up of the largest 3,000 equity securities in the U.S.

- **Russell 2000 Index™** – this index is a tricky one to remember. When you first see it, especially after reading the above other indices, you probably guessed that the index measured the largest 2,000 U.S. equity securities. That would be wrong. The Russell 2000™ index measures the smallest 2,000 securities that make up the Russell 3000™ index. This makes it the index that focuses primarily on small capitalization securities.

- **Dow Jones Industrial Average™ ("DJIA")** – the top 30 most influential equity securities in the U.S. Dow Jones determines what makes a stock influential enough to become part of the DJIA. The DJIA is price weighted, meaning that higher priced securities in the index make up a bigger percentage of the index than lower priced securities.

These are examples of commonly cited indices that are composed of equity securities. It is easier to use indices for equity securities as the equity market is much small in comparison to the bond market. There are indices for bonds as well, though they are not as well known to the general public.

One note on indices and benchmarks - typically an investor would not compare the performance of their municipal bond with the performance of the S&P 500™ index, as the S&P 500™ index does not include municipal bonds. When using indices and benchmarks, be sure you are comparing two similar things. Comparing the performance of AAPL (Apple) equity stock over the last 12 months with the performance of the Russell 2000 would not be a fair comparison. AAPL is a large capitalization equity stock and the Russell 2000™ is an index that tracks the performance of small capitalization securities. A better benchmark for AAPL would be the S&P 500™.

End of Chapter Quiz

Complete these end of chapter questions to assess your understanding of the subject matter discussed in this chapter. The answers follow on the next page. For those questions you have answered incorrectly, review the appropriate section of the chapter again to make sure you understand the concepts.

1. Over a year ago, you purchased 100 shares of XYZ security at $55. Today, you sold your 100 shares of XYZ security at $75. What type of investment return is this?
   - a. Interest
   - b. Unrealized gain
   - c. Capital gains
   - d. Ordinary income

2. Which of the following represents a long term capital gain if you buy 100 XYZ on 1/3/18 at $99?
   - a. sell 100 XYZ 1/2/19 at $110
   - b. sell 100 XYZ 7/3/18 at $89
   - c. buy 100 XYZ 1/5/19 at $110
   - d. sell 100 XYZ 1/5/19 at $102

3. Jane Investor has decided to sell short ABC stock. She sells 100 shares short at $78. The price of the stock decreases the next day to $75 when she sells the stock. Jane Investor has a(n) _____.
   - a. Realized loss
   - b. Realized gain
   - c. Unrealized loss
   - d. Unrealized gain

4. Which of the following represents a long term capital loss if you bought ABC on 6/1/18 at $40?
   - a. sell 5 ABC call options on 6/2/19
   - b. sell 500 ABC on 6/2/19 at $39
   - c. sell 400 ABC on 5/31/19 at $39
   - d. sell 400 ABC on 6/2/19 at $42

5. Jane Investor has decided to sell short ABC stock. She sells 100 shares short at $78. The price of the stock increases the next day to $80. Jane Investor has a(n) _____.
   - a. Realized loss
   - b. Realized gain
   - c. Unrealized loss
   - d. Unrealized gain

6. You own 1000 shares of XYZ equity stock. XYZ has recently announced a stock dividend of 10%. On the day prior to ex-dividend date, the stock closes at $56. On payment date, XYZ stock closes at $57. What will you receive from the issuer as your dividend payment?
   - a. 100 shares
   - b. $5.70
   - c. $5,700
   - d. $5.60

7. Which of the following is TRUE regarding payment of dividends to equity shareholders?
    a. Future dividend payments are guaranteed
    b. Dividends are typically authorized by the company Board of Directors
    c. Dividends cannot be paid in less than penny increments
    d. Companies cannot pay dividends if they carry debt on their balance sheet

8. Which of the following represents a short term capital loss?
    a. Buy 500 ABC on 6/1/18 at $40, sell 5 ABC put options on 5/31/19
    b. Buy 500 ABC on 6/1/18 at $40, sell 500 ABC on 6/2/19 at $39
    c. Buy 500 ABC on 6/1/18 at $40, sell 400 ABC on 5/31/19 at $45
    d. Buy 500 ABC on 6/1/18 at $40, sell 400 ABC on 5/31/19 at $39

9. Please review the following selected bonds, rating, and yields.

    State of New York Municipal Bond, BBB rated: 4.20%
    State of Georgia Municipal Bond, BB- rated: 4.40%
    ABC Corporate Bond, BBB rated: 5.58%
    XYZ Corporate Bond, BB- rated: 5.88%

    Assuming a 25% marginal tax rate, which bond has the highest after-tax yield?

    a. New York Municipal Bond
    b. Georgia Municipal Bond
    c. ABC Corporate Bond
    d. XYZ Corporate Bond

10. Which of the following is TRUE regarding the tax treatment of stock dividends?
    a. Long term capital gains taxes must be paid on stock dividends in the year received
    b. Short term capital gains taxes must be paid on stock dividends in the year received
    c. The appropriate dividend tax rate must be paid on stock dividends in the year received
    d. Taxes must be paid when the stock dividend is sold

End of Chapter Quiz Answers

1. C

An unrealized gain is a gain that has not actually occurred yet because the asset, in this case the stock, has not been sold. It is a loss only on paper because the stock is worth less than what you paid for it. Interest income is typically earned off of cash balances, not stock investments. Ordinary income would be earned through employment. Capital gains, are earned in the short run (less than a year owning the investment) or long-term (more than a year owning the investment).

2. D

Capital gains are earned in the short term (less than a year holding the investment) or long term (more than a year holding the investment). A gain means that the investment is worth more today than when you purchased it. Buying more of the same security would not result in a realized long term capital gain. Selling at $89 would result in a loss, and selling prior to 1/3/19 would classify the gain as short term.

3. B

Jane has a realized gain because she made money on her stock sale. In a short sale, an investor makes money when the price of the stock drops in price, not increases in price. An unrealized gain would occur if Jane did not sell the stock, but the price still dropped to $75. Jane would have realized gain if she sold the stock for more than she purchased it for, and an unrealized loss if the stock went up above her purchase price, but she did not sell it yet. Again, this is because she is selling short.

4. B

When an investor holds a security position for more than a year and then sells that position, that sale is considered a long term gain or loss. Sales that occur within one year of purchase are considered short term capital gains or losses. If the investor makes money after the sale of the position, it is considered a gain. Losing money after the sale of the position is considered a loss.

5. C

Investors who sell short are hoping that the price of the security decreases. Since the price of the security has increased, this means that the short seller is losing money and therefore has a loss. However, because the investor has not yet bought back the security (this would be how an investor gets rid of their short position), this loss would be an unrealized loss.

6. A

When the issuer declares a stock dividend to shareholders, shareholders receive shares of stock, not cash. A 10% stock dividend is then paid to the shareholder based on current holdings, or 1,000 shares.

7. B

Dividend payments are never guaranteed and must be declared by the company's board of directors. Dividends can be paid in cash or stock, in whatever increments the board of directors determines is appropriate. There are not typically limitations on paying dividends if there is debt on a company's balance sheet.

8. D

Both choices B and D are sales that generate a loss for the investor, as the price they are selling at, $39, is below where they purchased the security, $40. However, only one of the sales occurred in less than one year from the date of the purchase. Short term capital gains and losses can only occur within one year from the original purchase date. Anything over a year would be considered a long term capital gain or loss.

9. D

On their face, the XYZ corporate bond has a higher yield at 5.88%. However, this is a before tax yield. Recall that most municipal securities are not subject to federal taxes, and may be exempt from state taxes. To compare the yields, you must convert the corporate bond yield to an after tax yield. You do this by taking 4.40%/(1-.25) = 5.87%. In this case, the XYZ bond has a higher yield. Although not part of this answer, note that the yield is higher on bonds that are rated lower.

10. D

Stock dividends, unlike cash dividends, are not taxed in the year they are received. Instead, an investor is required to pay taxes on those stocks dividends when the stock dividend position is sold. This makes D the only possible choice.

Chapter 13:   Corporate Actions and Trade Settlement

The term "corporate actions" means that the issuer is taking some action that has a direct impact on shareholders. Corporate actions are typically authorized by the company's Board of Directors. For some corporate actions, like buybacks and stock splits, the shareholder cannot do anything to alter or change the corporate action. Other corporate actions, like rights offers, require the shareholder's active engagement. For all corporate actions however, the issuer must notify FINRA, or other SROs as applicable, at least 10 calendar days prior to the record date of an upcoming corporate action. This 10 day period allows FINRA time to make the necessary notifications to market participants, updates technology systems, and helps to ensure a fair and equitable marketplace. If you recall from our earlier discussions about dividends (also considered a corporate action), the record date is the date where ownership interest is essentially measured, determining in essence who does and who does not participate in the corporate action. If you are an owner of the security on the record date of the corporate action, then you can participate in that corporate action. Also recall that buying something on Monday does not mean you own the equity security on Monday (outside of a same day settlement). If you were to buy a stock on Monday this means, in a typical situation, that you will own the equity security on Wednesday (settlement date). SEC rules require that the issuer provide the following information to FINRA on upcoming corporate actions:

- additional details relating to stock or reverse splits
- for distribution of securities, generally the amount of the security outstanding immediately prior to and immediately following the dividend or distribution and the rate of the dividend or distribution
- the title of the security

- date of declaration
- record date
- payment or distribution date; for cash distributions, the amount to be paid per share
- details of any conditions that must be satisfied to enable the payment or distribution

Lastly, securities firms are required to notify their customers of upcoming corporate actions in writing, which can be in email or through hard paper copy correspondence. There are several important types of common corporate actions that we will review in this section:

- Stock splits
- Reverse stock splits
- Buybacks

- Tender offers
- Exchange offers
- Rights offerings

- M&A

Stock Splits and Reverse Stock Splits

When a stock splits, there are more shares after the split than there were before the split. The reason a company splits it's stock is to lower the overall price of the stock, in theory making it more affordable for retail investors to purchase. The thing to remember about any type of stock split is that the owner of the security is no better or worse off after the stock split than they were before the stock split. The best way to understand stock splits is to review an example. Let's say Google decides to split its stock. Prior to the stock split, Google has 100 million shares outstanding. The stock split is noted as a 3:2 split, or for every 2 shares of Google that you own, you will receive 3 shares. Sounds like a good deal, right? If you own 100 shares of Google that were trading at $200 before the split, how many shares would you have after the split?

The answer? 150 shares. So why is150 shares the correct answer?
Start with 100 shares. Take the 100 shares and multiply those shares by the numerator 3, then divide by the denominator 2. Expressed mathematically, it looks like this: 100 x 3/2.

What happens to the share price however? If you, the stockholder, are in no better shape financially after the split than you were before the split, what was the value of the shares before the split then? 100 shares x $200 per share = $20,000. If after the split the investor is no worse off, the investor would also then have $20,000 worth of Google stock. An individual share of stock is only worth $133.33 after the split. Here is the math behind the answer: $200/per share x the inverse of the split, or $200/share x 2 / 3 = $133.33. Every investor who owns shares is impacted by the stock split – an investor can neither opt in nor opt out of the split. All owners of the stock are impacted based upon their ownership of the stock, regardless of how many shares the investors own. One thing to note is that in the event of stock split, the records are typically kept by the transfer agent as to which shareholders are eligible to receive the additional shares.

Stock dividends work the same, but instead of cash, the shareholder receives additional stock. If a company pays a cash dividend of 10% and you have 100 shares, after the stock dividend you now have 110 shares. The share price would then be reduced by 10$.

For reverse splits, the concept works, well, in reverse. In a normal stock split remember that the share price decreases while the number of shares increases. In a reverse split, the share price increases while the number of shares decreases. Let's say that XYZ Company wants to execute a reverse stock split. The shares of XYZ Company currently trade for $2 per share. The company announces that the reverse split will be executed at a ratio of 1:10. For every 10 shares that you own, you will receive instead one share. The stock price will not be trading at $2 however – it will now trade at $20 per share, or $2 per share x 10 shares / 1 share = $20.

Stock splits will reduce your cost basis per share equivalent to the proportion of the stock split. The cost basis for reverse stock splits work in the opposite fashion – an investor's cost basis is increased, but again, the overall cost basis of the investor's position does not change. Your overall cost basis will not be impacted in either circumstance, because the overall monetary value of your position is not impacted by a stock split.

Lastly, a bit on general corporate actions. When there is a corporate action on a security, there is often an adjustment that must be made to either that security or any open order to purchase or sell that security. For instance, when a company issues a dividend of $.50 per share, any open order is reduced in price by that same $.50 per share. This is necessary because after payment of a dividend, the company is worth slightly less due to payment of the dividend (distribution of cash, an asset, to shareholders). Customers who do not want their orders adjusted for dividends must provide specific instructions to their broker-dealer firm holding their account. Typically, these special instructions are called DNR, or Do Not Reduce.

Buybacks

A buyback, or share repurchase occurs when a public company issuer purchases the shares or bonds of its own company. The most typical use of the term buyback exists when equity shares of a company are repurchased by the public company issuer. A company may also repurchase bonds in the same manner. When a company affects a buyback of equity securities, it must do so under strict securities laws to avoid being perceived as manipulating their own stock. Generally speaking, this means that companies have limits as to the number of shares they can buy in a given day or week, and when they can buy those shares. Companies conducting equity buyback transactions usually repurchase their shares during normal market hours.

Why would a company do this? Shares repurchases are conducted by companies for many indirect reasons, but the direct reason is to reduce the number of outstanding shares held by the public. This means that earnings paid out through dividends, for instance, are paid out to fewer shareholders, because there are fewer shares outstanding.

Tender Offers

"A tender offer is a broad solicitation by a company or a third party to purchase a substantial percentage of a company's Section 12 registered equity shares or units for a limited period of time. The offer is at a fixed price, usually at a premium over the current market price, and is customarily contingent on shareholders tendering a fixed number of their shares or units.[44]"

A tender offer can either be made by the issuer of the securities or by an existing shareholder of the securities. When making a tender offer, there are several filings and notices that must be made to the SEC. If the entity making the tender offer is not the issuer of securities but is going to acquire more than 5% of the outstanding shares, that person or entity will need to make a filing with the SEC. If the acquirer is purchasing less than 5% of the outstanding shares, the tender is considered a 'mini-tender'.

Exchange Offers

An exchange offer is an offering of securities whereby one security is exchanged for another. Practically speaking, an exchange offer could look something like one of the following:

- Exchange the issuer's bonds for new bonds;
- Exchange the issuer's bonds for the issuer's common stock; or
- Exchange the issuer's common stock for the common stock of a new company being split off from the original issuer.

An exchange offer often occurs as part of or a condition of a merger or acquisition between two separate companies.

Rights Offerings

A rights offering is another type of securities offering. In Chapter 4, we discussed various types of offerings – IPOs, secondary, and seasoned offerings. The basic premise between the offerings from Chapter 4 and a rights offering is the same – the issuer is looking to raise capital. Instead of going to the public markets though, a rights offering means that the shares are offered to the issuer's existing shareholders. To entice existing shareholders to purchase additional shares, the issuer prices the rights offering at a discount to the market price of the issuer's publicly traded security. Rights are offered to existing owners of the security as of a specific record date. The price at which the rights' offering is sold is called the subscription price. The rights' offering gives the existing shareholder the opportunity to maintain their existing ownership percentage of the issuer through the 'right' to purchase more shares. The rights' offering only lasts for a limited or fixed period of time. The value of the rights depend on many factors, including market volatility, how many days are left in the rights offering fixed period, market factors, and interest rates. If the rights holder does not exercise their rights within the fixed period of time outlined by the rights offering, those rights expire.

Some existing shareholders will purchase additional shares through the rights offering. Other shareholders will not, and instead, will sell their rights on the open market to other market participants. Rights offerings that are allowed to be sold to non-owners are called transferable rights offerings. Rights offerings that are NOT allowed to be sold are called non-transferable rights offerings. Whoever agrees to use the rights offering to purchase shares before the expiration of the fixed offering period will receive their new shares as of a specified settlement date.

Mergers and Acquisitions ("M&A")

At a basic level, a merger is simply two firms combining into one. An acquisition is one firm buying all or a part of another. The distinction is often hard to notice in many situations, as it can be easier to accept selling to someone if that sale is viewed as a merger instead of an acquisition! If a firm wants to sell all or part of its business, that firm will often hire an investment banking firm to do so. An investment banker who works with the firm selling all or part of their business is known as a sell-side advisor. It is the job of the sell-side advisor to understand the goals of its client (the firm selling) and to focus on meeting those goals. Sometimes the selling firm is looking to sell 100% of itself. Other times, the selling firm is only looking to sell a department or a group of assets it holds on its balance sheet. The selling firm usually wishes to receive the highest price possible; in other situations perhaps, the speed of the deal completion is the primary goal. Another goal of the sell-side advisor is to perform a valuation exercise. In other words – whatever is being is sold – how much is it actually worth? This value is often described as a range instead of a specific number. Once a value is established by the sell-side advisor, the sell-side advisor approaches potential acquirers. The potential acquirers are often represented by a buy-side advisor from another investment bank. The mechanics and steps of how this is performed are beyond the scope of the SIE. However, the M&A work typically involves many months with many discussions, meetings, and proposals along the way. If the buyer and seller can agree on price and terms a transaction, then the M&A transaction is completed. In exchange for advising the firm selling or the firm buying, both the sell side advisor and the buy side advisor receive a fee. This fee typically depends on the amount of work involved and the size of the sale or purchase.

It should be noted that the M&A transaction can involve only private companies, only public companies, or a mix of both. M&A activity involving a public company can result in more shares being issued, or a once-public company being absorbed into another public or private company. If a public company is being bought through an M&A process, the transaction is announced to the public, and typically requires approval of one or both of the involved company's Board of Directors. Once Board approval is obtained, a closing date for the transaction is announced, along with any final terms. Final terms include compensation to the shareholders whose ownership interest is being purchased.

For instance, the common equity shareholders of a Public Company X, who have an ownership interest in Public Company X, have just been notified that Public Company X's Board of Directors has approved the buyout offer from Public Company Y. Public Company Y will give all Public Company X shareholders $10 per share in cash and .75

shares of equity stock of Public Company Y in exchange for the common equity shareholder's stock in Public Company X. In more basic terms, shareholders of the selling company are typically compensated for selling their shares by receiving cash and stock in return. The mix of cash and stock is one of the terms negotiated between the buy-side and sell side advisors, each representing a different company. On the closing date, Public Company X will cease to exist, and all Public Company X shareholders will receive their compensation in cash and/or new stock in Public Company Y.

Figure 36: Two Sides of an M&A Transaction

As public companies have obligations to the securities market, sensitivity around M&A activity is extremely important. Those using information about pending M&A transactions for personal gain can subject themselves to insider trading liability, discussed further in Chapter 17.

Proxies and Voting

Occasionally, a public company needs shareholder approval to take an action like approving a merger or changing corporate bylaws. Direct owners of the company's stock are able to vote on these company matters by casting their votes. One share of stock is equal to one vote, or proxy vote. When company shareholders are asked to vote on important company matters, they typically do so through a proxy. A proxy is essentially a representative vote, in lieu of attending a meeting or vote in person. The process is similar to how a U.S. citizen would vote in their local, state, or national elections for political office. Think of a proxy like an absentee ballot, with the vote like going to the actual polling place to case your ballot for the President of the United States!

Not all stocks are owned directly by individual or institutional investors, however. In many cases, mutual funds own the shares of the underlying companies. Although retail or institutional investors may own shares of the mutual funds, these investors are not the direct owner of the underlying company shares themselves. Instead, the direct owners of the shares are the mutual funds themselves. In the case where a mutual fund owns shares of a company that has an open proxy vote, the mutual fund's board of directors is expected to vote on behalf of the interests of the mutual fund owners.

Trade Settlement

Trade date is the date the security was bought or sold. This is noted simply as "T". T+2 is therefore two days after trade date. Most securities settle on a T+2 basis, including equities, bonds, municipals, mutual funds, and exchange traded limited partnerships. Other securities bought or sold for settle on a next day, or T+1 basis, including options and government securities. It is assumed that if an order is placed to buy or sell securities and that order ends up executed, the order placed was for a standard settlement cycle. Figure 37 shows the specific settlement periods, broken down by type of security.

The above table lists the standard settlement of the most common security types. A customer may request the broker-dealer to agree to a shortened or extended settlement. A shortened settlement is anything sooner than the standard settlement. For an equity trade, a shortened settlement could be same day settlement (T+0), next day settlement (T+1), or T+2. If marked to settle on T (again, also known as trade date), this would indicate a *same day settlement*. An extended settlement would therefore be any settlement date after the standard settlement date. For a municipal trade, this could be T+3, T+4, etc...

As there are two sides to any trade, if you are considered the owner of the securities on T+2 (settlement date for a regular-way equity settlement), you must therefore pay for the securities. On settlement date, the new owner is considered the owner of record but must compensate the seller by paying the agreed upon amount. The opposite of course is true if you are the party selling the securities - you must deliver the securities on settlement date to receive your proceeds (cash) in the transaction.

Physical vs Book

Most securities are held in book form or book-entry form. This simply means that the broker-dealer that holds your account (or more precisely, your broker-dealer's clearing firm) also holds your securities on their books. Each broker-dealer and/or clearing firm must keep a list of securities owners on their books, thus the term 'book form' or 'book entry form'.

In some cases, the owner of the securities does not hold the securities in book entry form with a broker-dealer. For these cases, a physical certificate is used to denote ownership of the security.

Figure 37: Standard Settlement Cycle of Various Security Types

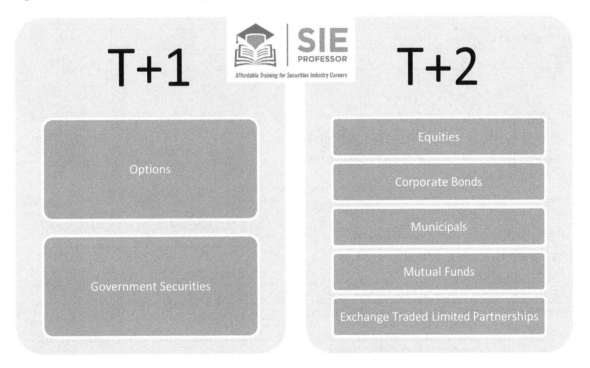

Owning a security in physical form as opposed to book entry form makes the process of selling the security much more cumbersome and time consuming. This is because selling a security in physical form typically requires the use of a transfer agent to verify the validity of the owner, as it is easier to fraudulently claim ownership with a counterfeit piece of paper (physical stock record) versus owning the shares in book entry from through your broker-dealer.

A security held in book entry form will typically settle on a normal settlement cycle for that particular security. A security held in physical form, however, will typically take longer to settle, due to the fact that the owner needs to find the physical certificate, deliver it to the broker-dealer, who then needs to work with the transfer agent to verify the valid ownership of the physical certificated shares.

End of Chapter Review Exercise

Lookup Security MSFT (Microsoft) on Yahoo! Finance's Quote Lookup.   Fill in the following:

Bid Ask (only during market hours)	
What is the size for each bid and ask?	
Volume	
52 Week Range	
Dividend date	
Ex-Dividend Date	
Market Cap	
What is the bid and ask?	
Previous Close	

Under the statistics link, note the following:
- What was the most recent press release?
- What is the declaration and payment date?
- What is the last sale

Select the options link next, and complete the following:

Select a series of options that expire in the near future.	
What is the first strike price listed?	
What are the bid and ask for the first strike price listed?	
What is the % change from the prior day?	
What is the last sale?	

End of Chapter Quiz

Complete these end of chapter questions to assess your understanding of the subject matter discussed in this chapter. The answers follow on the next page. For those questions you have answered incorrectly, review the appropriate section of the chapter again to make sure you understand the concepts.

1. XYZ Company has declared a 4-2.5 stock split. If you own 200 shares before the split, how many shares will you own after the split?
    a. 120 shares
    b. 200 shares
    c. 320 shares
    d. 800 shares

2. ABC Company has declared a 3-1 reverse stock split. You currently own 300 shares before the split, and the stock is worth $5. After the reverse stock split, what is your total position in ABC worth?
    a. $0
    b. $500
    c. $1,500
    d. $2,000

3. Which of the following is true regarding an exchange offer?
    a. IPO listed on a U.S. Exchange
    b. Quote published by a market marker to purchase or sell securities
    c. Condition of a merger or acquisition between two separate companies
    d. Issuer offers to exchange the issuer's bonds for options

4. Which of the following securities settle on a T+1 basis?
    a. Corporate Bond Securities
    b. Government Securities
    c. Municipal Securities
    d. Equity Securities

5. A public company equity issuer would likely be required to put which of the following to a shareholder proxy vote?
    a. Hiring of a Chief Operating Officer
    b. Filing of annual tax returns
    c. Approve a merger
    d. Issuing new stock

6. XYZ Company has declared a 4-2.5 stock split. If you own 200 shares before the split, how many additional shares will you own after the split?
   a. 120 shares
   b. 200 shares
   c. 320 shares
   d. 800 shares

7. You are considered the owner of the security on what date?
   a. Order date
   b. Trade date
   c. Settlement date
   d. Ex-date

8. Existing shareholders are permitted to do which of the following in an equity rights offering?
   a. Sell their rights on the open market
   b. Buy stock in another company
   c. Buy the issuer's bonds instead of the stock
   d. Buy their rights from the issuer

9. You have researched and decided to purchase XYZ security by placing a limit order at $55. XYZ security has declared a $.50 dividend. After ex-date, what will happen to your limit order?
   a. It will be cancelled
   b. Reduced in price to $54.50
   c. Increased in price to $55.50
   d. Price remains unchanged at $55

10. An equity security position held in physical form will typically settle:
    a. T+0
    b. T+1
    c. T+2
    d. Greater than T+2

End of Chapter Quiz Answers

1. C
To figure out the total shares you own after the split, take the number of shares you own and multiply it by 4, then divide by 2.5 (200 * 4 / 2.5 = 320). Because the first number (4) is larger than the second number (2.5) in the split you know it is a normal stock split. If the second number was larger than the first number, then you would know that this is a reverse split.

2. C
In either a reverse stock split or a normal stock split, your overall stock position is worth exactly the same both before and after the split. In a reverse split, the number of shares you own decreases, but the value of the stock increases. Your position is worth $1,500 both before and after the split.

3. C
An exchange offer typically occurs when one company is buying another. The purchase is made through all stock, a combination of cash and stock, or all cash. In an exchange offer, a certain ratio of securities is exchanged as compensation for the sale. Published quotes occur in the secondary market, not as part of the acquisition process. Listing an IPO is part of going public and would not be part of an exchange offer. Exchanging bonds of options would not be part of an exchange offer typically, but could exist as part of a convertible bond indenture.

4. B
Government securities settle T+1, while everything else listed settles T+2.

5. C
Typically, only the most important and atypical things require the approval of shareholders. What shareholders must approve directly is outlined in the company's corporate charter and bylaws. Mergers typically require approval of shareholders. The other items listed are more routine and are handled by the board of directors or the company's management team.

6. A

A stock split increases the number of shares owned and decreases the share price of the security being split. In this question, the investor starts with 200 shares. Given a 4-2.5 split, the math works like this: 200 x 4 / 2.5 = 320. The question asks for additional shares owned, which in this case is 120 shares (320-200 = 120).

7. C

An investor is considered the owner of a security on settlement date. This is the date that the cash to purchase the security and the ownership rights are exchanged. The date you place the order and the date you trade the security do not determine ownership. Ex-date refers to the date by which a security trades without an upcoming corporate action, like a dividend.

8. A

A rights offering allows existing shareholders to purchase an additional position in the existing company. These rights, if not used, can be sold onto the secondary market. A rights offering does not require the existing shareholder to buy their rights from the issuer, but the security itself is purchased from the issuer.

9. B

Limit order, absent instructions otherwise, are typically adjusted for payments of cash dividends. As the issuer is paying out a dividend, which comes from the issuer's cash account, the market value of the issuer will drop by the corresponding amount of the dividend. Since this is a purchase, the limit order will be adjusted downward by the amount of the dividend.

10. D

Equity securities held in book entry or electronic form will typically settle T+2. Because these securities are held in physical form, they will normally take more than two days to settle. Government securities and options normally settle T+1.

Chapter 14:   Customer Accounts and Compliance Considerations

Account Types and Characteristics

There are seven main account types:

1. Cash
2. Margin
3. Options
4. Discretionary/Non-discretionary
5. Fee-based vs commission
6. DVP vs. RVP accounts
7. Education accounts

For the SIE Exam, the specifics around account types are straightforward. When distinguishing between Account Types and Customer Account Registrations, keep in mind 'the what/how' and 'the who'. Account Types have to do with *the what* or *the how – what* types of securities, *what* types of collateral (cash and margin) or *how* the registered representative from the firm holding the account is actually paid (fee based or commission). Customer Account Registrations have to do with *the who - who* can open these accounts and *who* can be the account holder of record.

Cash Accounts

In a cash account, securities transactions are fully paid for by settlement date in cash. Customers are free to buy and sell securities as long as those transactions are 100% paid for by settlement date. In a cash account, the customer is not permitted to borrow money for transactions.

Margin Accounts

In a margin account, a customer is permitted to borrow money from the brokerage firm carrying the customer account. How much money can be borrowed depends in part on how much risk the brokerage firm wants to take, and what federal law limits. This means that part of the purchase in a margin account is paid for in cash, and part of the purchase can be made in credit. As with any loan, you have to pay interest back to the lender for the privilege of using their borrowed funds. The maximum amount that can be loaned in a margin account is 50% of the account value on an initial purchase, with a minimum of $2,000. This limit is set by the Federal Reserve under Regulation T. Customers do not have to borrow at that limit – they could choose to borrow much less, say 10 or 20%. In addition, not all securities can be purchased using margin. These prohibited securities include penny stocks, non-listed securities such as OTCBB (Over the Counter Bulletin Board) and Pink Sheets/OTC Equities, or IPO (Initial Public Offering) securities. These are prohibited under rules – the brokerage firm carrying the account can make more restrictive decisions about which securities you can purchase on margin, and which you cannot.

Under Regulation T, if a customer buys and sells a security in a cash account without paying for the stock in full, the firm must place a 90 day restriction on the position. This is called freeriding and covered in more detail in Chapter 17.

Given that customers are borrowing money, there is typically special approval required to open up a margin account, usually including steps such as checking the creditworthiness of the customer, and the customer's history with the firm carrying the account.

Upon opening up a margin account, the firm and the customer must agree to a margin account agreement, outlining how the margin account will work. In conjunction typically with the margin account agreement, the customer must also receive a margin disclosure statement. This margin disclosure statement makes customers aware of the risk of using margin.

Let's go through a few margin concepts to deepen our understanding of margin.
- **Initial Margin** – The initial margin requirement is 50% according to Regulation T. So, if an investor wanted to purchase 100 shares of security XYZ at $50, the total purchase amount would be $5,000. The maximum amount an investor could borrow on margin is 50%, or $2,500. Remember the $2,000 minimum.
- **Maintenance Margin** – The maintenance margin is just like the initial margin requirement, except that the margin requirement percentage is typically lower. Currently, regulators have maintenance margin set at 25%. Many firms who loan funds to investors may have the maintenance margin set higher. Following our earlier example, the investor's cash amount in the margin account must stay above 25%, otherwise the firm would exercise a margin call.
- **Margin Call** – When a customer's account falls below the maintenance margin level, that customer receives a margin call. A margin call requires a customer to deposit enough cash into the account to bring the account back into compliance with the maintenance margin requirement.
- **Hypothecation** – When a customer uses securities in a margin account as collateral for a loan, this is referred to as hypothecation. If the assets in the customer's account were to fall below the maintenance margin requirement, the firm carrying the account (and loaning the customer the margin) could sell the pledged, or hypothecated, assets to bring the account within allowable margin levels.
- **Re-Hypothecation** – A customer who permits rehypothecation allows collateral in their securities account to be used by the firm carrying the account. These securities are essentially loaned out to others in this arrangement. Customers who allow rehypothecation of securities are compensated through lower fees or margin loan rates in some fashion.

Now that you have some basic understanding of margin, what accounts can you use margin in? The list is short:

1. Individual;
2. Joint

3. Entity - Corporation, partnership, or association;
4. Partnerships

Each of the above account types are further described below. One last point on margin accounts - you cannot use margin in custodial accounts, like UGMA or UTMA accounts, retirement accounts (IRAs), 401k, 403b and other qualified plans, or trust accounts. Remember, using margin is risky. It can only be used in certain accounts and within certain federal and FINRA defined limits.

Options Accounts
Options accounts have a separate purpose in the securities world. If an individual investor or an entity wishes to trade in options, they must open up a specific options account. All options trades must occur within the options account. Options trades must be fully paid for by settlement date, which for options trades is T+1.

Discretionary and Non-Discretionary Accounts
Discretionary and non-discretionary accounts are another important account type to understand. In a discretionary account, a customer turns over decision making about what securities to buy and sell and when to buy and sell those securities to their broker (registered representative). The default setting for customer accounts is non-discretionary, meaning that the customer is the one making the decisions on the account activities. Some customers prefer to have their registered representative use their expertise to direct activity within their account – that is the primary reason customers may choose to open up a discretionary account.

Fee Based and Commission Accounts
Depending on how the customer wants to compensate their registered representative, the customer could choose to open up a fee-based account or a commission-based account. In a fee-based account, the registered representative (or more often the investment advisor) is not paid on a transaction basis, but instead on a percentage of the assets in the account, typically quarterly or annually. Fee based accounts are most often associated with investment advisors which are separate and apart from a registered representative at a broker-dealer, although registered representatives at broker-dealers could utilize a fee-based account in some circumstances.

If your account has a market value of $50,000 and you pay 1% for the fee-based account, you would pay approximately $125 per quarter, depending on the market value of the account. Here is the math:
$50,000 x 1% / 4 = $125

The 1% fee is divided into 4 parts for the quarterly fee. The fee would be assessed for each account that is managed on a fee basis.

Knowing that the market value of the account changes daily means that the fee charged will change each quarter. The level of assets are sometimes referred to as Assets Under Management, or AUM.

In a commission-based account, there is no quarterly or annual fee assessed. Instead, the customer pays on a transaction basis. For each transaction in a customer's account, the customer pays the registered representative a fee, calculated as a percentage of the trade, or as a flat amount. Typically the fee as a percentage of the account is smaller as the total transaction size is larger. The fee as a percentage of the account is larger as the total transaction size is smaller. Commissions (or commission equivalents) are charged to customers where the firm executing the customer's order in that account acts as an agent or risk less principal. When the firm executing the customer's order buys or sells to the customer at a different price in which they transacted with the customer, the fee paid to the registered representative is referred to as a markup or markdown. When a customer is buying, the fee is called a markup because the firm buys at a lower price at the customer buys.

Let's go through an example. Firm ABCD accepts an order from Customer A to buy 100 XYZ security. The customer's order is executed at a price of $50. This makes the total transaction value equal to $5,000 (100 shares x $50). Since Customer A is transacting in a commission account, the customer will pay 2% of the transaction, or $100. The commission could be a flat fee instead – the decision is up to the broker-dealer holding the customer account and the customer. The compensation that the registered representative and broker-dealer holding the customer account will receive is typically agreed to and disclosed to the customer at the time the customer account is opened.

In the event of a markup or markdown, the broker-dealer executing the order would for instance pay $49 to acquire the XYZ security, then turn around and sell the security to the customer at a price of $50. This difference in price of $1.00 is called the markup. So, $1.00 x 100 shares = $100. The compensation to the registered representative and the broker-dealer is roughly the same. When a customer sells, the process works in the opposite direction, with the firm selling high and the customer selling lower. This is referred to as a markdown. A transaction in a commission account is any purchase or sale of securities. There is no commission charged for wiring funds in or out of the account, although firms may charge a separate fee for these types of services. Customers can only be charged a commission or a markup/markdown, but not both.

DVP and RVP Accounts

DVP and RVP accounts are, simply put, one way to settle transactions. They are primarily used by institutional customers, but can be used by retail customers as well. They allow a customer to trade with multiple broker-dealers, but maintain a central account, known as a Prime Brokerage Account, where all of the customer's positions are held.

DVP = Deliver Versus Payment   RVP = Receive Versus Payment

Most retail customers maintain an account with only one broker-dealer. Institutional customers, however, usually maintain accounts at multiple broker-dealers. A retail account is usually a cash or margin account, meaning securities bought and sold within the account are bought and sold either for cash, or with funds borrowed from the broker-dealer (margin).

DVP and RVP accounts are mostly used by institutional investors. In a DVP/RVP account, securities are purchased and sold just like in a retail cash account. However, in a DVP/RVP account, the institutional investor does not maintain a cash balance nor does the institutional investor borrow money to pay for securities transaction like in a margin account. Instead, the securities purchased are delivered to the account on settlement date when the corresponding cash transfer payment is made to the same account, thus offsetting each other. The opposite is true for a RVP transaction. In a RVP transaction, the opposite occurs. The institutional investor sells shares of a security, but those shares of that security are not held in that account. Remember, a DVP/RVP account does not maintain security or cash positions on an ongoing basis. The cash and securities that exist in the account only exist for a short window – essentially settlement day, if everything goes well.

Education Accounts

It is important to note that education accounts are an important account type. However, because there is a lot of detail required for these accounts, these are covered in Chapter 8. Here are the specific education account types you should be aware of and familiar with:

- 529 Account
- Coverdell Savings Account
- ABLE Account

Types of Customer Account Registrations

Customer accounts can be registered in seven primary ways. A customer account can be registered or named to (a) an:

1. Individual
2. Joint
3. Entity
4. Partnership
5. Trust (revocable, irrevocable)

6. Custodial (UGMA/UTMA)
7. Individual retirement accounts (IRAs), 401k, 403b and other qualified plans, RMDs, contributions

FINRA provides a good summary of opening up new accounts, documents required, and reviewing brokers in a short overview[45].

Individual

An individual account is opened for *one person*, not for an *entity*, or *more than one person*. An individual account would be opened as that person's legal name, for instance, "John H. Smith". Only the individual named on that account may provide instructions to the firm handling the account, unless specific written instructions have been provided to the contrary in the form of a written Power of Attorney or written discretionary authority. This limitation helps to ensure the security and privacy of the account owner. A Power of Attorney provides another individual the ability to transact in another person's or entity's account without prior approval of the individual named on the account. A Power of Attorney can range from limited to full, depending on what the individual on the account wants. A limited Power of Attorney could provide authorization to buy and sell securities, decide when and how to invest dividend or interest payments, etc. A full Power of Attorney includes all capabilities authorized in a limited Power of Attorney, but also includes more expansive powers, like authorization to wire money out of the account to a third party.

Joint Account

A joint account is just like an individual account, except that there are two individual names listed on the account instead of one. A joint account cannot be opened on behalf of an entity. A joint account would be opened under both names, such as John H and Jane T. Smith. Although joint accounts are typically opened for two parties, these accounts can be opened for more than two parties. There are a few flavors of joint accounts to be mindful of here – Joint Tenants with Rights of Survivorship ("JTWROS") account and Tenants in Common ("TIC") account. In a JTWROS account, the death of one of the joint owners means that all assets in the account at death immediately pass to the joint owner still alive. For TIC accounts, the death of one of the owners means that their proportional ownership of the account passes to their estate, not to the other joint owner(s) of the account. The ownership of the assets is then governed by the will or state law. For two owners of a TIC account, each owner would own 50% of the account. For three owners of a TIC account, each owner would own 33%, and so on. Joint account owners must decide at account opening and update as necessary thereafter, where they would like notice of account activity, such as account statements and trade confirmations, to be sent.

Entity Account

An entity would have to open up an account to match their structure – Limited Liability Corporation (LLC), C-Corporation, Public Issuer, sole proprietorship, etc. To open up an entity account, the entity would need to provide documentation verifying the legitimacy of the entity such as corporate charter, corporate resolution, by-laws, or articles of incorporation. The specifics on what type of documentation is required depend entirely on the entity type. Regardless of entity type, however, the entity must provide documentation on who at the entity is authorized to take action regarding the account. Otherwise, anyone at the entity could try to place orders to buy and sell securities in the entity's account! Entities must indicate, through their authorized person on the entity's account, where they would like notice of account activity, such as account statements and trade confirmations to be sent.

Partnership Account

Partnership or Limited Liability Partnership ("LLP") accounts work in very similar fashion to some combination of joint accounts and entity accounts. Partnership and LLP accounts are for an entity that is formed by two or more persons. Just like our earlier authorization instruction discussions for individual and entity accounts, all partners must authorize which partner or partners are able to place transactions in the account, or transfer money in and out of the account. Upon account opening and updated as necessary thereafter, the partnership or LLC must indicate to whom and where they would like account statements and trade confirmations sent.

Trust Account

In a Trust account, the account is titled not in the name of an individual, joint individuals, or entity; it is titled in the name of the trust. For instance, the account name would read as: "John H. Smith Revocable Trust Dated November 1, 2018". The date refers to when the trust was established or created. If the trust had more than one individual, the account name would read as: John H. and Jane T. Smith Revocable Trust Dated December 1, 2018. Much like other accounts, an individual must be specified that can handle the affairs of the Trust account. The trustee(s) is/are often those people that the trust is named after if they are still alive. If that individual(s) have deceased, the trustee(s) may be a family member or an attorney who set up the trust to begin with. Upon account opening and updated as necessary thereafter, the trustee must indicate to whom and where they would like account statements and trade confirmations sent.

Custodial Account

Custodial accounts are different than other account types, as the assets in custodial accounts are being held for someone else's benefit. There are two primary types of Custodial Accounts - Uniform Gift to Minors Act and Uniform Transfer to Minors Act.

- Uniform Gift to Minors Act ("UGMA") – can hold securities, cash, bank deposits, and insurance policies.
- Uniform Transfer to Minors Act ("UTMA") – can hold everything an UTMA account can hold, but can also hold real estate or fine art.

In UGMAs and UTMAs, the assets in the account are owned by the minor child but controlled by the custodian (typically the parent or guardian) until they reach the age of 21. *These accounts are opened under the tax ID of the minor.* Individuals under the age of 18 are considered minors and cannot make decisions regarding their account. Even between the ages of 18 and 21, the future account owner does often not have much ability to transact in the account. Once the minor reaches the age of 21, however, the account ownership AND control of the account change to the now non-minor (over the age of 21). This age limit does vary by state to some degree, although most use the age of 21.

Once a gift is given to a minor under UGMA or UTMA, that gift must be promptly placed within the UGMA or UTMA account by the custodian. Once a gift has been given to a minor under UGMA or UTMA, it cannot be revoked or taken back by the giver or the custodian. In addition, there is only one custodian per UGMA or UTMA account. That custodian must act solely in the minor's best interest, not the custodian or anyone else's best interest. State law governs the specifics of how UGMAs and UTMAs work for minors, custodians, taxes, successor custodians, etc.

IRA

Individual Retirement Arrangements, or IRAs are one of the most common forms of retirement accounts. The U.S. Government created these types of accounts over the years as a way to encourage individuals to save for their retirement. To incentivize individuals to contribute to the account, the U.S. Government has attached specific tax incentives to each type of account. IRA's come in several types, including:

- Traditional IRA
- Roth IRA
- SEP IRA
- SIMPLE IRA

For the purposes of the SIE Exam, we discuss the high level details of each type of account only. Contribution limits to IRA's are made on a calendar year basis, plus additional time up to the tax filing date for the prior tax year. For instance, Judy would like to make a contribution to her Traditional IRA for 2020. Judy can contribute to this account in 2020 or up until the IRS filing deadline for 2020 taxes, usually in April 2021.

Traditional IRA

Overview: A Traditional IRA is the most common type of IRA. With a Traditional IRA, the individual can contribute an amount up to the maximum, as long as that individual has earned income for the tax year. Earned income includes wages, tips, commissions, etc. Earned income does not include things like dividend income or capital gains. An important note for spouses who do not have earned income themselves (stay-at-home parents, for instance) – these individuals can still contribute to a Traditional IRA as long one of the spouses has an earned income sufficient to cover the entire contributions (earned income is greater than $6,000 per year for one contribution to one spouse's IRA, or $12,000 for two contributions to both spouse's IRAs).

2020 Contribution Limits: $6,000 per individual plus an extra $1,000 for anyone over the age of 50. Therefore, for anyone over the age of 50, that individual can contribute $7,000. The extra $1,000 contribution is called a 'catch up' contribution.

Tax Benefits: Contributions to a Traditional IRA are made pre-tax or after tax. Pre-tax contributions can be made for individuals in lower income tax brackets, where after tax contributions are required of individuals in higher tax brackets. Once the contribution has been made into the Traditional IRA, the growth and earnings compound tax-deferred, meaning the individual does not pay income taxes on any growth or earnings inside the IRA each tax year. Many individuals have a 401k, Roth 401k, 403b, or other similar Qualified Plan. If you leave your employer and had such a Qualified Plan, an individual could roll the Qualified Plan balance into a Traditional IRA or Roth IRA, depending on how the contributions were made. This is known as a Rollover IRA and is not subject to the annual contribution limits of $6,000 per individual. Mandatory withdrawals called *required minimum distributions* must begin after reaching the age of 72. This is way that the U.S. Government ensures that they begin to collect tax revenue on the withdrawals. There are allowances for hardship withdrawals prior the age of 59 ½ for things like buying your first house, or major medical bills.

Roth IRA

Overview: Roth IRA's are similar to traditional IRA's in that they provide tax benefits and the same notes on spousal IRAs, Rollover IRAs, and hardship withdrawals listed above in the Traditional IRA section are applicable to the Roth IRA. Also the same from the Traditional IRA – you can only contribute cash, the contributions need to be made by someone with earned income, and the contributions must be made in the same calendar year (until April 1 the following year) timeframe.

2020 Contribution Limits: The same contribution limits for the Traditional IRA apply.

Tax Benefits: In a Roth IRA (and Roth 401k), the account grows tax-free, meaning all earnings generated in the account can be removed without paying taxes after an individual has reached the age of 59 ½. In exchange for the benefit of tax-free growth and withdrawal, individuals contributing to a Roth IRA (and Roth 401k) do not get an upfront tax deduction on their contributions. An individual may rollover funds from a Qualified Plan, but those funds must have been contributed on an after-tax basis (Roth 401k for instance), and not on a pretax basis (traditional 401k). There are no *required minimum distributions for Roth IRAs.*

SEP IRA

Self-employed individuals or small business owners are permitted to contribute to a Simplified Employee Pension (SEP) IRA. A SEP IRA is a type of traditional IRA that only companies can contribute to, not employees and can be used for business that have one or more employees. Contributions made go into the SEP IRA and are considered tax deductible to the entity making the contribution. The contribution is not tax deductible to the employee and the employee does not pay any taxes on the contributions or balance until the employee withdrawals the money in the SEP IRA after they reach the age of 59 ½. Unlike a traditional IRA, however, the SEP IRA has significantly larger contributions limits. In 2019, an employer can contribute up to $56,000 or 25% of income, whichever is less. Other important facts about SEP IRA's – contributions are made on an all or nothing basis, meaning if an employer contributes to their own SEP IRA, they must also contribute the same amount to ALL OTHER SEP IRAs of employees.

SIMPLE IRA

The Savings Incentive Match Plan for Employees IRA, or SIMPLE IRA is another type of Traditional IRA plan appropriate for small businesses and self-employed individuals. With a SIMPLE IRA, an employee is permitted to make a contribution in addition to the employer contribution. This is one important difference between SIMPLE and SEP IRA (remember employees are not allowed to contribute to SEP IRAs). Contribution amounts in a SIMPLE IRA also work a bit different – employers must contribute to the SIMPLE IRA by contributing a flat 2% of compensation or by matching up to 3% of compensation. Employees and employers have separate contribution limits.

Qualified Retirement Plans

The term Qualified Retirement Plan includes several different types of account plans, including 401k and 403b. 410k and 403b are named such because they actually refer to the section of the IRS Code that allowed the specific plan's formation.

A 401k is a type of Qualified Retirement Plan that employers offer their employees. Employees can contribute to the plan up to an IRS maximum of $19,500 in 2020, plus an extra $6,500 for anyone over the age of 50. Therefore, for anyone over the age of 50, that individual can contribute $26,000. The extra $6,500 contribution is called a 'catch up' contribution. Employers may choose to match employee contributions but are not required to do so. With the 401k plan, the employer selects several different types of mutual funds for the employee to choose from. In some 401k plans, employees can also invest in single securities or stock in the employer company. The employee selects both the amount to contribute and in which mutual fund or other security to invest in, typically using automatic direct transfer from the employee's compensation. The IRS also places a maximum on the amount the employer and employee can contribute in total, which is driven by the contributions of all eligible employees. The IRS does this so the plan remains balanced, meaning both highly paid and non-highly paid employees contribute. If only highly paid employees contributed, the annual maximum contribution amount would shrink.

403b's are similar to 401k's, except 403b's are for non-profit organizations, where 401k's are only applicable to for-profit entities.

One note about withdrawals – only those employees over age 59 ½ may withdrawals funds from their 401k without penalty. The only exception that some plans allow is to withdrawals funds at age 55 if the employee still works for the employer sponsoring the 401k. Qualified distributions from Roth 401k and Roth IRAs are both excluded from federal income taxes. This would not be the case with traditional IRAs or 401ks.

SIPC and FDIC Coverage

FDIC and SIPC were both covered in Chapter 1. SIPC provides account holders insurance in the event the firm holding their securities positions becomes insolvent. The FDIC does the same for non-securities positions (demand deposits, time deposits, etc.). All firms that hold customer securities accounts are required to be members of SIPC. All firms that hold customer non-securities positions are required to be members of FDIC.

End of Chapter Quiz

Complete these end of chapter questions to assess your understanding of the subject matter discussed in this chapter. The answers follow on the next page. For those questions you have answered incorrectly, review the appropriate section of the chapter again to make sure you understand the concepts.

1. Which of the following account types obligate you to take a required minimum distribution?
   a. Defined Contribution
   b. Roth IRA
   c. Regular IRA
   d. Defined Benefit

2. If you are 40 year old employee you can contribute a maximum of _____ to a 401(k) and _____ to an IRA.
   a. $19,500, $6,000
   b. $26,000, $6,000
   c. $19,500, $7,000
   d. $26,000, $7,000

3. When one of the two account owners of a Joint Account with Rights of Survivorship account passes away, what happens to the account?
   a. The account assets must be transferred to an IRA within 60 days
   b. It becomes the sole property of the remaining account owner
   c. 50% of the account value passes to the heir(s) of the deceased account owner
   d. The account assets must be transferred to a trust account within one year

4. The maximum amount that can be loaned in a margin account is what percentage of the security being margined?
   a. 25%
   b. 40%
   c. 50%
   d. 75%

5. What must a customer do when they receive a margin call?
   a. Deposit cash into the account
   b. Purchase more securities
   c. Open up a new account
   d. Enter into a hypothecation agreement

6. In a UGMA account, at what age does control of the account ownership change to the now non-minor child?
   a. 16
   b. 18
   c. 21
   d. 25

7. The amount of margin that must be in the account when the account is first established is:
   a. 33%
   b. 40%
   c. 50%
   d. 75%

8. In which of the following accounts can a customer use margin?
   a. Custodian
   b. Trust
   c. Partnership
   d. IRA

9. You have placed an order to purchase 100 shares of XYZ security at a price of $75. The financial advisor's compensation is 2% of the total account value, calculated each quarter. This is an example of which type of account?
   a. Commission
   b. Fee-based
   c. Discretionary
   d. DVP

10. A deliver versus payment account is most common with which of the following types of customer accounts?
   a. Joint
   b. Institutional
   c. Individual
   d. Trust

End of Chapter Quiz Answers

1. C
Required Minimum Distributions, or RMDs, only apply to Regular IRAs. Defined benefit plans are a category of retirement account types, and include pensions.   Defined Contribution plans are another category of retirement account types, and include 401k and 403b plans. Roth IRAs do not have RMDs.

2. A
The contribution limits for this individual are $19,500 per year to the 401k and $6,000 to the IRA. If the individual was older than 50, they could make **additional catch up** contributions of $6,500 per year to their 401k and $1,000 to their IRA.

3. B
The right of survivorship aspect of the account means that all of the assets in the account will pass to the other person listed on the account. If the account was simply a joint account, the deceased account owner's heirs would inherit 50% of the account value, unless another ownership percentage was stated.

4. C
25% is the maintenance margin that must be applied once the position has been entered into. 50% is the amount of initial margin that must be deposited when a position is first entered into.

5. A
A customer has two basic choices when they receive a margin call – deposit more cash in their account, or sell some securities to raise additional cash. Purchasing more securities would not be permitted, as the customer already is short on margin. Opening up a new account or entering into a hypothecation agreement will do nothing to solve the margin call.

6. C

Although there can be some variances for state law and individual circumstances, the age at which assets transfer ownership in a UGMA is 21. Age 18 is considered an adult, but even between 18 and 21 the future UGMA owner does not have much ability to transact in the account.

7. C

The amount of margin that must be in the account at account opening is called initial margin, and is 50% of the account balance.

8. C

Margin can only be used in a few types of accounts, including a partnership account. Custodial, Trust and IRA account prohibit the use of margin.

9. A

This is an example of fee-based compensation. A commission is generated and paid out on a per transaction basis, not on the total value of the account itself. A DVP account deals with how trades settle with a prime broker and do not impact compensation type. A discretionary account means that the registered representative has the ability to make buy and sell decisions on behalf of the customer.

10. B

DVP/RVP accounts are most common with institutional firms, who choose to keep their assets with a prime broker, and not with individual executing broker-dealer firms. Retail accounts, such as joint or individual accounts are typically not DVP/RVP, as their assets are held by the firm where they execute their trades. Trust accounts will likely fall into this last category as well.

Chapter 15:   Anti-Money Laundering (AML) Compliance

AML is a wide ranging program within the securities industry that covers all areas of a firm's business and associated persons' activities. AML can be broken down into four key categories:

1. AML Basics
2. Structuring, Layering, and Other Money Laundering Activities
3. AML Compliance Program
4. AML Regulators

AML Basics

AML or anti-money laundering is a general term used to describe programs that are designed to prevent and/or detect money laundering. But what is considered money laundering? Money laundering is any attempt to disguise, mask, or conceal proceeds from criminal activity so that the unlawful proceeds appear to be from legitimate, non-criminal sources. When you think money laundering, think of a washing machine and paper currency – dirty cash goes in, gets washed, and clean cash comes out when the washing machine stops. It's the same exact cash, but it sure looks different!

Financial institutions are required under the U.S. Patriot Act and Bank Secrecy Act to have AML programs that attempt to discover and avert money laundering activity. Many other countries have similar laws with a wide range of obligations and requirements of those financial institutions. In the securities industry, the SEC, FINRA, SROs, Federal Reserve, and the Department of the Treasury all have a role to play in AML detection, oversight, and enforcement. Individuals or financial institutions that are found guilty of violating AML laws, rules, and regulations can find themselves subject to both criminal and civil penalties, including jail time, fines, suspensions, and terminations from the industry. In the securities industry, the term "AML" encompasses a wide range of activities, although not all of these activities are specific to money laundering.

Structuring, Layering, and Other Money Laundering Activities

There are typically three stages in a money laundering scheme – Placement, Layering, and Integration.

In the **Placement** stage, a money launderer attempts to introduce the dirty cash into the financial system. This can be done in multiple ways. Money launderers may attempt to combine dirty cash with cash from legitimate business ventures. Other possible Placement strategies could include currency exchanges, where dirty funds in one currency are simply exchanged for 'clean' funds in another currency.

Figure 38: The Three Stages of Money Laundering

Stage 1	Placement
Stage 2	Layering / Structuring
Stage 3	Integration

The **second stage** is the **Layering** or **Structuring** stage. In this stage, the goal of the money launderer is to obfuscate the origins of the illicit funds. This makes it harder for authorities to have a clear audit trail of where the dirty money came from and where it is going, as it becomes harder to tell the difference between legitimate and illegitimate transactions. Some examples of Layering include: (1) Electronically routing funds from one bank to another, splitting and combining funds intentionally, and (2) Entering into complex or unnecessary financial transactions or investments without a clear economic purpose, often without real concern for the outcome of the investment.

The **final stage** is the **Integration** stage. In the Integration stage, the now 'clean' money is back in the full possession of the money launderer. The money launderer can now use the cash for whatever purpose they desire. Purchasing assets like art work, real estate, jewelry, boats, and vehicles are typical ways a money launderer uses the now 'clean' money. Unlike the movement of cash in the banking system, using cash to purchase assets is harder for authorities to track, and therefore a popular outlet for money launderers.

AML rules, regulations, and regulatory enforcement actions have also helped further entrench the concept of *willful blindness* into the industry. Willful blindness refers to the idea that an individual or a group of individuals have taken steps to deliberately avoid or ignore the knowledge of the facts surrounding illegal or questionable activity, including red flags.

AML Compliance Program
AML rules and regulations require several important elements within an overall AML program. These include:
- AML Compliance Officer
- Customer Identification Program and Know Your Customer
- Suspicious Activity Reports
- Independent Testing
- Training for Employees and Managers

Anti-Money Laundering Compliance Officer

All securities industry firms are required to appoint an Anti-Money Laundering Compliance Officer ("AMLCO"). The AMLCO is an individual with overall responsibility for the firm's AML program. The AMLCO is required to develop and AML Compliance Program including WSPs reasonably designed to comply with all industry rules and regulations.

Customer Identification Program ("CIP") and Know Your Customer "(KYC")

In the securities industry, a Customer Identification Program is referred to as C.I.P. or 'CIP' (pronounced 'SIP'). All broker-dealers who have customers must conduct CIP reviews to reasonably ensure that they can identify each of their customers. The rules around CIP pertain not only to broker-dealers who have customers, but also to any financial services firm such as banks and credit unions. The FDIC has published an excellent overview that students should review[46].

In CIP, a firm must typically verify that customers identify through documentary or non-documentary means. Examples of documentary means include such items as a driver's license or passport for individuals, and trust documents or articles of incorporation for entities. Non-documentary means could include obtaining a customer's social security number or taxpayer identification number, date of birth, and address. Obviously, non-documentary means are likely to be less effective at identifying a customer's identity. For this reason, firms that have an AML obligation may choose to primarily use documentary means to identify customers as it is more reliable and presents less risk.

After verifying a customer's identity, the firm must both keep a record of how it was able to identify a customer, and then compare that customer's name against a specific set of government lists. There are several different types of institutions or entities that are exempted from CIP requirements. These include:

- States
- Municipalities
- Governmental authorities (e.g., FNMA, GNMA, FHMC, etc.)
- Publicly listed U.S. companies
- Financial institutions regulated by the SEC, Commodity Futures Trading Commission, Federal Reserve, FDIC, etc.
- Banks regulated by a state bank regulator

Suspicious Activity Report ("SARs") Protocol

SAR's are filed by financial institutions to alert regulators and other federal officials of potential suspicious activities that have occurred. The contents of SAR filing and even the fact that the SAR was filed by a firm must not be shared broadly, and only shared with those who have a need to know. SARs can be filed for a variety of reasons.

Some common reasons include suspicion of criminal activity, a transaction that has no business or legal purpose, or structuring transactions to avoid reporting requirements. SAR's are confidential when they are submitted to FinCEN for review. The information provided to FinCEN must be complete and provided within 30 days of the activity, or within 30 days of when the firm first learns of the activity.

What are some of the SAR report categories?

- Elder exploitation
- Insider relationships
- Embezzlement
- False statements
- Self-dealing
- Structuring

- Money laundering
- Check fraud
- Credit card fraud
- Identity theft
- Source of funds
- EFT/wire fraud

- Transaction patterns
- Beneficiary designations
- Market manipulation
- Altered documents
- Forgery

SARS are filed by financial institutions identifying red flags in account activity, money movements, trading patterns, customer information, or suspicious activities. What might some red flags be for potential AML activity? Let's say you are a broker who is trying to open up a new retail brokerage account for a new client. When opening up the account, you ask for the customer's address, phone number and date of birth. Because you live in the local area, the address given by the customer is not one with which you are familiar. In fact, after digging further, you learn that the customer has provided you with an address that does not actually exist! Now, perhaps the customer just made a mistake and provided the incorrect address. Whether that is the case or not, the fact that the customer has provided you an invalid address, is by itself a red flag. A red flag simply means that more verification and a closer review of the customer must be done. Here are some other examples of potential red flags:

Suspicious conduct from client's can be considered a red flag. For instance, you would consider behavior to be a red flag if the client:
- asks a lot of questions about your firm's AML policy
- provides false information or refuses to provide information
- uses a dead person's social security number

As we discussed earlier in this chapter, securities firms are required to have AML policies and procedures in place as well as systems to detect and prevent illegal activity. There are many information databases used by broker-dealers to verify customer information and determine if fake addresses are being used, or if an invalid social security number is being used to open an account. The *source of funds* can also raise some red flags during the review process. Some examples include:

- higher than expected deposits into an account. If a client has indicated that they makes $5,000 per month but regularly deposits $10,000 per month, this would be a red flag.

- All or some of the source of funds come from higher risk jurisdiction, including those jurisdictions identified by regulators as such
- Client is reluctant or refuses to identify where the funds are coming from

Lastly, certain types of *account activity* can raise red flags. For instance:
- Third party wire requests can be suspicious, as fraudsters often try to get firms to wire money to a third party without the consent of the account owner. How is this possible? Fraudsters often hack your email account, and then send email instructions to your financial advisor in an attempt to sell securities and/or simply wire available cash to the third party account.
- There is a mandatory reporting threshold of $10,000, meaning that any cash transaction over $10,000 must be reported according to government guidelines by filing a Currency Transaction Report. Some fraudsters will try and break up larger money movements into smaller transactions in an attempt to evade AML systems and controls and cash transaction reporting requirements. For instance, instead of wiring $12,000 to another account, the fraudster will break up the wire into 3 parts, of approximately $4,000 each. Breaking up the wires, or deposits into smaller units is considered to be a red flag.
- Client uses starter checks (indicated by a low check number), has an out of state address, or has a Post Office Box on their checks.
- No trading activity occurs in the account. What sense does it make to open up an account, deposit money, but never actually make any trades or buy any securities at all? This would naturally be suspicious, especially if there is a lot of wire activity in and out of the account.
- Penny stocks are a common battlefield in problematic activity. Since penny stocks are trading at a low price, it takes smaller amounts of cash to purchase large quantities of equity stock. Often penny stocks are targets of fraudulent promotions with someone's real ownership interests being concealed to the market.
- Price manipulation of a stock, meaning an attempt to drive the price of the stock up or down for illegal purposes.
- Activity not in line with proposed investment activity – If an investor says they is interested in corporate and government bond investments when they opens up an account, then suddenly become interested in trading options or penny stocks, this would be a clear red flag.

In fact, many of the fraudulent or prohibited behaviors identified in Chapter 17 may also have a SAR reporting component to them once they are identified by the financial institution.

Independent Testing
Independent testing of an AML program is important, as it allows an outsider of the firm to take an objective view of an individual firm's overall AML program. Independent

testing of a firm's AML program is required to be conducted annually. The independent testing is performed by an individual or entity with knowledge and experience in AML matters and is often familiar with the practices of other firms, and can therefore identify potential weaknesses much easier. There are a few exceptions to this annual testing requirement, such as Capital Acquisition Brokers ("CAB") and any other firm that does not execute transactions for customers or otherwise hold customer accounts or act as an introducing broker with respect to customer accounts (e.g., engages solely in proprietary trading or conducts business only with other broker-dealers), in which case such "independent testing" is required every two years (on a calendar-year basis).

Training for Employees and Managers

Employees need to be able to recognize red flags when dealing with customers and customer activities. When employees notice something unusual or a potential red flag, those employees typically have a duty to escalate their concerns to a manager. The Manager is often not dealing directly with a customer, but may in some cases. The Manager is usually responsible for supervising the employee and reasonably ensuring that they are following firm procedures and industry rules (like AML rules). Managers are trained on how to supervise, what to look for, and to whom they should escalate their concerns. In the AML context, a manager will be trained to escalate any potential AML concerns to the firm's AML Compliance Officer (or AML Compliance team). Training for employees and managers helps everyone to know how to handle AML-related situations with customers, how to recognize potential red flags, and to whom and when to escalate their concerns.

AML Regulators

There are several regulators and resources created by regulators involved in AML laws, rules and regulations. You should be able to distinguish between each of these regulators based upon what their primary focus is, plus their roles and responsibilities.

Office of Foreign Asset Control (OFAC) – The following is from the treasury.gov website and contains a great synopsis of what OFAC is and what OFAC does:

"The Office of Foreign Assets Control (OFAC) of the US Department of the Treasury administers and enforces economic and trade sanctions based on US foreign policy and national security goals against targeted foreign countries and regimes, terrorists, international narcotics traffickers, those engaged in activities related to the proliferation of weapons of mass destruction, and other threats to the national security, foreign policy or economy of the United States. OFAC acts under the Presidential national emergency powers, as well as authority granted by specific legislation, to impose controls on transactions and freeze assets under US jurisdiction.

Many of the sanctions are based on United Nations and other international mandates, are multilateral in scope, and involve close cooperation with allied governments."

Specially Designated Nationals and Blocked Persons (SDNs) List

The following is again from the treasury.gov website and contains a great synopsis of the SDN list:

"As part of its enforcement efforts, OFAC publishes a list of individuals and companies owned or controlled by, or acting for or on behalf of, targeted countries. It also lists individuals, groups, and entities, such as terrorists and narcotics traffickers designated under programs that are not country-specific. Collectively, such individuals and companies are called "Specially Designated Nationals" or "SDNs." Their assets are blocked and U.S. persons are generally prohibited from dealing with them."

Financial Crimes Enforcement Network (FinCEN)

The following is again from the treasury.gov website and contains a great synopsis of FinCEN:

"FinCEN is a bureau of the U.S. Department of the Treasury. The Director of FinCEN is appointed by the Secretary of the Treasury and reports to the Treasury under Secretary for Terrorism and Financial Intelligence. FinCEN's mission is to safeguard the financial system from illicit use and combat money laundering and promote national security through the collection, analysis, and dissemination of financial intelligence and strategic use of financial authorities.

FinCEN carries out its mission by receiving and maintaining financial transactions data; analyzing and disseminating that data for law enforcement purposes; and building global cooperation with counterpart organizations in other countries and with international bodies.

To fulfill its responsibilities toward the detection and deterrence of financial crime, FinCEN:

- Issues and interprets regulations authorized by statute;
- Supports and enforces compliance with those regulations;
- Supports, coordinates, and analyzes data regarding compliance examination functions delegated to other Federal regulators;
- Manages the collection, processing, storage, dissemination, and protection of data filed under FinCEN's reporting requirements;
- Maintains a government-wide access service to FinCEN's data, and networks users with overlapping interests;
- Supports law enforcement investigations and prosecutions;
- Synthesizes data to recommend internal and external allocation of resources to areas of greatest financial crime risk;

- Shares information and coordinates with foreign financial intelligence unit (FIU) counterparts on AML/CFT efforts; and
- Conducts analysis to support policymakers; law enforcement, regulatory, and intelligence agencies; FIUs; and the financial industry."

The collection of and amendments to of various laws, rules, and regulations that FINCEN acts under is commonly referred to as the Bank Secrecy Act (BSA). The BSA provides FINCEN with wide-ranging powers in the area of anti-money laundering enforcement.

Financial Action Task Force (FATF)

FATF is a collective group of about 37 or so nations that come together to try and address a more global approach to anti-money laundering. FATF passes recommendations that are then considered by the FATF membership within their own country as laws, rules, or regulations. Think of FATF as an entity that promotes common laws, rules, and regulations between member governments with the goal to reduce the differences in what these laws, rules, and regulations say and in how they are applied. From an anti-money laundering perspective, it is important that as many countries as possible have very similar frameworks for dealing with money laundering. If there are material differences in countries with how money laundering is required to be detected and enforced, criminals will more likely use these differences to have a better chance at avoiding detection by government officials.

SEC, FINRA and other SROs

Each of these regulators has rules and regulations pertaining to AML that are enforced on a regular basis. Most regulators, during the course of routine examinations or if there is a reason to ask questions pertaining to AML, will review a securities firm's AML Compliance Program to make that program is reasonably designed to detect AML violations.

End of Chapter Quiz

Complete these end of chapter questions to assess your understanding of the subject matter discussed in this chapter. The answers follow on the next page. For those questions you have answered incorrectly, review the appropriate section of the chapter again to make sure you understand the concepts.

1. Which of the follow correctly places the three stage of money laundering in the correct order, from first stage to last stage?
   a. Placement, Layering, Integration
   b. Integration, Placement, Layering
   c. Layering, Integration, Placement
   d. Placement, Integration, Layering

2. Financial institutions are required to report cash or cash equivalent transactions over what amount?
   a. $3,000
   b. $10,000
   c. $50,000
   d. $100,000

3. Which of the following is considered layering?
   a. Exchanging one currency for another
   b. Splitting and combing funds by electronically routing funds between banks
   c. Purchasing assets like jewelry and real estate
   d. Opening up a brokerage account and depositing funds

4. When evaluating KYC and CIP documents, which of the following would be considered non-documentary?
   a. Driver's license
   b. Trust documents
   c. Passport
   d. Social security number

5. Which of the following may be considered suspicious behavior, and therefore be considered an AML red flag?
   a. Asks a lot of questions about your AML policy
   b. Moved 2 times in the last year
   c. Has been married 3 times
   d. Wants to open up an account for their niece

6. Which of the following would be suspicious from an AML perspective?
    a. The customer has moved 2 times in the last 5 years
    b. The customer was born in a foreign country
    c. The customer wants to make large cash deposits
    d. The customer used to own a business that went bankrupt

7. Which of the following is an example of the Integration stage of money laundering?
    a. Creating complex financial transactions
    b. Sending cash outside the country
    c. Buying a business
    d. Exchanging small dominated cash bills for large denominated cash bills

8. When evaluating KYC and CIP documents, which of the following would be considered documentary?
    a. Social security number
    b. Date of birth
    c. Address
    d. Trust documents

9. Which of the following is an example of the Placement stage of money laundering?
    a. Making investments in a brokerage account
    b. Creating complex financial transactions
    c. Sending cash outside the country
    d. Buying a house or a commercial property

10. Which of the following would be least likely to be considered a suspicious activity under AML rules?
    a. Customer provides false information
    b. Telephone number provided matches another unrelated client
    c. Customer is unwilling to provide required information
    d. Bank account was just recently opened

End of Chapter Quiz Answers

1. A

Placement, Layering, and Integration is the correct of money laundering stages. Placement is the first stage, and involves getting the illicit funds into the financial system. Next comes layering, and involves routing the funds to different banks in an effort to mix the dirty money with clean money, or make it appear that the dirty money is clean money. Lastly is integration, where the funds are used for legitimate purposes are often brought out of the financial system.

2. B

Cash transactions over $10,000 are required to be reported on a CTR, or currency transaction report. If a customer made a series of transactions of $3,000 four times in a day, a CTR would be required to be submitted as well because the total would be $12,000, which is over the $10,000 reporting limit.

3. B

Routing the funds and splitting them up is an indication of layering. Opening up a brokerage account and depositing funds and exchanging one currency for another currency occurs at the placement stage. Purchasing assets occurs at the integration stage.

4. D

A driver's license, trust document, and passport all involve a type of document, implying those are documentary means of satisfying KYC and CIP requirements. A social security number is a non-documentary way to help meet KYC and CIP requirements.

5. A

Asking questions about a firm's AML program is a certain AML red flag. Although the other options could be viewed as red flags under certain circumstances, they are not obvious red flags that would cause an immediate AML concern.

6. C

By itself, the most suspicious item of the choices is the large cash deposits. One aspect of AML review is knowing the source of funds, and cash is hard to track and determine where it came from. Moving or being born in a foreign country are not red flags from an AML perspective, nor would owning a business that went bankrupt (again, by themselves).

7. C

Creating complex financial transactions or sending cash outside the country are two examples of the layering or placement stage of money laundering. Exchanging small bills for large bills is an example of the integration stage of money laundering. Buying a business is the only listed example of the integration stage of money laundering. This stage is where the money launderer uses the illicit funds to purchase legitimate assets.

8. D

The only documentary item listed is the trust document. The other items are all examples of non-documentary means of KYC and CIP.

9. C

Buying a house or commercial property is the only listed example of the integration stage of money laundering. This stage is where the money launderer uses the illicit funds to purchase legitimate assets. Creating complex financial transactions or sending cash outside the country are two examples of the layering or placement stage of money laundering. Making investments in a brokerage account is the money launderers attempt to integrate their dirty funds into the financial system, and is an example of the integration stage of money laundering.

10. D

This is a 'least likely' question. Just having opened up a bank account is not suspicious by itself and is something that happens every day without concern. Customer's providing false information or not wanting to provide all requested information are certainly red flags that warrant AML concern.

Chapter 16: Books and Records, Privacy, Communications with the Public, and Suitability

Customers may receive many types of communications from the broker-dealer where they hold their account. In addition, the broker-dealer is required to maintain many types of books and records pertaining to their business and their written or electronic interactions with their customers.

These books and records include anything from accounting records, electronic communications, and evidence of supervision and review of transactions to policies and procedures. These documents are required to be retained for varying lengths of time. Books and records rules are among the most fundamental and basic rules that apply to firms in the securities industry.

Books and Records Requirements

Broker-dealers that are FINRA or exchange members are required to maintain books and records for a specific period of years after they have been created. Although FINRA, SEC, MSRB, and the exchanges all have slightly different requirements, all regulators have some type of tiering, depending on the required book and record. For instance, the general requirement is to keep books and records for a period of 6 years. This includes information about customer trades and orders. Other books and records are only required to be kept for a period of 3 years, such as bank statements, or communications sent and received. Still others are only required to be kept for 18 months, such as evidence of supervision. Knowing the intricate details of which record you need to keep and for how long is beyond the scope of the SIE Exam. Focus instead on the requirement to keep records pertaining to the business of the firm, including records about customers and their activities.

In addition to books and records, there are two types of communications most relevant for customers - customer confirmations of trading activity and customer statements.

Account Statements

The look of account statements will vary among broker-dealers. Each account statement shows the record of the account as of the end of statement period, as well as all activities in the account occurring within the statement period. This allows the customer to review the transactions in the account to ensure that all activity is appropriate.

Customers are required to be provided statements on a regular basis. If there is trading activity (the buying or selling of securities) within a customer account, that customer must receive a statement representing that activity on a monthly basis. This is referred to as a 'monthly statement'. If there is no activity in the customer account, the customer only needs to receive a statement each quarter. This is referred to as a 'quarterly statement'. Broker dealers must deliver a statement to a customer within ten days after the close of the monthly or quarterly period, depending on the level of activity.

Customer statements include several important elements that customers use to review their purchases, sales, position holdings, or other account activity. Even though each broker-dealer does things a little bit differently, there are several common elements that all account statements will include, such as:

- Name of the customer
- Name of the registered representative that covers the account
- Name of the firm carrying the account
- Name of the firm clearing the account, if different
- Positions held in the account, including both cash and securities
- Total account value
- Change in value of positions
- Transactions, including the sale or purchase of securities, movements of cash, incoming or outgoing wire of funds to/from third parties

Customer Confirmations

There are many pieces of information that a broker-dealer must include on a customer confirmation. This information is important because it allows the customer to not only be aware of the transaction itself, but to verify that the details of the trade are consistent with their information about the transaction. Several items required to be included on the customer confirmation include, but are not limited to:

- Name of the security bought or sold
- Security symbol (if applicable)
- Sales or purchase price
- Any applicable fees, taxes, or additional charges associated with the transaction
- Net price paid or received
- Trade and settlement dates
- Typically, the confirmation will include a series of legal disclosures surrounding the trade and the broker-dealer
- Capacity of the trade, whether agent or principal
- Where the trade occurred, whether on an exchange or over the counter
- Applicable disclosures, such as whether:
  - the firm trading the security makes a market in the security
  - the trade was solicited or unsolicited
  - whether the trade represents an average price confirmation
  - if the trade had a markup or markdown, the amount of the markup or markdown
  - that the customer can request additional information about the trade, such as time of the trade

- Although not required to be disclosed on the confirm, the broker-dealer must offer the following information upon request:
  - where the trade was executed
  - the time that the trade was executed
  - if more than one trade makes up the full customer execution price, the individual execution prices
  - other items include access equals delivery, meaning where the customer can access a prospectus, official statement, or other similar document related to a new offering of securities

Confirmations are required to be delivered to a customer immediately upon the completion of a transaction, but no later than settlement date of the transaction. The confirmation can be in hard copy (paper form), or electronic form if the customer has consented in writing to the electronic delivery of the confirmation in that manner. There is no difference in the content of the confirmation, whether it is electronic or hard copy form.

In some cases, with the prior consent of the customer, duplicate statements and/or customer confirmations may be generated and sent to a third party. This third party could be the customer's employer if the customer is an employee of a broker-dealer. Or, duplicate statements and confirmations could be sent to a third party if the account is set up as a trust or to a bank if the account has been pledged as collateral for a loan.

Holding Customer Mail
FINRA member firms may hold physical mail for customers in some circumstances. To hold customer's mail, the customers registered representative ("RR") must receive written instructions from the customer pertaining to the length of time the mail is to be held. If the requested time period will be longer than three months, the customer will need to provide justification for the greater than three month time period, other than simple convenience. Another thing the RR must inform the customer of is how they can get information about their account activity while their mail is being held. This could simply be a notification about the firm's website, or electronically mailed copies of account statements or activity. Lastly, the RR must be able to communicate with the customer about important notices and activity. Periodically, the RR must check to make sure the mail is not being tampered with or otherwise used in an inappropriate manner and that the customer's instructions are still valid.

Business Continuity Plans
Business Continuity Plans ("BCP") require firms to plan for worst case scenarios that have a material potential impact on their businesses. In the real world, this has meant

planning for floods, hurricanes, terrorist attacks, loss of electrical power, etc. Anything that causes the business to materially change its operations or the employees of that firm to have to work from another location (including their homes) would be covered under a BCP. According to FINRA[47], a BCP must have the following elements:

- Data backup and recovery (hard copy and electronic);
- List of all mission critical systems;
- Regulatory reporting;
- Financial and operational assessments;
- Alternate communications between customers and the firm, and between the firm and employees;
- Alternate physical location of employees;
- Critical business constituent, bank, and counterparty impact;
- Communications with regulators; and
- How the firm will assure customers' prompt access to their funds and securities in the event that the firm determines that it is unable to continue its business.

By reviewing and having a plan in place to address each of these core areas FINRA has identified, firms are in a better position to address whatever comes their way. Although BCP's have often have specific contingencies for specific events, there is also some flexibility designed into the plan because the firm cannot predict every possible event. Bigger firms will often have a more complex BCP due to their size and complexity (types of products offered, number of offices, etc...). Smaller firms may have a simpler BCP because of their smaller size and less complexity.

Customer Protection and Custody of Assets

Assets in customer accounts are required to be custodied, or held, by the firm that maintains the accounts. The custodian has a duty to protect those assets which are being custodied. Since customer accounts can contain both cash and securities, it is of utmost importance that the custodian protects those underlying customer assets. For this reason, firms must keep separate customer cash and securities from firm cash and securities. Firms are not allowed to use customer cash for any reason. Customer securities can be loaned out to other customers or industry participants, but only with the express permission of the customer. To ensure that firms treat customer securities and other assets properly, firms that loan out customer securities are subject to regular and rigorous reporting requirements and examinations by industry regulators.

Privacy Requirements

The purpose of privacy rules involves three parts, according to SEC Regulation SP:
- Requires a financial institution to *provide notice to customers* about its privacy policies and practices;
- Describes the *conditions under which a financial institution may disclose nonpublic personal information* about consumers to nonaffiliated third parties; and

- Provides a *method for consumers to prevent a financial institution from disclosing* that information to most nonaffiliated third parties by "opting out" of that disclosure, subject to certain exceptions.

The SEC's privacy requirements help to protect customer information from being shared with a third party that does not have a need or right to know that information. As noted above, these privacy requirements note appropriate sensitivity to nonpublic personal information. To be more specific, industry regulations help define nonpublic personal information more narrowly as personally identifiable information. Such personally identifiable financial information includes:

- Information that a consumer provides on an application to obtain a loan, credit card, or other financial product or service;
- Account balance information, payment history, overdraft history, and credit or debit card purchase information;
- The fact that an individual is or has been a customer or has obtained a financial product or service from the firm;
- Any information about the consumer if it is disclosed in a manner that indicates that the individual is or has been the firm's consumer;
- Any information that a consumer provides to the firm or the firm's agents otherwise obtain in connection with collecting on a loan or servicing a loan;
- Any information you collect through an Internet "cookie" (an information collecting device from a web server); and
- Information from a consumer report.

Not all information about customers, however, is considered personally identifiable financial information. For instance, personally identifiable financial information does not include:

- A list of names and addresses of customers of an entity that is not a financial institution; or
- Information that does not identify a consumer, such as aggregate information or blind data that does not contain personal identifiers such as account numbers, names, or addresses.

If information is already publicly available, the firm does not have an obligation to keep that information secure or private. *Publicly available information* means any information that you reasonably believe is lawfully made available to the general public from:
- Federal, State, or local government records;
- Widely distributed media; or
- Disclosures to the general public that are required to be made by federal, State, or local law.

Unless considered publicly available information as defined above, any customer information would likely then be considered nonpublic personal information. Financial firms have a duty of confidentiality to maintain and store such information in a manner that keeps the nonpublic personal financial information to themselves.

Securities firms are required to notify customers of their privacy rights under industry rules. This is typically done at the opening of a customer account and annually thereafter. Customers have the ability to opt out of receiving marketing information form the firm (or any affiliate) that holds their account. Customers must simply notify their firm of their wishes.

When the SEC created Regulation S-P, it also noted that securities firms would be required to put in place many safeguards, through policies and procedures, to help reasonably ensure customer nonpublic information was protected. These policies and procedures are required to:
- insure the security and confidentiality of customer records and information;
- protect against any anticipated threats or hazards to the security or integrity of customer records and information; and
- protect against unauthorized access to or use of customer records or information that could result in substantial harm or inconvenience to any customer.

Communications with the Public

Industry rules require strict adherence to rules for how, when, and what communication is used with customers. There are a few broad categories that you should be aware of when talking about communications with the public in the securities industry that are covered below. All types of communications with customers are required to be supervised and reviewed. Communications with retail investors are subject to the most supervision, training and review, while communications with institutional investors require the least amount of supervision, training, and review. It is generally not acceptable to use past performance as a predictor or promise of future results, regardless of the type of communication.

Institutional Investor – The definition of an institutional investor encompasses many different types of entities and a few individuals. Each of the following are considered institutional investors for purposes of communications with the public:
- a bank, savings and loan association, insurance company or registered investment company;
- an investment adviser registered either with the SEC or with a state securities commission;
- any other person (whether a natural person, corporation, partnership, trust or otherwise) with total assets of at least $50 million;
- FINRA member or registered person of such FINRA member;

- person acting solely on behalf of any such institutional investor;
- Government entity; and
- Employee benefit plan

Retail Investor – any investor other than an institutional investor

Communications – includes Correspondence, Retail Communications, and Institutional Communications

Correspondence – any written or electronic communication that is sent or made available to 25 OR FEWER retail investors within 30 calendar days. This type of correspondence has a review and supervision standard that is stricter than that of Institutional Communications, but not as strict as Retail Communications.

Institutional Communications - any written or electronic communication that is sent or made available to only institutional investors. Institutional Communications have the least strict review and supervision standard. The institutional Communications standard only requires a sample review of these communications after the fact. Institutions are expected to be more sophisticated and knowledgeable about the securities markets and therefore in less need of regulatory protections.

Retail Communications – any written or electronic communication that is sent or made available to MORE THAN 25 retail investors within 30 calendar days. Retail communications must be pre-approved by a firm principal (e.g., a registered supervisor) and FINRA's Advertising Department within 10 days of first use. This is the most strict review and supervision standard.

Do Not Call Registry
Customers and potential customers can subscribe to the U.S. Do Not Call registry if they do not wish to be solicited for their securities business.

Only individuals may place their names on the Do Not Call registry. Once an individual's name is on the Do Not Call Registry, securities firms are not permitted to call that individual for business solicitation. In fact, securities firms must check the list prior to soliciting individuals that they do not have an existing relationship with, or those that have not inquired about the securities firm's services in the last 6 months. Financial firms are permitted to call individuals who are:
- Not on the Do Not Call registry
- Existing customers
- Have inquired with the financial firm in the past 6 months about their available service or product offerings

Suitability/Know Your Customer Requirements

FINRA member firms owe their customers a suitability obligation. This means that an investment option must be suitable for that customer based on the customer's unique blend of characteristics. These characteristics include things like a customer's risk tolerance, age, and investment time horizon. These characteristics are identified by the customer at the time the account is opened, and updated whenever the customer changes. Let's go through an example.

Customer A is a 65 year old, married, prefers little risk, wants to receive an income off of the investments, and is expected to retire in 3 years. If a registered representative were to recommend purchase of XYZ technology stock that pays no dividend, the recommendation would likely be unsuitable for this customer. However, if the registered representative recommended a bond-focused mutual fund made up of short term bonds that paid out monthly income, this investment would likely be suitable for this customer. Neither product is a bad product. XYZ technology stock may be a perfectly suitable investment for another customer who wants to take more risk and does not need the investment to produce an income. For Customer A, however, the product is a poor match to the investment objectives – little risk and income producing. When a registered representative is familiar with their clients, knows exactly the types of investments they are looking for, is familiar with their financial history and expectations, knows their tax bracket, and is knowledgeable about the customer's investment objectives, that registered representative has meet their Know Your Customer obligations under industry rules.

A customer's investment profile includes, but is not limited to, the customer's age, other investments, financial situation and needs, tax status, investment objectives, investment experience, investment time horizon, liquidity needs, risk tolerance, and any other information the customer may disclose to the member or associated person in connection with such recommendation.

In more detail, industry suitability obligations have three parts:
- **Reasonable-basis suitability** – this is the minimum bar for recommendations of the purchase or sale of securities – any recommendation made by a registered representative must be suitable for at least some customers of the registered representative. If the recommendation is suitable for no one, then obviously it cannot be suitable for anyone.
- **Customer specific suitability** – the registered representative must believe that the recommendation is suitable for the specific customer to whom the recommendation is being made.
- **Quantitative suitability** – registered representatives have an obligation to reasonably ensure that the series of recommendations in their totality for a customer in aggregate are suitable, not just the individual recommendations. A customer's investor profile is used to make sure this important suitability test is met.

When thinking through suitability based questions, consider what is reasonable given the investor's financial profile and investment objectives. Consider the relative riskiness, as defined by liquidity, ability to produce income, etc. So what is not covered under suitability rules? Anything very general in nature would count. Specifically, general financial and investment information includes the following:

- basic investment concepts, such as risk and return, diversification, dollar cost averaging, compounded return, and tax deferred investment,
- historic differences in the return of asset classes (e.g., equities, bonds, or cash) based on standard market indices,
- effects of inflation,
- estimates of future retirement income needs,
- assessment of a customer's investment profile,
- Descriptive information about an employer-sponsored retirement or benefit plan, participation in the plan, the benefits of plan participation, and the investment options available under the plan, and
- Asset allocation models

A recommendation occurs when a registered representative, unsolicited, provides a security or list of securities to an individual for their consideration as a purchase or sale of that investment. In some circumstances, telling a customer not to sell a security may be deemed to be a recommendation.

Institutional customers are not treated the same as retail investors under the suitability rules. Industry rules assume that institutional investors are more sophisticated, better capitalized, and have more industry experience. For these reasons, institutional investors receive less protection under industry rules and broker-dealers have much greater flexibility in how, when, and why they interact with them. This flexibility is evident in the different suitability rules for retail and institutional customers.

For example, a registered representative fulfills the customer-specific suitability obligation for an institutional customer if the registered representative:

- has a *reasonable basis* to believe that the institutional customer is capable of evaluating investment risks independently, both in general and with regard to particular transactions and investment strategies involving a security or securities, and
- receives an *affirmative indication from the institutional customer* indicating that the institutional customer is exercising independent judgment in evaluating the registered representative's recommendations.

Recall earlier that we noted the higher level of sophistication and knowledge about the securities markets that institutional investors are assumed to possess, and therefore in less need of regulatory protections in some areas. The retail investor is much more likely to take the registered representative's recommendations, whereas the institutional investor may hear the recommendation, but will likely only consider the recommendation to be one data point among many in their overall decision making process.

Updating Customer Account Records

Customer account records are required to be updated as needed, but no later than every three years. The registered representative (or firm) responsible for the account should update customer account records when there is a change to any of the information obtained from a customer during the account opening process. A customer account must have the following information on file:

- Risk tolerance
- Name
- Address
- Social security number
- Income
- Level of assets
- Value of home, if applicable
- Investment objectives

Asking for updated customer information every three years (or changing information on file when the customer advises them of a change) helps the customer's registered representative to know their customer and make better recommendations. For instance, if the customer's investment objectives have changed, from less risk to more risk, the registered representative would consider a slightly more aggressive portfolio mix. Likewise, if the customer was thinking of retiring soon, the registered representative may want to recommend a less risky portfolio overall.

End of Chapter Quiz

Complete these end of chapter questions to assess your understanding of the subject matter discussed in this chapter. The answers follow on the next page. For those questions you have answered incorrectly, review the appropriate section of the chapter again to make sure you understand the concepts.

1. How often is a customer required to be provided a statement if there is trading activity in the customer's account?
   a. Weekly
   b. Monthly
   c. Quarterly
   d. Semi-annually

2. Which of the following is NOT required on a customer confirmation?
   a. Name of the security purchased or sold
   b. Trade date
   c. Settlement date
   d. Dividend date

3. A customer must be delivered a statement within how many days of the end of the period?
   a. 5 days
   b. 10 days
   c. 20 days
   d. 30 days

4. Which of the following would typically be considered personally identifiable information?
   a. widely distributed media
   b. local government records
   c. information from a customer on a financial service application
   d. disclosures to the general public that are required to be made by federal, State, or local law

5. Which of the following is required on a customer confirmation?
   a. Amount of taxable gain or loss
   b. Trade capacity
   c. Capital gain
   d. Dividend date

6. Policies and procedures related to SEC Regulation SP are NOT required to include which of the following?
    a. insure the security and confidentiality of customer records and information
    b. insure that customer requests for wire transfers are made within 5 business days
    c. protect against any anticipated threats or hazards to the security or integrity of customer records and information.
    d. protect against unauthorized access to or use of customer records or information that could result in substantial harm or inconvenience to any customer.

7. In order to hold a customer's physical mail, the registered representative must receive _____ instructions and can only hold the customer's mail for _____ months without justification.
    a. Written, three
    b. Written or verbal, three
    c. Written, six
    d. Written or verbal, six

8. According to FINRA, a Business Continuity Plan must have which of the following?
    a. Procedures that address at least 50% of mission critical systems
    b. Regulatory reporting
    c. Alternate international physical location for employees
    d. Communication between firm management and owners

9. Which of the following is typically found on a customer statement?
    a. Incoming wires
    b. Average price disclosure
    c. Customer net worth
    d. Where the trade was executed

10. How often is a customer required to be provided a statement if there are no trading activity in the customer's account?
    a. Weekly
    b. Monthly
    c. Quarterly
    d. Semi-annually

End of Chapter Quiz Answers

1. B

The requirement to provide statements to customer is one of two frequencies - monthly or quarterly. If there is activity in the customer account during the month, the firm must send the customer a statement for that month. If there is no activity in the customer account for the month, the firm is only required to deliver a statement to the customer on a quarterly basis.

2. D

A customer confirmation is generated after every customer purchase or sale. Customer confirmations must include the name of the security purchased or sold, trade date, and settlement date (amongst several other items). The date a dividend was or will be paid is important information, but not required on the customer confirmation. Dividend payment information about a security held by a customer would typically show up on a customer statement instead.

3. B

Statements must be provided to customers within 10 days of the end of the reporting period. This applies to statements delivered quarterly or monthly.

4. C

Widely distributed media, local government records, and disclosures to the general public required by law are NOT considered personally identifiable information. This type of information should not be categorized the same as specific information about a customer, such as information provided on an application.

5. B

The amount of a taxable gain or loss, and the amount of the capital gain may be included on a customer statement, but not on a customer confirmation. The dividend date would also be on a customer statement, as this would show the dividend paid from the issuer to the investor. Only the trade capacity would exist on the confirmation, informing the customer of which capacity that particular trade was executed (agency or principal).

6. B

Regulation SP deals with customer privacy. Although important, wire transfers being completed within 5 days is not something covered under Regulation SP. The remaining answers are all required elements under Regulation SP that firms must comply with on an ongoing basis.

7. A

The customer must provide written instructions to the registered representative when seeking to have the registered representative hold their mail. Without further justification this is limited to 3 months.

8. B

Business Continuity Plans must include a communication plan between firm management and employees, and an alternate physical location (this does not need to be an international location). Regulatory reporting is required as part of the plan to keep regulators informed about issues, problems, progress, and status.

9. A

Average price disclosures and where the trade was executed can typically be found on a customer confirmation, not a customer statement. Customer net worth is not located on either a customer statement or a customer confirmation, although a customer statement will have the level of assets held within a customer's account(s). Incoming wires represent money coming into the account, which would show up on a customer statement.

10. C

The requirement to provide statements to customer is one of two frequencies - monthly or quarterly. If there is activity in the customer account during the month, the firm must send the customer a statement for that month. If there is no activity in the customer account for the month, the firm is only required to deliver a statement to the customer on a quarterly basis.

Chapter 17:   Prohibited Activities

Industry regulators have created a series of rules over the years that address conduct and behavior that negatively impacts both investors and the overall integrity of the financial markets. For the SIE Exam, the larger category of Prohibited Activities has been broken down into three subcategories:

- Market Manipulation
- Insider Trading
- Other Prohibited Activities

Each of these subcategories has listed of specific behaviors or actions that are prohibited either by industry rules or federal laws.   It is important that you can distinguish between the specific behaviors and recognize each one from the larger group.

Market Manipulation

Market manipulation is a general term used to describe any behavior that is intended to unfairly or illegally control or influence the market. There are numerous types of market manipulation that industry regulators like the SEC and FINRA have passed rules to prohibit over the years. Some of the most common types of market manipulation activities include the following:

- Spreading of Market Rumors
- Pump and Dump
- Front Running
- Wash Sales & Excessive Trading
- Marking the Close/Open
- Backing Away
- Payments to Publications to Influence the Market Price of a Security
- Freeriding

These types of market manipulation all have one thing in common - they unfairly advantage one party over another. There are several types of activities that individuals or firms may try to conduct that laws, rules, or regulations have deemed to be fraudulent or manipulative. On the examination, you may be asked to identify and distinguish between different types of manipulative or fraudulent activity. One also thing to note - several of these activities have an 'intent' component to them. In other words, individual or group conducting the activity must have intent to manipulate another individual, firm, or the market.

Spreading of Market Rumors

The securities markets move up and down on a daily, weekly, monthly basis. Some of the market movements are explained by facts, such as a publicly traded company's equity securities increase in price after their quarterly earnings announcements. Some of the market movements are explained by what individuals think will happen in the future (e.g., profits will increase, the FDA will approve a new drug that cures cancer, etc...).

Example 1: John works for Broker-Dealer A and owns 100 shares of equity security XYZ, a pharmaceutical company. Since John owns, or is long XYZ, he will benefit if the price of XYZ increases. John does not want to wait and see if the price of XYZ appreciates, he wants to sell XYZ in the next few days for a profit. To ensure this happens, John goes onto a popular message board and fabricates a story about how 'XYZ has recently created a breakthrough breast cancer drug'. For good measure, John goes onto several different platforms and repeats the same story. At the open the next day, XYZ stock increases dramatically, allowing John to sell his position for a nice profit. Spreading knowing false rumors is against the rules. Industry participants should have a basis for making the statements that they make, and those statements must be made on platforms or through services approved by their employing firms.

Registered persons of broker-dealers must be particularly sensitive to these matters. It is important to note, however, that some degree of speculation, based on reasoned analysis, is permitted. Will a company go bankrupt? Will a company meet their earnings guidance or will they fall short? These are unknowable questions about the future to some extent, and it is the job of many in the industry to try and predict what will happen in the future. In these types of situations, it is not a violation of the rules to speculate on what might happen, as this is different than spreading rumors.

Pump and Dump

Pump and dump is a classic market manipulation tactic used by unscrupulous individuals trying to make a quick profit for themselves. The pump and dump works best in small capitalization equity securities that are thinly traded. Thinly traded means that very few shares trade in the secondary market on a daily basis. Because of the small number of shares available in the market and the small number of shares that trade each day, any increase in demand will cause the price to shoot up quickly.

Think of someone putting slow and steady air into a balloon. Over time, that balloon will inflate, getting progressively bigger and bigger the more air that is put into the balloon. Eventually, the balloon gets to a rather large size. This is the 'pump'. Then you let go of the balloon. All of the balloons' air rushes out of it, and the balloon returns to its original shape. This is the 'dump'.

In the securities world, it works like this – an unscrupulous investor holds 10,000 shares of a very thinly traded equity security that they bought at an average price of $2.00 per share. The unscrupulous investor wants to make some money, but cannot really make any serious money if they sold the stock at the current market price of around $2.08. So what do they do? They go onto the internet into some popular stock forums or send out spam emails and start talking up the stock, saying things like:

"This stock is hot"

"This company is about to announce a big new product – I should know, I work there!"
"One of their key competitors is about to go out of business"
"They just landed a HUGE new client – a grand slam for the management team!"

The truth here does not matter to the unscrupulous investor. Their only objective is that people buy the stock – 'pumping up' the stock price in the secondary market. Remember about inflating the balloon! Only a small number of duped investors need to buy the stock for the stock to increase in price. Because these securities are illiquid, there are few shares outstanding and few shares trading each day. Any abnormal buying pressure will increase the price of the stock rapidly. This buying can take place over a few days or only a few hours. Our stock now trades at $15.75. Once the stock price has increased and reached the level desired by the unscrupulous investor, that investor sells, or dumps all of their shares. Selling 10,000 shares at $15.75 is a lot higher of a price than selling those same shares for $2.08! All of the new investors that bought the stock between $2.08 and $15.75 quickly realize that they have been duped as the price drops quickly back to where the stock was before the pump and dump.

Front Running
Front running at a high level refers to trading prior to some event, of which you have material nonpublic information. The event can be one of many things, such as the knowledge of a large order that is likely to move the market up or down. When an individual or entity is buying a large number of shares in a stock, the price of that stock is likely to increase for the duration of the order. Think of this effect as basic supply and demand – whenever more of something is desired, the price of that something tends to go up. Another event would be the publication of a research report that is likely to move the market up or down. The same impact is felt here – a research report that increases the price target on the share of an equity security is likely to increase the price of that security. If you know about the order or the research report before is entered or published, you can take advantage of that fact. If any individual or entity does take advantage of this fact by trading in front of the event, the behavior is illegal and called front running.

Example: Jamie, a research analyst is about to publish a research report downgrading company XYZ. Jamie has decided that the company is not worth $70 per share like she said in her old research report. XYZ company is now only worth $50 per share due to increased competitive pressures. Jamie is looking to publish this new research report on Friday, two days away. Jamie want to make sure her good friend Alex who trades XYZ for his trading firm can sell his shares of XYZ that the firm owns before her research report is published. Jamie knows that once her research report is published, the price of the stock will likely drop quickly. Therefore, she decides to tell Alex about her pending research report. Alex sells the firm's shares the next day, one day ahead of the research report's publication. This is an example of front running of research reports. The same basic premise in this example exists whether you are publishing reports or taking larger orders from clients. It is the knowledge of material nonpublic information (i.e., publication of the research report or acceptance of a larger order) and then doing something improper with that knowledge (trading on that information for you or passing along the information to someone else so they can trade on that information).

Wash Sales and Excessive Trading

There are two types of wash sale activities – one is related to IRS rules, another related to security industry rules. From the IRS perspective, the term wash sale means not being permitted to take tax losses due to the sale and then subsequent repurchase of the same security within a 30-day period. There is nothing wrong with rebuying a security you sold last week, you just cannot take a loss on your taxes for the sale, that's all.

Wash sales related to the overall trading activity through purchases and sales of securities are something different altogether. In this type of wash sale, the intent of the individual or entity buying and selling the security is to make it appear as though there is trading volume in the security. This is accomplished by purchasing and selling the security in a short time span, at about the same price, with the intent to create additional volume, absent a real change in beneficial ownership. Sometimes this can also be called simply excessive trading. There should be an economic purpose to the trading activity, not simply trying buy and sell to make the market look bigger than what the market actually is on a regular basis.

Marking the Close/Marking the Open

Equity and options exchanges have standard opening and closing times. Normal market hours on U.S. equity exchanges are from 9:30a.m. to 4p.m. EST. Many people and entities inside and outside of the securities industry depend on the opening and closing prices of specific securities on the exchange. They use these prices to evaluate their holdings and perform historical analysis of market data (including opening and closing prices). For these reasons, some market participants may try to manipulate these important prices for their own benefit. Therefore, marking the close and marking the open are prohibited in the securities industry. Let's go through an example to get a good understanding of this activity.

Bob, a trader at Broker-Dealer A is worried about his long position in XYZ security. He has 10,000 shares of the stock on his inventory account and is coming up on quarter end. Each quarter, traders are evaluated at how well they are performing, which impact their compensation. Bob's average cost per share of XYZ is approximately $55.24, but the stock is trading at $55.01. He would like to see the stock get up at least to his average cost of $55.24 before the market closes today. That way, Bob will receive a more favorable performance review, given that his long position in XYZ will not be worth less than what he paid for the stock. So what does Bob do to make sure the stock closes at or above $55.24? He places several small buy orders within one minute of the market close. The increased buying pressure in the stock in such a short time pushes the price of the stock up to a close of $55.25. Right after the market close, Bob sells all of the new stock he acquired right before the close. Now, when Bob goes into his performance review, his long position in XYZ will not be held against him, because he has now made money!

All that said, marking the close and marking the open are intent based rules – merely trading near the open or close is not by itself a rule violation. An individual must possess intent to break the rules and typically must receive a benefit or avoid a loss.

Backing Away

A market maker or trader who posts a quotation to purchase or sell a security must honor the quotation if it is accessed by another party. If the market maker or trader does not honor the quotation, the market maker or trader may be found to have violated the prohibition on backing away from their quotation.

Payments to Publications to Influence the Market Price of a Security

Market participants often use media outlets for various types of communication, like newspapers, magazine, online publications, television, video channels, etc... to advertise their products. Advertising to customers, as long as the advertising is labeled as such, is permitted under industry rules. However market participants can get into trouble when they accept compensation and use any means of written communication that is designed to impact the market price of the security.

Under FINRA rules, these types of payments are not strictly prohibited. However, there are onerous disclosure requirements that accompany any publication designed to influence the price of a security (or to solicit orders in such security), where the person or entity creating the publication has been compensated for creation or publication. These types of publications are not typically used for securities with higher market trading volumes. Instead, these are typically used in a thinly traded security to increase interest. The use of these publications in thinly traded securities makes them very dangerous to the investing public, which is why regulators require onerous disclosures including details on payments to the publisher, typically by issuer or large owner of the securities.

Do you remember our discussion earlier about the pump and dump scam that is used by unscrupulous market participants? This rule is designed to make it clear to potential investors the difference between advertisements which are legitimate, and someone getting paid to try and pump up the market price of a security.

Other permitted activities include research reports and any communication that discloses the receipt of compensation in exchange for the communication.   In summary – research reports, advertisements, and communications that disclose payment in exchange for the communication are ok.   All other written communications are prohibited if those communications are designed to influence the market price of the security which they are written about.

Freeriding

If you break apart the word freeriding, you simply get 'free' 'riding', right? As in getting a free ride. Although we all like being given a free ride at the amusement park or even on the latest ride share app, in the securities industry, this is against the rules. Free riding in securities industry terms means that you are not paying for the trades that you execute in your accounts[48].

Specifically, freeriding takes place when a customer buys a security, and before that purchase settles, the customer sells that same security without ever depositing the money to cover the purchase. If a customer does this, the firm holding the customer's account is required to freeze that account from specific activities. The customer is still permitted to buy a security in the frozen account, but the customer must fully pay for the purchase on trade date.

Insider Trading

Insider trading occurs when an individual or group uses material nonpublic information. Insider trading has two main individuals involved: the tipper and the tippee. The tipper is the individual that has the inside information. The tipper passes along the information to the tippee. If the tippee did nothing with the information, there would be no insider trading case to be made. In an insider trading case, the tipper then trades on the information to either make a profit or avoid a loss. Consider the following scenario:

Buddy works at a pharmaceutical company that is going to announce a significant breakthrough in cancer treatment. The company would stand to make millions of dollars once the new cancer drug hits the market. Buddy knows about the new cancer drug and that the company will announce the cancer drug to the market in two weeks. Buddy also knows that once the announcement is made, the stock price is likely to go up significantly. To take advantage of this inside information, Buddy tells the information to, or tips off, his friend Charley. Charley (the tippee) decides to buy 1000 shares of XYZ and 10 XYZ January calls, both long positions ahead of the public announcement.

A quick review:
Tipper: Buddy
Tippee: Charley

Inside Information: New cancer drug will be very profitable

There are two concepts relating to insider trading: nonpublic and material. In the above scenario, the information relayed to the tippee was both material (defined as information for which there is a substantial likelihood that a reasonable investor would consider it important in making his or her investment decisions, or information that is reasonably certain to have a substantial effect on the price of an issuer's securities) and nonpublic. To contrast, the color of the carpet in XYZ Public Company's board room may be nonpublic information. However, that nonpublic information is not material and the sharing of that information would not be considered insider trading. One example of public information that you could use to trade your stock is if an independent research analyst publishes a report projecting lower earnings, an insider could be permitted to trade on the basis of that information. Another example of public information is a declared stock dividend.

What are the penalties if you are guilty of insider trading? These penalties can be quite harsh – a certain incentive to not insider trade in the first place. Penalties for insider trading can result in treble damages – 3x the gain or 3x the loss avoided. So if you made $1 million on your insider trading scheme and you get caught, you may have to pay a fine to the U.S. government of up to $3 million! Money is not the only punishment though – a suspension from the industry if you are registered and criminal charges can be levied as well, which means jail time.

Other Prohibited Activities

If you recall, prohibited activities in the securities industry are those activities that have specific rules in place to prevent or limit their scope. Prohibited activities more likely impact individual retail customers than any other group of market participants.

You can expect these prohibited activities to be covered on the SIE Exam:
- Restrictions for Associated Persons Purchasing IPOs
- Use of Manipulative, Deceptive or other Fraudulent Devices
- Improper use of Customer Securities or Funds and Making Guarantees
- Financial Exploitation of Seniors
- Prohibition Against Solicitation of Customers and Taking Orders
- Falsifying or Withholding Documents and Books & Records matters
- Churning
- Selling Away
- Prohibited Breakpoint Sales
- Best Execution & Interpositioning
- Telemarketing
- Payments for Market Making

When reviewing these prohibited behaviors, you should consider who is impacted and why the prohibitions are in place.

Restrictions for Associated Persons Purchasing IPOs

An associated person of a broker-dealer is not permitted to purchase shares in an Initial Public Offering (IPO). Why is this rule in place? This rule is in place to allow the investing public to receive shares in the IPO instead of the associated persons. This limitation exists only for IPO shares. Once the shares trade in the secondary market, an associated person is permitted to purchase shares.

Use of Manipulative, Deceptive or other Fraudulent Devices

Industry rules seek to have fair, open, and free securities markets. Individuals or entities that get in the way of these goals can be charged under the rules relating to manipulative, deceptive, or other fraudulent devices. Often times, there is no specific rule addressing the improper activities or behavior. If that is the case, the industry regulators will then look to charge market participants under these broad rules. Market participants that deal in good faith with other market participants, are truthful in their interactions, and retain good documentation about their decisions and activities would not usually be charged under the manipulative, deceptive, or other fraudulent device rules.

As an example, these rules and regulations were used by the SEC in the 1990's to punish equity market makers who were found to have illegally attempted to and succeeded in intimidating other market participants to change their quotations or not post quotations in certain securities. In other cases, some equity market makers were found to have coordinated their behavior in certain securities around trading and quotations, improperly colluding to dominate and control certain markets. The collective behavior was in fact so egregious that the SEC required FINRA (then called NASD) and Nasdaq to create the Series 55 (Equity Trader) Examination. It is now known as the Series 57 Examination. These behaviors violate prohibitions on anti-intimidation and coordination.

Let's go through a few examples to get a better feel for this type of activity.

Example 2: A trader at Market Maker A is looking to make money trading one of his favorite stocks. The problem (from his perspective) is that another firm (let's call them Market Maker B) keeps narrowing the bid-ask spread, thereby reducing any opportunity for the trader to buy low and sell high. So, the trader at Market Maker A calls up Market Maker B and tells them to widen their quote out a bit and not trade at the inside. Industry rules state that this activity is prohibited, as it is intimidation-style behavior. Even if Market Maker A asks Market Maker B 'nicely', it does not matter; the behavior is still considered intimidation and runs afoul of the anti-intimidation rules.

Example 3: If we change the scenario slightly, and Market Maker B agrees to move their quote at Market Maker A's request, this could be construed as coordination, which is also prohibited. Market participants are generally not permitted to work together or work either verbally or in writing to intimidate other market participants. The only exception to this kind of behavior exists inside a syndicate during an offering of securities.

Improper Use of Customer Securities or Funds and Making Guarantees
Generally speaking, employees of a securities firm are not permitted to borrow funds from customers. In the same vein, employees are not permitted to share an account with a customer. Sharing an account means that the account has both the customer and employee's name on it, thus allowing either party to make a transaction in the account. Investing in securities carries some degree of risk, even when an investor has taken steps to mitigate that risk. If a registered person were to make a guarantee about an investment, a customer may be more inclined to invest with that registered person. A registered person does not have control over the markets or an individual security's performance, so it would clearly be improper for that registered person to make a guarantee about their recommendations or the potential performance of their investments. Another prohibited activity would be if a broker-dealer participating in a public offering agreed to repurchase the shares sold to its customers at no less that the original offering price. This activity would be considered fraudulent and manipulative as it would be used to increase the amount of securities sold to the firm's customers who could then immediately sell the stock back to the broker-dealer.

Sharing with customers carries a similar risk. Sharing sounds reasonable, but it carries some of the same risks that guarantees do. If you were to share an account with a customer, how much does each person put into the account? What if one person wants to sell the investment and the other one does not? Does the registered person have an unfair advantage over the customer because of their industry knowledge experience? Each of these question raise serious concerns – enough concern that industry rules prohibit the activity, if for no other reason than to avoid all of these headaches in the first place.

Financial Exploitation of Seniors
The exploitation of seniors is a real and growing problem. The problem will likely only get worse, as the baby boomers continue to age and head into their retirement years. Senior have less time to recover from losing money in any form – from a market

downturn or being exploited out of their hard earned money.   Financial exploitation of seniors can take may shapes –

- Putting them into financial products that are very expensive and make no sense for their stage in life;
- Using sketchy financial seminars or lunches that are not really designed to educate or enlighten, but to sell senior investors products they do not need; or
- Churning their accounts (more on that below).

Due to this troubling development, industry rules now allow seniors to designate a trusted contact that can step into handle their financial affairs (including their securities accounts) in the event they are unable to do so. Regulators also look very closely at customer complaints involving seniors, or referrals from broker-dealers through a firm's Suspicious Activity Reporting and AML processes that allege financial exploitation of seniors.

Prohibition Against Solicitation of Customers and Taking Orders

There are two general types of employees within a securities firm - unregistered and registered. Industry rules require that commissions can only be paid to registered persons. To be registered, an individual must have passed the SIE Exam, a top off exam like the Series 7, and be current on their Regulatory Element training. If you are not registered and current on your training, you cannot accept commissions from your firm, nor interact with clients on a meaningful basis.

An unregistered individual does not hold any securities licenses. Someone who is unregistered is limited to the following types of interactions:

1. Administrative or ministerial functions (setting up appointments, making copies, forwarding documents, etc...)
2. Processing requests, and
3. Providing requested information.

Unregistered individuals are not permitted to accept orders in securities, solicit customers, make buy or sell recommendations, or provide advice to customers.

Falsifying or Withholding Documents and Books & Records Matters

In order to perform their duties effectively, regulators often make requests of individuals, broker-dealers, or exchanges for information. This information helps regulators determine if there has been customer harm, or rule violations such as market manipulation or even outright fraud. To make these determinations, regulatory rules require certain market participants to keep books and records about many types of activities – trades, orders, account activity, financial information, plus many other things.

As members of the securities industry, it is incumbent on all industry participants to maintain accurate books and records and to respond to regulatory requests on a timely and accurate basis. Regulatory requests must be answered within a specific number of days, usually outlined in the written request. The number of days can range from 1 day, up to several weeks, depending on the complexity and size of the request.

Creating fictitious records, altering existing records or failing to provide documents to regulators are all serious matters. Industry rules require its participants to maintain books and records of customer and firm activity. If these records are inaccurate, it may indicate poor recordkeeping or other rule violations. Some firms have been cited for not only altering documents, but signing a customer's name on a document, or allowing one customer to sign for another (so-called 'signature of convenience').

In addition, broker-dealers that are FINRA or exchange members are required to maintain books and records for a specific period of years after they have been created. Although each regulator has slightly different requirements, all regulators require different records to be kept for different periods of time, depending on the type of record required to be kept. For instance, the general requirement is to keep records for a period of 6 years. This includes information about customer trades and orders. However, other books and records are only required to be kept for a period of 3 years or 18 months. Knowing the intricate details of which record you need to keep and for how long is beyond the scope of the SIE Exam. Focus instead on the requirement to keep records pertaining to the business of the firm, including records about customers and their activities for 6 years.

Churning

Also referred to as excessive trading, *churning* refers to a practice whereby a broker who has the ability to make investment decisions in a client account, buys and sells securities within that account for the purpose of generating commissions[49]. Remember that a commission is the compensation paid to a broker for the purchase or sale of securities. It is a transactional charge, meaning that the commission is paid on every purchase or sale. The practice of churning is illegal, but not always clear-cut, as some buying and selling of securities is normal. For churning to have occurred, the trades within the customer account will not have any relationship to the overall customer investment objectives or risk tolerance.

Selling Away

The purchase or sale of securities through a customer's brokerage account represents activity that a broker's member firm is aware of and can supervise. As the term implies, *selling away* occurs when a broker buys, sells, or solicits products or services to customers <u>away from</u> the broker's firm. By entering into transactions with customers off a broker's firm platform, the firm has no knowledge of the activity and therefore cannot supervise it. To a customer though, the distinction between selling on the firm's platform and selling away from the firm's platform may be hard to distinguish. A common product used in selling away cases is private placements where the broker solicits customers to invest in the private placement but does not conduct the transaction within his or her firm. FINRA rules prohibit selling away.

Prohibited Breakpoint Sales

Mutual funds are a popular way to invest in the securities markets. When investing in mutual funds, many investors choose to invest in various mutual funds within the same fund family, or branded mutual fund. Breakpoints are offered by Mutual Fund Families as a way to reward investors who choose to invest more and more money within the Mutual Fund Family[50]. Think of breakpoints as a 'bulk buying' discount – the more you buy, the more you save in mutual fund fees. The line where the customer saves money on fees is the breakpoint. A prohibited breakpoint sale would occur if the broker sold a customer a mutual fund in a different Mutual Fund Family for the purpose of avoiding the breakpoint savings to the customer.

Industry rules allow firms to accept a Letter of Intent from a customer, indicating that they intend to purchase additional mutual fund shares within the next 13 months. This Letter of Intent allows the customer to benefit from the lower costs at a higher breakpoint. In our example above, an investor purchased $3,000 worth of mutual funds. If that same investor signed a Letter of Intent to purchase another $2,000 worth of mutual funds in the same family during the next quarter, that investor would only be charged .50% instead of the .57% mutual fund fee for the $5,000 investment. The breakpoints will vary between mutual fund families, but will add up over time – every dollar not paid in fees goes into the investor's pocket as part of their total return.

Best Execution and Interpositioning

Broker-dealers regularly execute client orders to buy or sell securities. That is the business the broker-dealer is in, after all. However, when broker-dealers execute an order for their customers, regardless of security type, they owe that customer a duty of best execution. Best execution means that, given the market conditions, terms and conditions of the order, and the size of the order, the customer should receive the best price possible. Interpositioning is a fancy term that simply means purposefully inserting a third party into the execution chain for no real purpose or benefit to the customer. Let's see an example. A customer places an order with your firm, Broker-Dealer X. Broker-Dealer X gets some dollar rebates for every order they send to Broker Dealer Y. Broker-Dealer Z is a well-known market maker in the stock that the customer wants to trade. If Broker-Dealer X sends the customer order to Broker-Dealer Z, all is well. If

Broker-Dealer X sends the customer order to Broker-Dealer Y, who then sends the order to Broker-Dealer Z, Broker-Dealer X has just committed an Interpositioning rule violation!

Telemarketing

You will meet very few people who enjoy getting telemarketing calls regardless of who they are from – the phone company, cable company, furniture store, car dealer, etc... Getting a telemarketing call from a securities firm like a broker-dealer ends up in the same category as these other companies. Customers therefore, have the right to 'opt out' of receiving telemarketing calls from securities firms. Broker-dealers can call prospective customer during reasonable hours and attempt to solicit their business – you cannot call a prospective customer at 11pm at night, though! If a customer is already on a 'do not call' list, you cannot call them. If the customer requests that they not be contacted when you call them, you cannot call them again and must add them to your do not call list. The telemarketing prohibitions do not apply if you are already an established customer of the broker-dealer or if you have inquired with the broker-dealer about using their services. This makes sense, because the rules are not designed to prevent broker-dealers from calling their own customers or potential customers that have asked about the broker-dealer's services.

Payments for Market Making

A market maker is a market participant that holds itself out as willing to buy and sell a security at a price reasonably related to the market. Market makers are not permitted to accept payments from issuers so they will make markets in securities. Market makers must be free to choose which stocks to make markets in, and at what price they are going to buy and sell. Issuer payments to market makers give the appearance of a conflict of interest, which industry rules seek to avoid. An exception to this rule occurs when a market maker accepts a payment from an issuer in connection with investment banking transactions. This type of issuer is payment is not prohibited.

End of Chapter Quiz

Complete these end of chapter questions to assess your understanding of the subject matter discussed in this chapter. The answers follow on the next page. For those questions you have answered incorrectly, review the appropriate section of the chapter again to make sure you understand the concepts.

1. Tim Trader has been talking to his old college friends about the stock market. One of Tim's friends, Beth Banker is the CFO of ABC, a publicly traded stock, who is considering a big acquisition. Beth tells Tim about the big ABC transaction, and Tim buys ABC stock. Which of the following is TRUE?
    a. Beth is the tippee, Tim is the tipper
    b. Tim has not violated insider trading laws because the stock is publicly traded
    c. Beth cannot be held responsible for Tim's actions
    d. Tim would not have violated the law if he refrained from trading

2. An Associated Person may guarantee against customer losses in connection with a securities transaction:
    a. if the customer is a family member.
    b. under no circumstances.
    c. if the customer agrees in writing.
    d. under the condition that the loss does not exceed $1,000.

3. Which of the following would be a red flag concerning potential adult exploitation?
    a. A customer wants to donate some money to charity
    b. A family member or caregiver is added to an account
    c. There are funds wired out of the customer's account for routine bills
    d. The client forgot to sign some recent account paperwork

4. What type of penalty is typically levied against an individual guilty of insider trading?
    a. two times the gain only
    b. two times the gain or loss avoided
    c. Three times the gain only
    d. Three times the gain or loss avoided

5. Which of the following account types is most susceptible to churning?
    a. Fee based joint account
    b. Commission based non-discretionary account
    c. Fee based individual account
    d. Commission based discretionary account

6. When is a market maker permitted to receive compensation from an issuer?
    a. Under no circumstances.
    b. If the compensation is less than $1,000 per year.
    c. If the compensation is connected to an investment banking transaction.
    d. If the compensation is related to an issuer that is listed on a U.S. Exchange.

7. When prospecting for a new customer, Randal Representative prefers to use the phone. When Randal calls Connie Customer, Connie asks that Randal not call her again. What must Randal do?
    a. Randal cannot call Connie for 1 year.
    b. Randal must add Connie to the do not call list.
    c. Randal can call Connie back to make sure she was serious.
    d. Randal can ask another representative to call Connie instead.

8. Which of the following is not a factor in determining whether or not an executed order received best execution?
    a. Market conditions
    b. Executing firm
    c. Size of the order
    d. Terms and conditions on the order

9. A registered representative and his customer are considering an investment in a highly illiquid micro-cap stock. The customer is nervous about the investment, but the registered representative says he will split any losses with the customer as an incentive. Which of the following is TRUE?
    a. The registered representative cannot do this unless they receive their supervisor's approval.
    b. The customer can enter into this arrangement with the registered representative if they get the agreement in writing.
    c. The registered representative can do this if they determine if the investment is suitable for the customer.
    d. The registered representative cannot enter into this arrangement.

10. Which product is most likely to be part of a registered representative's efforts to circumvent the prohibition on selling away?
    a. Private placements
    b. Listed equities
    c. Corporate bonds
    d. OTC options

End of Chapter Quiz Answers

1. D
In this scenario, Beth is the tipper, Tim is the tippee. Beth can be held liable for Tim's actions because she passed along the information to Tim. The fact that the stock is publicly traded makes it more likely that insider trading is an issue. The only way for Tim not to violate insider trading laws is to refrain from acting on the information - he shouldn't trade based on it or pass it along to someone else.

2. B
A registered representative cannot guarantee against customer losses under any circumstances. This applies whether or not the customer is family member, agrees to it writing, or even if loss is relatively small like $1,000.

3. B
Adding a family member of caregiver to the customer's account is a red flag because the individual added could have undue influence on the likely elderly customer. This influence can be positive, but it could also be negative, in that the added individual could be using their influence to enrich themselves. The remaining items are routine in nature and would not cause any alarm by themselves.

4. D
Those individuals found guilty of insider trading are required to pay three times the gain or loss avoided. This acts as a deterrent to insider trading and does not distinguish between those trying to make money, and those avoiding losing money.

5. D
Commissions are earned on a per transaction basis, making them most susceptible to churning. Churning is when a registered representative makes a trade in a customer's account for the purpose of generating commissions. A discretionary account means that the registered representative has the ability to make buy and sell decisions on behalf of the customer. This combination is where churning is most likely to occur. A fee based account makes churning unlikely, because the registered representative is paid a fee based on total assets, not a fee based on number of trades.

6. C
Market makers are permitted to receive compensation from issuers only under very limited circumstances. One of these circumstances is when the market maker also happens to be the investment banker to the issuer. The compensation received from the issuer in this context is in relation to the investment banking transaction, not from making a market in the security.

7. B
Once the potential customer has indicated a desire not to be called again, the registered representative making the call must not call that potential customer again, nor can anyone else at the registered representative's firm.

8. B
Market conditions such as how volatile the market is or volume of the security for sale/purchase, the size of the order, and any relevant terms and conditions all have an impact on the overall execution quality of a customer order. The name of the firm that executed the order is not typically a relevant factor.

9. D
This is a hard no. Registered representatives cannot split losses with customers or promise to split potential future losses as an incentive. No amount of documentation, consent, or approval will suffice.

10. A
A private placement is a type of securities offering. A registered representative can invest in a private placement or in a private security outside of a broker dealer with relative ease. Listed equities, corporate bonds, and options can be sold away, but these are typically done through another broker dealer, making it much more difficult.

SIE Exam Study Guide 2020

Section 4: Overview of Regulatory Framework

Chapter 18:   SRO Regulatory Requirements for Associated Persons

In the securities industry, there are two types of people – those that are registered, and those that are not registered. When a person is said to be registered, it means that the individual has passed one or more licensing exams. As a candidate for the SIE Exam, you are on the path to becoming registered. Technically however, an individual needs the SIE plus a 'top off' examination, such as:

- **Series 6** – <u>Investment Company and Variable Contracts Products</u>
- **Series 7** – <u>General Securities Representative</u>
- **Series 22** – <u>Direct Participation Programs</u>

- **Series 52** – <u>Municipal Securities</u>
- **Series 57** – <u>Principal Trader</u>
- **Series 79** – <u>Investment Banking</u>
- **Series 82** – <u>Private Securities Offerings</u>
- **Series 87** – <u>Research Analyst</u>
- **Series 99** – <u>Operations Professional</u>

So, the SIE Exam, plus any of the above top-off exams will result in an individual being considered registered. Note however that although almost anyone can take the SIE Exam, a firm must sponsor you to take one of the top off examinations. Those individuals who held any of the top off examinations prior to the SIE Exam being launched are automatically waived-into the SIE Exam. This means that any individual who has a top off exam prior to October 1, 2018 will earn the SIE Exam without having to actually take it.

Registration of Associated Persons

Each SRO, including FINRA, creates licensing requirements appropriate for their members. These licensing requirements vary by position, as noted in the top-off examination discussion earlier. Basically though, SRO rules will require individuals to obtain licenses appropriate for the type of business they wish to conduct. Being registered simply means you can perform duties and functions consistent with your licensing. For instance, if you have the Series 7, you are permitted to interact with retail or institutional customers, solicit their business, accept orders and a host of other items. The same goes for other top-off examinations.

What this *does not* mean though is that as a Series 7 licensed associate only that you can act as an Investment Banker (Series 79) or a Research Analyst (Series 86/87). These are separate licenses entirely and unless you hold those licenses, you cannot act in the capacity as an Investment Banker or Research Analyst.

A non-registered person is anyone who does not currently hold an up-to-date securities license. Securities licenses lapse if a registered associate has failed to maintain their **Continuing Education** requirements, or if they have left the industry, or do not have their licenses currently held by a sponsoring firm. Once an individual leaves the industry and does not have a firm sponsoring their licenses for two years, their licenses expire and they must retake those licensing examinations if they ever want to become registered again in the future. FINRA does have a process in place for granting waivers to examinations. FINRA grants waiver exemptions in the following four categories (information from www.finra.org):

1. **Requests Based on Registration Filing Errors**
   These requests involve individuals working in good faith as representatives or principals in firms, but their registrations, for reasons related to the filing of the appropriate application forms, are not reflected in Web CRD. FINRA may waive the exam for such an individual provided the firm documents the filing error and confirms the individual has, in good faith, engaged in the securities business.

2. **Requests Based on Securities Industry and Related Investment Field Experience**
   These requests take into account an individual's experience in the securities industry and in related investment fields. These include, but are not limited to, investment banking, securities trading on behalf of a financial institution, securities research, portfolio management, investment advisory services or securities activities in a foreign broker-dealer. FINRA considers such factors as:
   o the length and quality of the applicant's securities industry experience or professional experience in investment related fields;
   o the specific registration the applicant requests and the type of business to be conducted in relation to the applicant's experience;
   o the applicant's previous registration history, if any;
   o the nature of the applicant's disciplinary, regulatory and criminal history, including any such matters that are disclosed on the applicant's Central Registration Depository record and, specifically, any arbitration awards or arbitration settlements; and
   o other examinations taken by the applicant, such as those for Certified Financial Planner or Chartered Financial Analyst, that may be acceptable substitutes in conjunction with experience and other factors above, for the normal securities industry qualification examination.

3. **Requests Based on Educational Achievement**
   FINRA will consider waiver requests from individuals who terminate their registrations and enroll in a master's or law program that substantially emphasizes finance and investments, and then promptly return to a firm after completing their studies. The applicant must return to a member firm promptly after completing the course of study and furnish a copy of the course transcript with the waiver request.

4. **Requests Based on Regulatory Experience**
   Individuals previously registered with a member firm, or whose most recent employment has been with a securities regulatory agency, may seek a waiver to have their registration reinstated. Those with no prior securities registration must have at least five years of regulatory experience for a waiver request to be considered.

If you recall from Chapter 17 – Prohibited Activities, someone who is not registered is limited to the following types of interactions:

- *Administrative or ministerial functions* (setting up appointments, making copies, forwarding documents, etc...)
- *Processing requests*, and
- Providing *requested information*.

Upon starting with a sponsoring firm, a new employee will be fingerprinted by either the firm or a third party approved by the sponsoring firm. This is an industry requirement, and helps to ensure that the person being hired by the member firm is who they say they are upon hire. Once the fingerprints are collected, the sponsoring firm will run a background check and submit the fingerprints to FINRA to run additional checks with law enforcement officials. If there are any material issues that come up during the background check process, the sponsoring firm will need to consider those material issues, and determine if the issues uncovered qualify as statutory disqualification of the employee.

Statutory Disqualification

Statutory disqualification is one of the worst punishments an individual or firm can receive. Once you are statutorily disqualified, you cannot do much of anything in the securities industry – it means that you have been disqualified from participation. In sports terms, the referee has disqualified you from the match or game due to some behavior or violation. Market participants do not get statutorily disqualified for just any reason – there is a specific list of events. An individual or firm is considered statutorily disqualified if any of the following disqualifying events have occurred[51]:

- certain misdemeanor and all felony criminal convictions for a period of ten years from the date of conviction.
- temporary and permanent injunctions (regardless of their age) issued by a court of competent jurisdiction involving a broad range of unlawful investment activities.
- expulsions or bars (and current suspensions) from membership or participation in a self-regulatory organization (SRO), including bars with a right to re-apply.
- bars (and current suspensions) ordered by the SEC, CFTC or other appropriate regulatory agency or authority, including bars with a right to re-apply.
- denials or revocations of registration by the SEC, CFTC or other appropriate regulatory agency or authority.
- findings that a member or person has made certain false statements in applications or reports made to, or in proceedings before, SROs, the SEC or other appropriate regulatory agency or authority.
- any final order of a State securities commission, State authority that supervises or examines banks, savings associations, or credit unions, State insurance commission (or any agency or office performing like functions), an appropriate Federal banking agency, or the National Credit Union Administration, that bars such person from association with an entity regulated by such commission, authority, agency, or officer, or from engaging in the business of securities, insurance, banking, savings

association activities, or credit union activities; or
- a final order based on violations of any laws or regulations that prohibit fraudulent, manipulative, or deceptive conduct.
- findings by the SEC, CFTC or an SRO that a person: 1) "willfully" violated the federal securities or commodities laws, or the Municipal Securities Rulemaking Board (MSRB) rules; 2) "willfully" aided, abetted, counseled, commanded, induced or procured such violations; or 3) failed to supervise another who commits violations of such laws or rules.

State Registration Requirements

In addition to SRO (including FINRA) rules, U.S. states also have a role to play in this process. When registering an individual with a top-off examination, it is typically expected that the individual will also be registered in one or more states. States will typically require that anyone who is conducting business within their state, or contacting/soliciting customers within their state, to be registered in that state. Let's say Patricia is an SIE and Series 7 licensed representative with Broker Dealer XYZ. Patricia has customers, some of who reside in Maine, some who reside in Vermont, and some who reside in New Hampshire. Patricia's office location is in Vermont. Even though Patricia works in Vermont, her customers are in Maine, Vermont, and New Hampshire. Given this, Patricia must be state registered in all three states.

Upon seeking registration in a particular state, that state will conduct a review of the individual's background and application. To process that application, states require that individuals pass a state licensing examination, in addition to the SRO required examination. The options for state licensing examination are as follows:
- **Series 63** – Uniform Securities Agent State Law Examination
- **Series 65** – Uniform Investment Adviser Law Examination
- **Series 66** – Uniform Combined State Law Examination

Depending on an individual's business focus, any one of the three may be appropriate. The Series 63 only covers brokerage activities, and not any investment advisory activities. Investment advisory activities are covered under the Series 66. The Series 66 covers both brokerage and investment advisory activities.

So now that you understand registered and non-registered associates and the various licenses that individuals complete, we need to review how individuals keep those licenses up to date.

Continuing Education for Registered Associates

For securities industry professionals, continuous training plays an important role not only in keeping up to date on new rules, but also getting refreshed in existing rules. The obligation for registered persons to attend and/or receive training is referred to as Continuing Education. There are three primary ways Continuing Education manifests itself for registered individuals:

- Firm Element
- Regulatory Element
- Annual Compliance Meeting

These are not the only forms of training registered or non-registered individuals would typically receive as a result of their association in the securities industry. Many other forms of training are conducted on an as-needed basis, but these three areas are the training areas required under industry rules. In **Firm Element and Annual Compliance Meeting training**, the firm is required to create and deliver training content to all registered associates. In order for the training to be meaningful to registered associates, such training must be tailored to an individual's function and duties within the regulated entity. For instance, the **Firm Element** training for a registered retail Financial Advisor should include items such as suitability obligations, written communications with retail clients, and firm policies around the processing of checks and securities from customers. Each of these items is directly related to the duties and functions of the retail Financial Advisor. Relevant Firm Element training would not need to include research report disclosures, or trade reporting requirements for equity securities. These topics would be most relevant to Research Analysts and Equity Traders, respectively. **Annual Compliance Meeting and Firm Element** training must be conducted on an *annual basis*. These trainings must offer registered associates an opportunity to ask questions. In addition, a record of who completed the training, and when they completed the training is required to be maintained as part of a firm's books and records. This training may be delivered in-person, through use of an on-line training course, or some combination of the two.

Regulatory Element training is also an important aspect of industry training. This type of training is actually conducted by industry regulators such as FINRA. In this FINRA-led training, registered associates now access the training through a website, login, and go through a series of steps to complete the training. Since it is web-based, the training typically includes audio, video, and on-screen components to the Regulatory Element Training. FINRA tailors the training based upon an individual's securities licenses. For instance, a registered representative who holds the SIE and Series 7 will take the 'rep-level' Regulatory Element training. A supervisor of that registered representative will take the 'supervisor-level' Regulatory Element training. This training is required to be completed within two years of an individual first becoming registered with a top off examination (Series 7, 57, 79, etc...). After the first training has been completed, the registered person must take subsequent training *every three years thereafter*.

Failure to take training mandated by industry rules can result in disciplinary action, including fines, suspension, or termination. In addition, those associates who are behind on their training may not act in a registered capacity until their training is caught up.   For instance, Sam Smith is a Series 7 registered associate.   Sam was supposed to take his Regulatory Element training by the due date of March 1. Today is March 2 and Sam still has not found the time to take his training. Since Sam's training is not current, he cannot solicit clients, accept orders, or take any other actions that would require industry registration.   He also cannot receive compensation for any activities that would require industry registration.

End of Chapter Quiz

Complete these end of chapter questions to assess your understanding of the subject matter discussed in this chapter. The answers follow on the next page. For those questions you have answered incorrectly, review the appropriate section of the chapter again to make sure you understand the concepts.

1. Which of the following would NOT make an individual be considered statutorily disqualified?
    a. Findings by the CFTC that a person willfully violated commodity laws
    b. Any misdemeanor conviction
    c. Bar from membership in an SRO
    d. State order barring association with a firm engaging in insurance or banking activities

2. Which of the following is NOT a valid top-off exam to the SIE Exam?
    a. Series 4 – Options
    b. Series 86/87 – Research Analyst
    c. Series 57 – Principal Trader
    d. Series 52 – Municipal Securities

3. Which of the following is TRUE regarding an individual registered representatives state registration requirements? Registered representatives must
    a. pass the Series 63 Examination.
    b. register in all 50 states.
    c. register in all states where they have customers.
    d. register in the state they reside and work in only.

4. Firm Element training is required to be delivered to which employees of a firm?
    a. All employees
    b. All registered associates
    c. All associated persons
    d. All domestic employees

5. Which of the following must be recorded or included with a Firm Element training?
    a. An opportunity to ask questions
    b. Location of the training
    c. The date of birth of the registered representative
    d. In-person training element

6. Which of the following is true regarding required Continuing Education training if such training is not completed as required?
   a. Licensing examinations must be retaken by the registered representative.
   b. Registered representatives can solicit clients, but cannot get paid until their training is up to date.
   c. Registered representatives can get paid, but not accept customer orders until their training is up to date.
   d. Registered representatives cannot accept customer orders or solicit clients until their training is up to date.

7. Which of the following is NOT a required training component for registered representatives?
   a. Firm Element
   b. Regulatory Element
   c. Annual Compliance Meeting
   d. Exchange Element

8. Regulatory Element training must first be completed _____ years after first becoming registered, and every _____ years thereafter.
   a. Three, two
   b. Two, three
   c. Three, three
   d. Three, one

9. The Series 66 Examination covers which of the following?
   a. Uniform Investment Adviser Law Examination
   b. Uniform Combined State Law Examination
   c. Uniform Securities Agent State Law Examination
   d. Uniform Securities Principal State Law Examination

10. Regulatory Element training for registered representatives is most typically completed how?
   a. In a session led by a law firm
   b. Through an online course
   c. In a session led by a firm principal
   d. By attending a testing center

End of Chapter Quiz Answers

1. B
Some misdemeanor convictions may cause an individual to become statutorily disqualified, but not all of them. A willful violation of the securities or commodity laws and bars from association with an SRO or from a state are clear ways an individual would be considered statutorily disqualified.

2. A
The SIE exam is not a prerequisite for the Series 4 Exam. All of the other exams - the Series 86/87, 57, and 52 all require the SIE Exam first.

3. C
Although a registered representative may choose to register in all 50 states, you do not need to register in any state where you do not have a customer in that state. Although a registered representative will be registered in the states they live and work typically, these are not the only states where they need to be registered, as they also need to be registered wherever they have a customer account. The Series 63 is one of the possible exams, but not specifically required as the only exam.

4. B
Although all employees may receive Firm Element training, only registered associates are required to take it. Firm Element must be delivered annually. Registered employees who work outside of the US are still required to take the Firm Element.

5. A
In person training, the location of the training, and the date of birth of the registered representative may be important in some respects, but these have no bearing on Firm Element training and are not required to be recorded or included as such. However, a registered representative must be given the opportunity to ask questions, either in person or through electronic contacts.

6. D

By not taking required Continuing Education Training, a registered representative is prohibited from interacting with customers in any meaningful way. This includes accepting customer order, soliciting customers, or getting paid on customer trades/activity. Licensing examinations do not typically need to be retaken, outside of formal disciplinary action taken by a regulator who requires the retake.

7. D

Firm Element, Regulatory Element, and Annual Compliance Meetings are all required to be completed. Firm Element and Annual Compliance Meetings are done annually, while the Regulatory Element must be completed every 2 or 3 years.

8. B

Regulatory Element training is not taken every year. It is required to be completed 2 years after first becoming registered with an exam such as the Series 7 or 79. After this initial Regulatory Element training, the registered representative must take the training every three years thereafter.

9. B

The Uniform Investment Adviser Law Examination is the Series 65. The Uniform Securities Agent State Law Examination is the Series 63. The Uniform Combined State Law Examination is the Series 66. The Uniform Securities Principal State Law Examination is not an actual licensing examination.

10. B

Regulatory Element training used to be completed through a testing center and technically could still be done that way. However, most firms have their associates complete their Regulatory Element training through an online course. Law firm sessions are typically used for Legal Continuing Education Credit, which is outside the scope of FINRA and SEC requirements. Principal led training is important and is often a part of Firm Element training, but not Regulatory Element training.

Chapter 19:   Employee Conduct and Reportable Events

Securities industry rules contain many specific obligations for members of the securities industry. Some of the most important securities industry rules surround conduct of those securities industry employees. Chapter 17 covered many different types of prohibited activities, many of which involved employee conduct. Employee conduct rules were established to provide transparency to the market, clients, and potential clients about an employee's past conduct, minimize or disclose potential conflicts of interest, and identify red flags.

Employee Conduct

One of the ways securities industry regulators uses to push for higher-quality individuals to join the industry is through a thorough background and disclosure check process.

Form U4

Upon joining an industry firm, a new employee is required to complete the **Form U4** - Uniform Application of Securities Registration or Transfer. Form U4 is used by securities industry firms to register their employees and is a comprehensive, detailed form that asks the employee numerous questions about their personal background, financial activities, education, prior employment, and many other areas. According to the Form U4 Instructions:

"Representatives of broker, investment advisers, or issuers of securities must use this form to become registered in the appropriate jurisdictions and/or SROs. These instructions apply to the filing of Form U4 electronically with the Central Registration Depository ("CRD (R)")...."

"An individual is under a continuing obligation to amend and update information required by Form U4 as changes occur. Amendments must be filed electronically (unless the filer is an approved paper filer) by updating the appropriate section of Form U4[52]. The Sections of the Form U4 are as follows:

1. General Information
2. Fingerprint Information
3. Registration With Unaffiliated Firms
4. SRO Registrations
5. Jurisdiction Registrations

6. Registration Requests With Affiliated Firms
7. Examination Requests
8. Professional Designations
9. Identifying Information/Name Change

10. Other Names
11. Residential History
12. Employment History

13. Other Business

14. Disclosure Questions Criminal Disclosure (Questions 14a, 14b) Regulatory Action Disclosure (Questions 14c, 14d, 14e, 14f, 1 14g) Civil Judicial Disclosure (Question 14h) Customer Complaint/Arbitration/Civil Litigation Disclosure (Question 14i) Termination Disclosure (Question 14j) Financial Disclosure (Questions 14k, 14l, 14m)

15. Signature

   15a. Individual/Applicant's Acknowledgment And Consent

   15b. Firm/Appropriate Signatory Representations

   15c. Temporary Registration Acknowledgment

   15d. Amendment Individual/Applicant's Acknowledgment And Consent

   15e. Firm/Appropriate Signatory Amendment Representations

   15f. Firm/Appropriate Signatory Concurrence Disclosure Reporting Pages (DRPs U4) Criminal DRP Regulatory Action DRP Investigation DRP Civil Judicial DRP Customer Complaint/Arbitration/Civil Litigation DRP Termination DRP Bankruptcy/SIPC/Compromise With Creditors DRP Bond DRP Judgment/Lien DRP

The contents of the Form are listed here so you can begin to understand what is requested when an employee is initially registering in the industry. As that employee's employment or ANYTHING ELSE on the Form changes, that employee must notify their employer and update the relevant sections of the form promptly. The standard for making updates is within 30 days from the date of the change. For instance, let's say you moved from one state to another. You would be required to update Form U4 removing your old address and including your new address as the location of your current residence. Practically speaking, an employee's sponsoring firm makes the actual updates to the Form U4 through internal processes. However, informing the sponsoring firm as to the contents and accuracy of Form U4 remain the responsibility of the employee.

To get registered, an employee will need to be registered by submitting a Form U4. Once becoming employed at a broker-dealer or SRO, that entity will typically begin the Form U4 registration process, with the employee reviewing the Form prior to the Firm submitting it through the CRD system. The employee is ultimately responsible for the accuracy of the content on the Form. An accurate completion of the Form U4 is extremely important. When completing the Form U4, all appropriate disclosures must be made, including involving those surrounding general information like name and address, Outside Business Activities, prior employment, financial items like bankruptcy or liens, and current industry licenses. Leaving relevant information off of Form U4 is a serious matter. Industry regulators and the investing public use the information provided to evaluate those working in the securities industry. If the information is not materially accurate, those users will not derive the same level of benefit had the information been accurate. If an employee or an employer submits false or misleading information, they would be subject to disciplinary action within the industry, including fine, suspension or termination of employment. An employer would be subject to disciplinary action, including fines and potential business limitations.

Someone working in the securities industry as a registered or associated person is required to file a Form U4 with FINRA, exchanges, and state regulators. Those people employed in the securities industry that file a U4 are required to notify the regulators of certain pieces of information, and update the Form U4 when any information changes. An example of this is for liens, bankruptcy, and debt. When filing the U4 form, an individual must disclose if they have ever filed for bankruptcy, or have liens against them or their property.

In reviewing the information on Form U4, it is important to be aware of potential red flags that a regulator or the investing public might raise questions about. Although numerous items might be considered a red flag, a few common red flags would include:

1. Recent *bankruptcy*
2. Liens or significant debt
3. *Outside Business Activity* that could be a potential conflict of interest
4. Employment with several employers within a short period of time
5. *Negative* reason for termination from prior employer

Form U5

Now you know that Form U4 is filed by an employee when they begin employment with a new securities industry firm. On the other hand, **Form U5 -** Uniform Termination Notice for Securities Industry Registration is used when an employee terminates employment for any reason. Form U5 can be used to fully terminate an employee, or partially terminate single or multiple securities industry licenses or state registrations. By filing Form U5, the filing firm provides notice to relevant regulators of the change in an employee's employment. Just like we did for Form U4, let's now take a look at the Form U5[53] instructions to get a better sense of what exactly the securities industry regulators are asking for when filing this form. According to the Form U5 Instructions:

"Broker-dealers, investment advisers, or issuers of securities must use this form to terminate the registration of an individual in the appropriate jurisdictions and/or self-regulatory organizations (SROs)."

"If the Form U5 has been completed for a full termination, a copy of this form and any subsequent amendments thereto, must be provided to the terminated individual. Firms are under a continuing obligation to amend and update Section 7 (Disclosure Questions) until final disposition, including reportable matters that occur and become known after initial submission of this form." The Sections of the Form U5 are as follows:

1. General Information
2. Current Residential Address
3. Full Termination
4. Date Terminated
5. Partial Termination
   5a. SRO Partial Termination
   5b. Jurisdiction Partial Termination

6. Affiliated Firm Termination
7. Disclosure Questions (Full Terminations And Amendments Only) Investigation Disclosure (Question 7a)
   Internal Review Disclosure (Question 7b)
   Criminal Disclosure (Question 7c)
   Regulatory Action Disclosure (Question 7d)
   Customer Complaint/Arbitration/Civil Litigation Disclosure (Question 7e)
   Termination Disclosure (Question 7f)
8. Signature
   8a. Firm Acknowledgment
   8b. Individual Acknowledgment and Consent Disclosure Reporting Pages (DRPs U5) (Full Terminations And Amendments Only) Criminal DRP Customer Complaint/Arbitration/Civil Litigation DRP Internal Review DRP Investigation DRP Regulatory Action DRP Termination DRP

As you can see from the contents of Form U5, it is quite a bit shorter than Form U4. In a practical sense, a full or comprehensive Form U5 is filed as an employee changes firms voluntarily, involuntarily, or is deceased. A reason for termination must always be given when filing Form U5. It is up to the employer/sponsoring firm to complete the Form U5, and then send a copy of Form U5 to the employee for their records. Of course, Form U5 must be truthfully and accurately completed by the firm making the filing. If there is anything inaccurate on Form U5, the now former employee can contest the inaccuracy.

Differences between Forms U4 and U5
There are a few differences between Forms U4 and U5 with which you should be familiar:
1. Form U4 is used to *register or transfer an employee*; Form U5 is used to *terminate* an employee, in whole or in part.
2. Form U4 may be started by the employer, but must be *completed and signed off on by the employee*; Form U5 is only completed and signed off by the *employer*. However, the employee must receive a copy of Form U5.
3. Firm has to approve and submit both the U4 and U5 filings.
4. Form U4 must be updated as an *employee's information changes*; Form U5 is only used for a *termination* of employment.
5. Form U4 must be made within 30 calendar days from the *date of the change*. Form U5 must be filed within 30 calendar days of the *full/partial termination*.

Reportable Events
There are several different types of reportable events in the securities industry that pertain to employees. Some items are required to be reported to both the employer

and to regulatory authorities within a certain period of time. It is important that employees follow the rules in this area. Disclosure and prior approval (as required) of these reportable events helps to reduce potential conflicts of interest, discloses materially relevant items to customers and potential customers, and helps to reasonably ensure that no undue influence is being used to win future customers. These reportable events include:

- Outside Business Activities
- Private Securities Transactions
- Political Contributions and Activities
- Gifts and Entertainment

Outside Business Activities

An **Outside Business Activity** ("OBA") as defined in FINRA Rule 3270 is a type of activity that an associated person of a broker-dealer conducts outside the scope of their employment with the broker-dealer. An OBA includes forms of paid activities as an employee, contractor, part time worker, etc... for an entity other than the associated person's broker dealer. For instance, John works for Broker-Dealer ABC as a Financial Advisor. John gets paid by Broker-Dealer ABC for the work he does for ABC. If John decides to also become a real estate agent in addition to his work as a Financial Advisor, John's work as a real estate agent makes this activity an OBA with his employer, BD ABC. Paid employment from a party other than an individual's BD employer is the most straightforward example. An OBA also exists for non-paid activities in certain circumstances. For instance, an associated person would have an OBA if they were on the Board of Directors (or similar role/level with that type of decision making) of a charitable organization.

A few common examples of OBAs:
- Member of the Board of Directors (or similar) for a local or national charity, school or religious organization
- Part time job as a real estate agent, web designer, blogger, car washer, etc... (anything where you get paid)
- Owner of an outside business

All OBA's must be preapproved by the associated person's employer. Firms will have requirements for associates to disclose potential OBAs to them under FINRA rules, then make a determination whether or not that OBA meets the regulatory threshold for disclosure on an individual's Form U4.

So, why does an associated person need to get their employers approval to have an OBA anyway? The regulatory guidance is clear – securities industry regulators like the SEC and FINRA want the firm to evaluate potential conflicts of interest with the employer's business and the associated person's duties. If the associates' firm approves the OBA, the OBA may be included on the associates' Form U4, allowing current and potential customers of the associate to be aware of the OBA. The preapproval process also allows the employer to review the employee's request to make sure that other industry rules are followed – like prohibitions against selling away (a prohibited activity from Chapter 17) or operating a business in competition or direct conflict with the associate's current employer.

Private Securities Transactions

Private Securities Transactions, as noted in <u>FINRA Rule 3280</u> are also required to be preapproved by a registered person's employer by disclosing to the firm the activity and the compensation structure. By the name itself, you should be able to deduce that this does not include any publicly traded securities, like those listed on an exchange. A Private Securities Transaction would include transactions such as:

- Purchasing shares in a privately held company
- Owning all or part of an LLC, partnership or similar venture
- Owning real estate for investment or rental purposes

Unlike OBA's, **Private Securities Transactions** are not included on an employee's Form U4. They are however reviewed for very similar risks, like conflicts of interest and completion with the employer's business. For that reason, a registered representative must provide relevant information about the private securities transaction and get the approval of their employer prior to engaging in the transaction. Note that an activity could be considered both an OBA and a Private Securities Transaction. Owning a company or business could be considered a Private Securities Transaction. Running the business would be considered an outside business activity. Industry rules do not want to encourage direct competition with an employer's business in this way, because from the customer's perspective, it makes it very hard to distinguish which is the 'normal' business, and which is the outside business or private securities transaction.

Political Contributions and Activities

The securities industry has very important rules and regulations on political contributions or participating in political activities. In the securities industry, the MSRB specifically has written important rules governing political contributions and activities. The number you need to remember here is that the limit is $250 per election, with the primary and general elections considered separate elections. Why are securities regulators interested in where and to whom industry members contribute money or time? It all comes down to the concept of pay to play. Back in Chapter 5, we discussed municipal securities as a type of debt security. Municipalities access the capital markets to fund roads, schools, buildings, etc... The people that typically make the final decision on raising money from the capital markets through a bond issuance are elected officials – mayors, city council, governor, etc... These local and state officials play an important role in the decision making process of what, when and how much to borrow. The firms that arrange the financing through the capital markets are underwriters. Underwriters try to make money in a bond issuance by buying from the municipality at one price, then selling to the investing public at another price. This is called the underwriting spread.

Now that we are refreshed a bit on municipal securities and underwriting basics, what does this have to do with political contributions? Let's say a mayor was up for reelection this coming fall. The mayor has a lot of influence in determining who the town will select as their underwriter for an upcoming municipal bond issuance. Municipal Underwriter, Inc., a firm who underwrites municipal securities, really wants to be the underwriter for town's upcoming municipal bond issuance. So Municipal Underwriter, Inc.'s best underwriter, Chris Smith decides the best thing to do would be to personally contribute $50,000 to the mayor's reelection campaign. That way, the mayor will think favorably of Municipal Underwriter, Inc. and Chris Smith, and will hopefully select them as the municipal underwriter for the upcoming bond issuance. Chris Smith lives in the mayor's town, and is therefore entitled to vote for the mayor in the election. Are you with me so far?

Municipal Underwriter, Inc.'s profit on the upcoming municipal bond issuance is expected to be $250,000 as underwriter. Seems like a smart move, right? Spend $50,000 up front; make $250,000 down the line, for a net profit of $200,000! What's the problem with that?

This is a textbook example of pay to play. The pay component is the contribution of $50,000. The 'play' component is the awarding of the role of underwriter in the municipal securities offering, worth an expected $250,000.

For individuals that violate the political contribution limits, the firms that those individuals work for now, or in the next two years are not permitted to engage in municipal securities business with that issuer. In our above example, the contribution is above $250, so Municipal Underwriter, Inc. would be banned from engaging in activities with that municipal entity within two years from the date of the contribution. Any political contributions equal to or under $250 are excluded from the political contribution prohibition.

There are a few other quick points about political contributions to cover before moving on to the next topic. Only state and local officials, either currently in office, or running for those offices, are subject to the MSRB's political contribution rule. The political contribution rule does not apply to existing federal office holders, or those running for federal office so long as those seeking those offices are not currently state or local municipal officials. Federal offices include, U.S. Senator, President, Vice President, or U.S. House of Representatives. State offices include, but are not limited to mayor, school district superintendent, town or city council, alderman, deputy mayor, governor, state senate, state representative. Let's go through a real-life example.

In the 2016 U.S. Presidential election, the two major party candidates for President and Vice President were as follows:
- **Democratic Party** – Hillary Clinton, *President*; Tim Kaine, *Vice President*
- **Republican Party** – Donald Trump, *President*; Mike Pence, *Vice President*

Both Clinton and Trump were not then municipal office holders nor were they seeking municipal office at the time of the election. Kaine was an office holder, but he was a U.S. Senator at the time of the election, which is a federal office. Pence however was the sitting Governor of Indiana, a U.S. state. As a municipal official of an issuer (the state of Indiana), those individuals subject to MSRB rules were limited to $250 in contributions in the election. If these individuals gave more than $250 to the Trump/Pence campaign, they would be banned from engaging in municipal securities activities for two years with the state of Indiana. Political contributions are not Form U4 reportable.

Gifts and Entertainment

Gifts and entertainment are often thought of together for good reason. When giving someone a gift, entertainment is sometimes included in the form of dinner, drinks at a restaurant, etc... A gift however is separate and distinct from entertainment.

FINRA Rule 3220 defines a gift as indirectly or directly giving another individual something of value *in relation to the business of the employer of the recipient of the payment*. The limit for gifts is $100 per individual per year. Gifts cannot include cash or cash equivalents.

Industry regulators generally accept that items branded with a firm's logo like pens, mugs, t-shirts, etc... are de minimis or not considered 'something of value', and therefore not considered a gift. In addition, giving some type a gift for a life event like a wedding, birth of a child, or life event is generally not considered a gift that is in relation to the business of the employer of the recipient of the gift.

A quick example: Jon works for Broker-Dealer A and Susan works for Broker-Dealer B. Jon is trying to get Susan to send more orders from Broker-Dealer B to Broker-Dealer A where Jon works. If Jon gives Susan a signed baseball worth $75, Jon has not violated the gift rule. If Jon gives Susan an iPad worth $600, he has violated the gift rule.

The line between gift and entertainment can be blurry in some cases. Entertainment is typically an experience, outing, dinner, or some other type event. For instance, if you were to give someone tickets to a football game and attend the game with them, the tickets would be considered entertainment. However, if you gave two tickets to the same individual, and said, "have a great time at the game" and did not attend the game with them, then the tickets would be considered a gift. To comply with the gift and entertainment rules, a firm would typically require an employee to report all gifts and record such gifts on a firm or department gift log. For entertainment, many firms would require an employee who entertained clients to be present at the event, helping to reasonably ensure that the event is not a gift, but instead entertainment.

Entertainment is subject to the extravagance standard. Although there is no specific dollar limit for entertainment, any form of entertainment cannot be so lavish or excessive that it calls into question the propriety of the entertainment. Taking a client to see a baseball game would generally be acceptable and not considered lavish or excessive. Taking a client to all 82 home games that season would likely be considered lavish and excessive, and therefore a violation of the entertainment rule. Gifts or entertainment are not Form U4 reportable.

A quick recap on gifts and entertainment:
- The gift giving limit is $100 per individual per year
- Gifts must involve giving something of value. Life event or de minimis (in other words – of little real value) logo gifts do not fall within the purview of the gift rule
- Paying for meals or lodging for a client is entertainment. Giving a client a certificate to go to dinner with their spouse is a gift. This distinction is important.

End of Chapter Quiz

Complete these end of chapter questions to assess your understanding of the subject matter discussed in this chapter. The answers follow on the next page. For those questions you have answered incorrectly, review the appropriate section of the chapter again to make sure you understand the concepts.

1. Which of the following activities would likely be considered an Outside Business Activity?
    a. Volunteering at a local food pantry
    b. Driving for a rideshare company
    c. Selling items in a garage or rummage sale
    d. Passive investment made in a real estate LLC

2. When must a registered representative seek approval for an Outside Business Activity?
    a. 30 days prior to engaging in the activity
    b. Within 30 days from starting the activity
    c. On the day the activity begins
    d. Prior to engaging in the activity

3. In order to be considered a de minimis political contribution, the contribution must not exceed which amount per election?
    a. $0
    b. $100
    c. $250
    d. $500

4. Which of the following is TRUE regarding a Form U5?
    a. Reason for termination is optional.
    b. A copy must be sent to the employee.
    c. Form U5 is not required if an employee is deceased.
    d. The employee must complete the Form U5 before departing the firm.

5. Which of the following is TRUE regarding permissible gifts to customers by registered representatives under the FINRA gift rules?
    a. Gifts must not exceed $0 per calendar year.
    b. Gifts must not exceed $50 per calendar year.
    c. Gifts must not exceed $100 per calendar year.
    d. Gifts must not exceed $200 per calendar year.

6. Tony Smith, an MFP, would like make a political contribution to a mayoral candidate in his local town. What is the maximum amount Tony can contribute in both the primary election and general election combined without subjecting his firm from a ban on municipal securities business?
   a. $0
   b. $125
   c. $250
   d. $500

7. Which of the following is TRUE regarding permissible gifts to customers by registered representatives under the FINRA gift rules?
   a. Gifts not exceeding $200 would be permissible under FINRA gift rules.
   b. Gifts for life events, such as a wedding, would be permissible under FINRA gift rules.
   c. Attending a sporting event with a customer would not be permitted under FINRA rules.
   d. Gifts to customers by registered representative are not permitted under FINRA rules.

8. Which of the following information is NOT on the Form U4?
   a. Fingerprint information
   b. SRO registrations
   c. Residential history
   d. Account balances

9. Updates to a Form U4 must be made timely and are the responsibility of the:
   a. Employee
   b. Employer
   c. Supervisor
   d. FINRA

10. Which of the following is NOT required to be disclosed on the Form U4?
    a. Outside Business Activity
    b. Private Securities Transaction
    c. Bankruptcy
    d. Lien

End of Chapter Quiz Answers

1. B

Passive investments would likely not be considered an outside business activity, but would be considered a private investment. This is because you are not actively managing or working on the business. Selling items in a garage sale is not a business and is not consistent, so this would not be an outside business activity. Volunteer activities are not considered outside business activities typically, unless you are on the board of directors (or similar). Only driving for a ridesharing company would likely qualify because you are getting paid and you are working for another company.

2. D

Outside business activities must be preapproved by a firm prior to the employee engaging in the activity. This gives the firm an opportunity to review the proposed activity, ensure it is consistent with industry rules and firm policy, and review for potential conflicts of interest.

3. C

Although not all contributions above $250 will necessarily get a firm banned from engaging in business with a municipal issuer, $250 is the cutoff for a contribution to be considered deminimis. Contributions above $250 are not considered deminimis. The limitation is per election, so $250 applies to the primary election, and another $250 applies to the general election.

4. B

To ensure that the individual has an opportunity to review the U5 and the reason for termination, a copy must be provided to the individual. The U5 is completed by the firm and must be sent for all terminations, even if the employee is deceased. A reason for the termination is required, and a copy of the U5 is not required to be sent to the employee before it is finalized.

5. C

FINRA's gift limit is $100 per year per customer. Any gifts given in excess of this limit would be a rule violation.

6. D

For a single election, the limit is $250. This limit applies separately to the primary and general elections. Therefore, Tony (the Municipal Finance Professional, or MFP) could contribute $250 to a candidate in the primary election, and another $250 to the same candidate in the general election for a total of $500.

7. B

Life event gifts, such as weddings, births, and funerals would be ok under FINRA rules. Attending a sporting event with a customer would be ok under FINRA rules as long as it was not excessive or lavish. The general FINRA gift limit is $100 per year per customer.

8. D

The U4 contains information about the registered representative's job history, exams, prior residences, fingerprint information, and other personal-related items. An account balance, although perhaps known to the registered representative's firm, would not be on the U4.

9. A

Although a firm, an employee of the firm, or a supervisor of the firm makes updates to a U4, it is the responsibility of the employee to make sure these updates are made timely and accurately.

10. B

Although private securities transactions are required to be disclosed to the firm, they are not reportable on Form U4. Outside business activities, liens, and bankruptcies must be disclosed to the firm and on Form U4.

Table of Figures

Additional Resources

Primary Securities Industry Regulator Websites
- Financial Industry Regulatory Authority (FINRA) - www.finra.org
- Securities and Exchange Commission (SEC) - www.sec.gov
- BATS Exchange - www.batstrading.com
- New York Stock Exchange – www.nyse.com
- Nasdaq – www.Nasdaq.com
- Chicago Board Options Exchange – www.cboe.com
- Municipal Securities Rulemaking Board – www.msrb.org
- MSRB's EMMA portal – emma.msrb.org

Other Securities Industry Regulator Websites
- Internal Revenue Service – www.irs.gov
- Federal Reserve - www.federalreserve.gov
- North American Securities Administrators Association - www.nasaa.org
- Securities Investor Protection Corporation (SIPC) - www.sipc.org
- Federal Deposit Insurance Corporation – www.fdic.gov

General Industry Rules and Sources:
- SEC Fast Answers: http://www.sec.gov/fast-answers
- List of Investor Educational Sites: http://www.sec.gov/investor/links.shtml
- FINRA Regulatory Notices: https://www.finra.org/industry/notices
- FINRA Rules: http://finra.complinet.com/
- MSRB Rules: http://www.msrb.org/Rules-and-Interpretations/MSRB-Rules.aspx
- SEC Rules: https://www.sec.gov/about/laws/secrulesregs.htm

Additional Information on Specific Products and Concepts
- Municipal Bonds:
  http://www.sec.gov/investor/alerts/municipalbonds.htm
  http://www.finra.org/investors/alerts/municipal-bonds_important-considerations-individual-investors
- Municipal Bonds: Understanding Credit Risk:
  http://www.sec.gov/investor/alerts/municipalbondsbulletin.pdf
- Corporate Bonds: http://www.sec.gov/investor/alerts/ib_corporatebonds.pdf
- High Yield Corporate Bonds: http://www.sec.gov/investor/alerts/ib_high-yield.pdf
- Private Placements: http://www.finra.org/investors/alerts/private-placements-risks

- Closed End Fund: http://www.finra.org/investors/alerts/closed-end-fund-distributions-where-money-coming
- REITs: http://www.sec.gov/investor/alerts/reits.pdf
- ETFs: http://www.sec.gov/investor/alerts/etfs.pdf
- Target Date Retirement Funds: http://www.sec.gov/investor/alerts/tdf.htm
- Hedge Funds: http://www.sec.gov/investor/alerts/ib_hedgefunds.pdf
- Mutual Fund Classes: http://www.finra.org/investors/alerts/understanding-mutual-fund-classes
- American Depositary Receipts: http://www.sec.gov/investor/alerts/adr-bulletin.pdf
- Variable Annuities: http://www.sec.gov/investor/alerts/ib_var_annuities.pdf
- College Savings Plans: http://www.finra.org/investors/alerts/college-savings-plans-before-invest
- Investing in an IPO: http://www.sec.gov/investor/alerts/ipo-investorbulletin.pdf
- Accredited Investors: http://www.sec.gov/investor/alerts/ib_accreditedinvestors.pdf
- Pump and Dump: http://www.sec.gov/investor/alerts/ia_pumpanddump.htm
- Customer Confirmation Statements: http://www.sec.gov/investor/alerts/ib_confirmations.pdf
- Margin Accounts: http://www.sec.gov/investor/alerts/ib_marginaccounts.pdf
- Credit Ratings: http://www.sec.gov/investor/alerts/ib_creditratings.pdf
- MSRB Fact Sheets: http://www.msrb.org/EducationCenter/library/pdfs.aspx

Now, onto the Final Exams!

Final Exams

In the pages that follow, you will find two Final Exams. You should only attempt these final exams once you have read each chapter, reviewed the Table of Figures, and successfully completed each of the End of Chapter Questions.

When attempting the final exams, use the Final Exam Answer Sheets located after each of the two Final Exams. Complete Final Exam #1 first, then check your answers using the answers without explanations. For those that you have incorrect, go back to the material in the book and see if you can figure out where you went wrong. If you can't figure out why you got the answer wrong, use the answers with explanations.

After you have completed the first Final Exam, repeat the process with the second Final Exam. Then, go back and retry Final Exam #1 and #2 to see if you can improve your score. At this point, read (o re-read) all of the answers with explanations.

Read any of the material not clear at this point another time, and review each of the figures in each of the chapter to make sure you have a detailed understanding and recall of the facts.

Your last step is to try the FINRA SIE sample exam, linked at the end of book. This sample exam can only be done online.

Good luck!

Final Exam #1

1. The FINRA Form that requires current or prospective registered representatives to provide information pertaining to their personal background, financial activities, education, and prior employment is called:
a. Series 7
b. CRD
c. U4
d. U5

2. A political contribution made by a firm employee in violation of the MSRB's political contribution rule may result in which of the following penalties?
a. The employee making the contribution could be suspended.
b. The firm the employee works for would be prohibited from doing business for two years with the municipality involved.
c. The firm would not be permitted to conduct municipal securities business for two years.
d. The employee would have his municipal securities license suspended.

3. The death of an owner of which type of account means that their proportional ownership passes to their estate?
a. Joint Tenants with Rights of Survivorship
b. Tenant in Common
c. Custodial
d. LLC

4. Which of the following is NOT required to be completed when submitting a U4 to FINRA?
a. Fingerprints
b. Signed U4
c. Signed affidavit
d. Review of prior employment and work history

5. A potential new associate who is statutorily disqualified may be hired under which of the following circumstances?
a. They generally cannot be hired by FINRA member firm in any capacity.
b. They can be hired if the activity causing the statutory disqualification occurred more than 6 years ago.
c. An employee receives a waiver approval from all of their prior employers.
d. They can be hired if granted an exemption by a regulator.

6.   The CFO of publicly traded company ABC has been talking to her neighbor about her work. In a recent conversation, the CFO tells the neighbor that they will be releasing their quarterly earnings report next week. As a result, the neighbor decides to buy 1,000 shares of ABC in their individual account. What, if any, violations of insider trading laws have occurred?
     a. If the quarterly earnings report is positive, insider trading laws will apply.
     b. Insider trading laws will apply if the CFO knew the earnings numbers at the time of her conversation with the neighbor.
     c. If the neighbor subsequently sells their ABC stock for a profit, insider trading laws will apply.
     d. None, as the earning release information is not material or inside information.

7.   A retail investor has recently entered into the following transactions:

     5/1 - cash balance: $0
     5/2 – buy 100 shares of XYZ at $50 for a total of $5000
     5/3 – no activity cash deposits
     5/4 – sell 100 shares of XYZ at $50 for a total of $5000
     5/4 – cash balance $0

     If the above transactions were the only transactions in this account between 5/1 and 5/4, what form of market manipulation has the retail investor engaged in?

     a. Freeriding   c. Wash trading
     b. Pump and dump   d. Backing away

8.   Which of the following would be considered personally identifiable information?
     a. A list of names and addresses of customers of an entity that is not a financial institution.
     b. Information provided to one customer that does not identify another consumer.
     c. Information from widely distributed media mentioning your customer.
     d. The fact that an individual has obtained a financial service from your firm.

9.   Customer confirmations are required to be sent to the customer in _____ form no later than _____.
     a. Electronic or paper, settlement date.
     b. Electronic or paper, trade date.
     c. Electronic, settlement date.
     d. Electronic or paper, trade date.

10.   Which of the following entities are NOT exempt from CIP requirements?
       a. Revocable Trust   d. SEC   Registered   Investment
       b. Municipality   Advisor
       c. Listed equity issuer

11.   Which of the following is NOT required in an AML Program?
       a. Designation of an AML Compliance Officer
       b. AML specific policies and procedures
       c. Technology system that prevents money laundering
       d. Process for filings SARs

12.   Which of the following AML regulators must financial institutions submit SAR
       filings?
       a. FinCEN   c. OFAC
       b. FATF   d. SEC

13.   Which of the following retirement accounts grow tax free?
       a. Roth IRA   c. 401k
       b. Regular IRA   d. Joint account

14.   Which of the following accounts grow tax deferred?
       a. Roth IRA   c. UGMA account
       b. Spousal IRA   d. Trust account

15.   Which of the following is difference between Coverdell ESAs and 529 Plans?
       a. Only Coverdell ESAs are self-directed investments.
       b. Only 529 plans are used for education savings.
       c. Only 529 plans grow tax-exempt if used for qualified educational expenses.
       d. Only Coverdell ESAs have income based contribution limits.

16.   Which of the following is a defined benefit account?
       a. IRA   c. 401k
       b. Roth IRA   d. Pension plan

17.   Which of the following securities settle on a T+1 basis?
       a. Equity Securities   c. Corporate Bonds
       b. Option Securities   d. Municipal Bonds

18.   You own 75 shares of XYZ security which has just split 5-3. Your XYZ shares
       originally cost $54. You will own _____ shares after the split and your cost basis
       will be _____.
       a. 125 shares, $32.40   c. 125 shares, $54.00
       b. 45 shares, $90.00   d. 45 shares, $32.40

19. Which of the following is NOT considered and taxed as ordinary income?
     a. Wages   c. Interest
     b. Long term capital gains   d. Commissions

20. You have purchased shares in a listed equity security on a Friday. When will your
     trade settle under a normal settlement cycle?
     a. Saturday   c. Monday
     b. Sunday   d. Tuesday

21. A municipal finance principal (MFP) is any associated person
     a. who is municipal securities principal and a supervisor of any municipal
         finance representative
     b. who is a member of an executive or management committee
     c. who is a municipal solicitor
     d. primarily engaged in municipal securities representative activities

22. Most issuers that pay dividends typically pay them out how many times per
     year?
     a. 1   c. 4
     b. 2   d. 12

23. Which of the following is in the correct order, from the date that occurs first to
     the date that occurs last?
     a. announcement date, record date, ex-date, payment date
     b. ex-date, announcement date, payment date, record date
     c. announcement date, record date, payment date, ex-date
     d. announcement date, ex-date, record date, payment date

24. John Investor has decided to buy ABC stock. He buys 100 shares at $78. The
     price of the stock increases the next day to $80. John Investor has a(n)
     _____.
     a. Realized loss   c. Unrealized loss
     b. Realized gain   d. Unrealized gain

25. In a principal trade, the broker dealer effects a buy or sell transaction with the
     customer
     a. out of their own inventory account.
     b. without ever owning the security.
     c. after first purchasing it from a counterparty.
     d. and crosses it against another customer trade.

26.   A few months ago, you purchased 500 shares of XYZ stock at a price of $67. Recently, the stock has appreciated and traded yesterday around $114. Although you do not want to sell the stock now, you do want to protect your profits in the event of a severe price drop. What type of order should you enter?
      a. Market   c. Day
      b. AON   d. Stop

27.   Which of the following best describes a UIT?
      a. There are a variable number of shares of a UIT that typically changes over time.
      b. When the UIT reaches maturity or the end of its life, the underlying assets within the UIT are sold and the principal is returned to the owners/investors.
      c. Shares in UITs may be listed on U.S. Stock Exchanges such as NYSE or Nasdaq, or over the counter.
      d. Shares in the UIT are typically sold through the IPO process to public investors.

28.   Which of the following would be a bearish market indicator?
      a. Q1 Real GDP goes from $19 trillion to 19.2 trillion
      b. Unemployment rate decreases from 5.1% to 4.9%
      c. Retail sales increase by 4% year over year
      d. Durable goods orders drop by 2%

29.   The risk an investor takes when they use their money to purchase an asset is called:
      a. interest rate risk   c. credit risk
      b. capital risk   d. political risk

30.   Use the following information for this question.

Name	Bid	Name	Ask
MMA	89.56 x 4	MMB	89.60 x 2

      Which market maker is willing to buy and for how many shares?
      a. MMA for 400 shares   c. MMB for 200 shares
      b. MMA for 560 shares   d. MMB for 600 shares

31.   Which of the following best describes a default?
      a. Issuer has decided not to make preferred stock dividend payments.
      b. Issuer makes a partial coupon payment on an outstanding bond issuance.
      c. Issuer reduces the dividend on an equity stock.
      d. An increase in interest rates drops the price of the bond in the secondary market.

32. Of the following securities, which has the least amount of liquidity risk?
    a. 30 year Treasury Bond
    b. A-rated 10 year Corporate Bond
    c. AA-rated 15 year Municipal Bond
    d. OTC equity security

33. Which of the following is TRUE regarding hedge funds?
    a. Hedge funds could hold assets that are hard to value.
    b. Hedge funds have fees comparable to mutual funds.
    c. Hedge funds can be bought and sold at the end of market hours similar to mutual funds.
    d. Hedge funds only invest in equities or fixed income, but not both at the same time.

34. Which of the following is an accurate similarity between hedge funds and mutual funds?
    a. charge similar fee amounts
    b. can hold equity securities
    c. investors can sell their ownership stake at any time
    d. all retail investors can invest

35. Which of the following is TRUE regarding DPPs?
    a. Exist in lifespan similar to listed equities.
    b. Cannot be bought or sold on an exchange like listed equities.
    c. DPPs do not typically include REITs or BDCs.
    d. DPPs often invest in the consumer and manufacturing sectors.

36. Which of the following best describes a difference between ETFs and open-end (mutual) funds?
    a. ETFs invest in a many securities, but open end mutual funds invest in only a few securities.
    b. Open end mutual funds can be bought or sold throughout the day, while ETFs can only be bought and sold after 4pm EST.
    c. ETFs may charge fees to investors, while open end mutual funds may not charge fees.
    d. ETFs are traded on an exchange, while open end mutual funds are only redeemable to the fund company.

37. Of the following expenses, which are NOT considered legitimate uses of 529 plan funds and therefore taxable when withdrawn?
    a. Fees
    b. Computers
    c. Books
    d. Transportation

38. Absent a default, when would a bond have capital risk?
    a. investor intends to sell the bond prior to maturity
    b. bond was upgraded
    c. bond was called by the issuer
    d. investor put the bond to the issuer

39. Which of the following securities are not exempt from the SEC registration process?
    a. Municipal securities
    b. Offerings with maturities of less than 270 days
    c. U.S. Government securities
    d. Corporate bonds

40. Which of the following accurately describes a characteristic of a 529 Prepaid Tuition Plan?
    a. Locks in tuition rate
    b. Investments made into choices pre-selected by investment manager
    c. Can be opened through the U.S. government
    d. No penalty applied if funds are used for improper expenses

41. On January 1, an investor's portfolio has the following components:

    Equities: 50%
    Municipal Bonds: 20%
    Corporate Bonds: 20%
    Cash/Money Markets: 10%

    Due to changes in the market and the growth of the overall portfolio over the course of the year, the investor's portfolio now looks like this on December 31 of the same year:

    Equities: 40%
    Municipal Bonds: 25%
    Corporate Bonds: 25%
    Cash/Money Markets: 10%

    If the investor wants to maintain the portfolio composition that they had on January 1, which of the following actions should they take to rebalance their portfolio?

    a. buy equities, sell municipal bonds, sell corporate bonds
    b. buy equities, sell municipal bonds, buy corporate bonds
    c. sell equities, buy municipal bonds, buy corporate bonds
    d. sell equities, sell municipal bonds, sell corporate bonds

42. Which of the following mutual fund share classes often has a contingent deferred sales charge attached to their sale?
    a. Class A
    b. Class B
    c. Class R
    d. Class CDSC

43. Which of the following is TRUE regarding a 529 Savings Plan?
    a. Locks in tuition rate
    b. No specific investment choices made
    c. Deductions are never state-tax deductible
    d. Penalty applied to funds used for improper expenses

44. A mutual fund that seeks to mirror the performance of the S&P 500 is known as a(n):
    a. Income fund
    b. Index fund
    c. Hybrid fund
    d. Growth fund

45. Which of the following is required to be provided to a mutual fund investor upon purchase of a mutual fund?
    a. Prospectus
    b. Official Statement
    c. Preliminary Prospectus
    d. Private Placement Memorandum

46. Which of the following best describes a positive yield curve?
    a. Municipal bonds yield more than equivalent corporate bonds
    b. Municipal bonds yield less than equivalent corporate bonds
    c. Short term interest rates are greater than long term interest rates
    d. Short term interest rates are less than long term interest rates

47. Which of the following best describes a balanced mutual fund?
    a. 100% of the investments are made in a broad array of equity securities.
    b. The mutual fund incrementally shifts from 80% of the total mutual fund investment in equity securities to 80% of the total mutual fund investment in fixed income securities by a specified future date.
    c. 50% of the mutual fund is invested in growth stocks, 50% of the mutual fund is invested in income stocks.
    d. 40% of the mutual fund is invested in fixed income securities, 60% of the mutual fund is invested in equity securities.

48. Which of the following is true regarding a closed-end company?
    a. Must redeem shares with the closed end company upon sale
    b. There are only a fixed number of shares available
    c. A prospectus is always required to be sent to new purchasers
    d. New shares are offered all the time

49. Which of the following is NOT a SAR report category?
    a. Forgery
    b. Source of funds
    c. Identity theft
    d. High income

50. _____ must be sent the options disclosure document _____.
    a. All option accounts, annually
    b. All options accounts, upon account open
    c. Active options account, annually
    d. Active options accounts, upon account open

51. One option contract is typically equivalent to how many shares of the underlying security?
    a. 1
    b. 10
    c. 100
    d. 1000

52. In an options transaction, the premium must be paid to the _____ by _____.
    a. option writer, settlement date
    b. option writer, trade date
    c. option purchaser, settlement date
    d. option purchaser, trade date

53. You currently hold 10 ABC April 80 calls. Of the following, at what price does the underlying security needs to trade at to be considered away from the money?
    a. $82.50
    b. $75.00
    c. $80.00
    d. $85.00

54. Which piece of information is a rating agency unlikely to ask a municipality to provide when the municipality is seeking a rating?
    a. Balance Sheet and Income Statement
    b. Debt covenants
    c. Length of Mayor's term
    d. Proposed debt structure

55. You purchased 1 XYZ August 45 put a month ago. The option you purchased last month have now reached expiration date, which is today. If the stock is trading at $50, what will happen to your option?
    a. The option will expire worthless.
    b. The OCC will exercise the option on your behalf if you do nothing.
    c. You must pay the difference between $45 and $50 per share of underlying stock.
    d. The counterparty you bought the option from will pay you the $5 difference.

56.　In your investment account, you currently hold the following:

1 call option contract on ABC company
100 shares of XYZ company

Given these holdings, which of the following is true?
a. This is considered a covered options position.
b. A fully covered options position would only exist if you held 100 ABC option contracts.
c. The options position and stock position have nothing to do with one another.
d. If the price of XYZ equity shares are volatile, the option will tend to be worth more.

57.　A certificate of deposit purchased for $10,000 is considered a _____ deposit and a _____ instrument.
a. time, non-negotiable
b. fixed, negotiable
c. time, negotiable
d. fixed, non-negotiable

58.　What is the maximum amount of cash the FDIC will insure in the event of bank insolvency?
a. $150,000
b. $200,000
c. $250,000
d. $500,000

59.　Commercial paper is typically:
a. secured by corporate assets.
b. bought by investors seeking income.
c. issued by lower credit quality issuers.
d. sold on a discount basis.

60.　Assuming both bonds are otherwise equivalent, why should a municipal bond always yield less than a corporate bond?
a. Corporate bond coupon payments are taxable.
b. Municipal bonds are more interest rate sensitive than corporate bonds.
c. Municipal bonds have a shorter maturity than corporate bonds.
d. Corporate bonds are more risky than municipal bonds.

61.　Your local municipality is expecting to receive revenue near the end of the calendar year when property taxes are normally paid. However, the municipality has incurred some unexpected expenses they would like to pay for now. Which of the following is the most appropriate form of new municipal security issuance to address this problem?
a. TAN
b. GO
c. BAN
d. Revenue

62. Which of the following will the FDIC NOT cover in the event of a bank becoming insolvent?
   a. safe deposit boxes at the bank
   b. money market deposit accounts
   c. time deposits
   d. cashier's check

63. Which of the following is common between 529 Plans and Education Savings Accounts?
   a. Limit contributions per calendar year at $2,000
   b. Authorized by individual U.S. states
   c. Both can only be used for post-secondary educational expenses (i.e. college or university)
   d. Proceeds are exempt from federal taxes if used for qualified expenses

64. Which of the following is characteristic of common equity stock?
   a. Convertible
   b. Voting rights
   c. First right of bankruptcy after bond/debtholders
   d. First right of dividend

65. A trade in a listed equity security occurring on the listing exchange would be considered to be in the:
   a. Primary market
   b. Secondary market
   c. Third market
   d. Fourth market

66. An equity security with a market capitalization of $60 million is likely to be considered a:
   a. large cap stock
   b. mid cap stock
   c. small cap stock
   d. micro cap stock

67. In the event of a bankruptcy, equity holders may:
   a. be held personally liable for issuer debts.
   b. lose their entire equity stake.
   c. vote to move ahead of debtholders for liquidation.
   d. receive additional shares for additional risk.

68. If an investor holds an equity security in their individual account, this means that an investor
   a. has the right, but not the obligation to purchase the security in the future.
   b. has let the issuer borrow money from the investor.
   c. is considered an owner of the company.
   d. is guaranteed to received future dividend payments.

69. Which of the following is true about penny stocks?
    a. they are typically listed on an exchange
    b. low risk investments because of their low price
    c. must meet stringent listing requirements to be traded over the counter
    d. considered speculative investments

70. Which of the following places the members of the underwriting syndicate in the correct order, from largest role to smallest role?
    a. selling group, syndicate member, co-manager, lead manager
    b. lead manager, co-manager, selling group, syndicate member
    c. lead manager, co-manager, syndicate member, selling group
    d. lead manager, syndicate member, co-manager, selling group

71. Potential investors in an new securities offering may only be solicited after the Registration Statement has been:
    a. filed with the SEC
    b. approved by the SEC
    c. created by the issuer, but before it is filed with the SEC
    d. acknowledged by the potential investor in writing

72. Which of the following securities are not typically issued as a private offering?
    a. Municipal securities
    b. US Government securities
    c. Corporate bonds
    d. Offerings with maturities of less than 270 days

73. Which of the following directly takes money out of the money supply?
    a. Fed's purchase of securities
    b. Moral suasion
    c. Increasing the reserve requirements
    d. Decreasing the discount rate

74. Which of the following is considered contractionary economic factor?
    a. Decrease in Federal Funds rate
    b. Increase in the money supply
    c. Increase in the discount rate
    d. Higher interest rates

75. The rate at which member institutions charge each other for the use of funds is:
    a. Interest rate
    b. Discount rate
    c. Federal Funds rate
    d. 10 Year Treasury Bond Rate

76.   The entity that sells an ownership position in itself to a third party is known as the:
      a. Investment advisor   c. Underwriter
      b. Issuer   d. Transfer agent

77.   What is the maximum amount of cash and securities SIPC will insure per account in the event of a broker dealer becoming insolvent?
      a. $150,000   c. $250,000
      b. $200,000   d. $500,000

78.   M2 defines money as a:
      a. Store of value   c. Medium of exchange
      b. Price of good and services   d. Value of employment

79.   Which of the following accurately ranks from first paid out to last paid out in the event of a bankruptcy?
      a. debt holders, preferred stockholders, equity stockholders
      b. preferred stockholders, debt holders, equity stockholders
      c. debt holders, equity stockholders, preferred stockholders
      d. equity stockholders, debt holders, preferred stockholders

80.   Without justification, how long can a registered representative hold customer mail?
      a. 1 month   c. 6 months
      b. 3 months   d. 12 months

81.   You own 1000 shares of ABC security which has just reverse split 1-10. Your ABC shares originally cost $75. You will own _____ shares after the split and your cost basis will be _____.
      a. 100 shares, $750.00   c. 100 shares, $75.00
      b. 100 shares, $7.50   d. 10,000 shares, $75.40

82.   During the interview process, a potential new employee indicates that they may be statutorily disqualified. Which of the following facts would make this employee statutorily disqualified?
      a. The employee pled no contest to felony breaking and entering charges (non-financial related).
      b. The employee filed for bankruptcy on two occasions.
      c. The employee has outstanding child support.
      d. The employee has not paid their federal income taxes in two years

83. When are associated persons permitted to purchase a security in an IPO?
    a. If they have more than 5 years of experience in the industry.
    b. Under no circumstances can the associated person purchase an IPO.
    c. Only if other customers have passed on purchasing in the IPO.
    d. If the underwriter selling the IPO receives approval from the issuer.

84. In order to be exempt from the ban on future municipal securities business as a result of a political contribution made per election, which of the following must be true?
    a. Contribution must be $250 or less
    b. Contribution must be $250 or less and the contributor must be entitled to vote for the municipal candidate
    c. Contribution must be $500 or less
    d. Contribution must be $500 or less and the contributor must be entitled to vote for the municipal candidate

85. Which of the following is considered a U.S. Exchange?
    a. Securities and Exchange Commission
    b. NYSE
    c. FINRA
    d. MSRB

Final Exam #1 – Answer Sheet (First Attempt)

Place your answer in the space below that corresponds to each question. When you complete the Final Exam, check your answers against the answer key that follows.

1	_____	30	_____	58	_____
2	_____	31	_____	59	_____
3	_____	32	_____	60	_____
4	_____	33	_____	61	_____
5	_____	34	_____	62	_____
6	_____	35	_____	63	_____
7	_____	36	_____	64	_____
8	_____	37	_____	65	_____
9	_____	38	_____	66	_____
10	_____	39	_____	67	_____
11	_____	40	_____	68	_____
12	_____	41	_____	69	_____
13	_____	42	_____	70	_____
14	_____	43	_____	71	_____
15	_____	44	_____	72	_____
16	_____	45	_____	73	_____
17	_____	46	_____	74	_____
18	_____	47	_____	75	_____
19	_____	48	_____	76	_____
20	_____	49	_____	77	_____
21	_____	50	_____	78	_____
22	_____	51	_____	79	_____
23	_____	52	_____	80	_____
24	_____	53	_____	81	_____
25	_____	54	_____	82	_____
26	_____	55	_____	83	_____
27	_____	56	_____	84	_____
28	_____	57	_____	85	_____
29	_____				

Final Exam #1 – Answer Sheet (Second Attempt)

Place your answer in the space below that corresponds to each question. When you complete the Final Exam, check your answers against the answer key that follows.

1	_____	30	_____	58	_____
2	_____	31	_____	59	_____
3	_____	32	_____	60	_____
4	_____	33	_____	61	_____
5	_____	34	_____	62	_____
6	_____	35	_____	63	_____
7	_____	36	_____	64	_____
8	_____	37	_____	65	_____
9	_____	38	_____	66	_____
10	_____	39	_____	67	_____
11	_____	40	_____	68	_____
12	_____	41	_____	69	_____
13	_____	42	_____	70	_____
14	_____	43	_____	71	_____
15	_____	44	_____	72	_____
16	_____	45	_____	73	_____
17	_____	46	_____	74	_____
18	_____	47	_____	75	_____
19	_____	48	_____	76	_____
20	_____	49	_____	77	_____
21	_____	50	_____	78	_____
22	_____	51	_____	79	_____
23	_____	52	_____	80	_____
24	_____	53	_____	81	_____
25	_____	54	_____	82	_____
26	_____	55	_____	83	_____
27	_____	56	_____	84	_____
28	_____	57	_____	85	_____
29	_____				

Final Exam #1 – Correct Answers

Grading time! Check your answers against the answer key below.

First attempt score: _____　　**Second attempt score:** _____

1	c	30	a	58	c
2	b	31	b	59	d
3	b	32	a	60	a
4	c	33	a	61	a
5	d	34	b	62	a
6	d	35	b	63	d
7	a	36	d	64	b
8	d	37	d	65	b
9	a	38	a	66	d
10	a	39	d	67	b
11	c	40	a	68	c
12	a	41	a	69	d
13	a	42	b	70	c
14	b	43	d	71	a
15	a	44	b	72	b
16	d	45	a	73	c
17	b	46	d	74	c
18	a	47	d	75	c
19	b	48	b	76	b
20	d	49	d	77	d
21	a	50	b	78	a
22	c	51	c	79	a
23	d	52	a	80	b
24	d	53	b	81	a
25	a	54	c	82	a
26	d	55	a	83	b
27	b	56	c	84	b
28	d	57	a	85	b
29	b				

Final Exam #1 – Correct Answers with Explanations

1. C - The Series 7 is a licensing exam. CRD stands for Central Registration Depository, and is used by regulators to compile information about firms and those individuals within the securities industry. Form U4 and U5 are both submitted to regulators using CRD. Form U4 is used to collect information about individuals pertaining to their personal background, financial activities, education, and prior employment.

2. B - Political contributions made in violation of MSRB rules may result in firm the employee works for being prohibited from doing business for two years with the municipality involved.   MSRB rules would not prohibit all municipal securities business, nor would those rules require suspension of any kind.

3. B – An account with rights of survivorship means that upon death of the owner, those owner's rights pass to the other owner on the account. Custodial accounts are established for the benefit of usually a minor. The minor is the actual owner. Tenant in Common accounts pass the proportion ownership interest to their estate, and ultimately, the beneficiary.

4. C – All other items, except for an affidavit, are required to be submitted to FINRA via Form U4.

5. D – Being statutorily disqualified means that an individual cannot act in a registered capacity with any firm, without approval from regulators in the form of a waiver or exemption from those regulators.

6. D – All public companies release quarterly earnings numbers, so this fact would not be considered material. If the CFO told the neighbor the actual earnings numbers ahead of their public release, that would be material non-public information and subject to insider trading laws.

7. A – This is an example of Freeriding. Freeriding occurs when an account owner purchases securities without paying for them, then selling those same securities on or before settlement date. The account owner deposits no cash to pay for the purchase, in violation of industry rules.

8. D – Of the choices, only that an individual has obtained a financial service from your firm would be considered PII, or personally identifiable information. The remaining choices are all either general information widely available or not specific enough about customers.

9. A – Confirms must be sent to customers in either form by settlement date.

10. A – A listed equity issuer and SEC registered investment advisor would be considered regulated entities, one listed on an exchange and one registered with the SEC. Municipalities are also exempt from CIP. Only the revocable trust, of the choices given, would be subject to CIP.

11. C – Although technology based systems are often used in an AML program, they are not required to be used by law.

12. A – Financial institutions submit SARs to FinCEN. Other regulators may be involved in AML reviews and potential cases, but SARs are submitted to FinCEN.

13. A – In a Roth IRA, the investor pays taxes on the contribution before it is made. All gains in the account are not subject to further tax. Regular IRAs and 401ks grow tax deferred, with no taxes paid on the contribution before it is made. Joint accounts are not subject to any specific tax sheltering.

14. B – A spousal IRA is a type of Regular IRA, which grows tax deferred. Roth IRAs grow tax free. UGMA and Trust accounts have no tax advantages.

15. A – Coverdell ESAs can invest in any security type, while 529 plans are limited to investments offered by the plan sponsor.

16. D – A pension plan is a defined benefit plan, while the other choices are defined contribution plans.

17. B – Options settle T+1, while the other securities all settle T+2.

18. A – In a normal stock split, the number of shares owned increases, while the price of those shares decreases, both in proportion to the split, so the end financial position of the owner does not change. Here is the math: 75 shares x 5 / 3 = 125 shares. $54 x 3 / 5 = $32.40.

19. B – Long term capital gains are taxed at the long term capital gains rate, not as ordinary income. The remaining items would normally be considered ordinary income for tax purposes.

20. D – Equities normally settle on a T+2 basis. Weekends and market holidays do not count as settlement days. Friday would be Trade date, or T, Monday would be T+1, and Tuesday would be T+2.

21. A – Municipal solicitors, or members of an executive or management committee would not be considered MFPs. A municipal securities representative would not normally be considered an MFP either, as this is typically limited to retail customer activity.

22. C – Although dividend payments can vary, most issuers that pay regular dividends do so on a quarterly, or 4x per year basis.

23. D - Announcement date, ex-date, record date, payment date is the correct chronological order.

24. D – Jane has taken a long position by purchasing the stock. As the price increases, Jane now has a gain. Because Jane has not yet sold the stock, the gain is unrealized.

25. A – Principal trades mean that the broker dealer sells to a customer from the broker dealer's inventory account. When a broker dealer crosses two customer trades or never owns the security, the broker dealer acts in an agent capacity. Purchasing the security first from another counterparty then selling it to a customer is typically a riskless principal capacity.

26. D – A stop order allows an investor to protect profits or prevent losses. The investor enters the stop order below the current market, and the order is activated when the market drops below the stop price. Market orders are executed immediately, AON orders are executed all or none, immediately, and day orders are only good for that market day.

27. B – A UIT has a finite life. UITs are not exchange listed nor do they go through an IPO process like equity securities. UITs have a fixed number of shares as well to investors.

28. D – A drop in durable goods orders would be a bearish indicator, as this could mean a decrease in sales of durable goods. If fewer goods are sold overall, fewer needs to be produced, this leads to a decrease in the number of jobs. All of the other indicators are bullish.

29. B – Capital risk is the risk an investor takes when they use their own funds, or capital, to make an investment. Credit risk is the risk that someone will not pay you back. Political risk occurs when the government or regulator may decide to change the laws or rules, thereby impacting an investment. Interest rate risk is the risk that interest rates will change in an unexpected way.

30. A – Market makers buy at the bid and sell at the ask or offer. The x4 and x2 notation indicates the number of round lots (100s of shares) willing to be bought and sold at the specified price. X 4 represents 400 shares.

31. B – A default occurs when an entity who has borrowed does not pay as agreed. This could be a full or partial failure to pay – both would be considered a default.

32. A – Liquidity risk measures the ease with which an investor can be sold in the secondary market. Of the choices, a 30 year Treasury is the most liquid and widely traded security of those listed – it is highly rated and widely held by investors.

33. A – Hedge funds can hold assets that are hard to value. Hedge funds typically have higher fees than mutual funds, are illiquid, and hold a wide variety of assets.

34. B – Hedge funds can hold assets that are hard to value. Hedge funds typically have higher fees than mutual funds, are illiquid, and hold a wide variety of assets. Many hedge funds limit investments to QIBs.

35. B - Equities can be bought and sold on the secondary market through an exchange, while DPPs are not typically exchange listed. DPPs often include REITs and BDCs within their structure, and also have a lifespan similar to equities.

36. D - ETF's and mutual funds both charge fees to investors and invest in numerous security types. Mutual funds can only be bought/sold after 4pm ET, whiles ETFs can be traded throughout market hours.

37. D - Fees, computers and books are all considered legitimate uses of 529 funds, while transportation is not. If transportation would be paid from 529 funds, those funds would be subject to taxes and penalties.

38. A – Selling the bond prior to maturity means that the bond could have decreased or increased in price. The possibility that an investor may not receive all of their invested capital back when an investment is sold or called, is capital risk.

39. D – Corporate bonds are not exempt from SEC registration – all of the other securities would be exempt.

40. A – A prepaid tuition plan locks in tuition rates. These are opened through individual plans through states.

41. A – The portfolio now has a greater percentage of bonds and a lower percentage of equities. To rebalance, the investor should sell some bonds and buy some equities to get back to the target allocation.

42. B – Class B shares typically have a contingent deferred sales charged attached to their sale. Class A shares would typically not have this charge attached, but would have an upfront load charge.

43. D – Using 529 funds for non-qualified expenses means that those funds are subject to taxes and penalties by the IRS. Some states offer income tax deductions for contributions. A prepaid tuition plan locks in tuition rates, not a 529 Savings Plan.

44. B – Because the S&P 500 is an index, a mutual fund that seeks to mirror the performance of that index would normally be considered an index fund. The mutual fund would hold the same securities found within the S&P 500 index.

45. A – Investors who purchase a mutual fund must be provided a prospectus. Official Statements are used for new issue municipal securities, while Private Placement Memorandums are used for private placement securities.

46. D – A positive yield curve has a positive slope, meaning short term rates are lower than long term rates. The type of security normally does not matter when discussing the shape of the yield curve. When plotting a yield curve, the same type of security is used for short, medium and long term, such as US Treasuries.

47. D – A mixture of stocks and bonds inside a mutual fund would normally be considered a balanced mutual fund. Mutual funds that shift investments over time are called target date funds. Mutual funds may have a particular focus across the entire equity market, or just subsections of the equity market.

48. B – A closed end company only offers a fixed number of shares for sale. The remaining choices all are characteristics of open end companies.

49. D – High income is a not a SAR report category. The other categories are all SAR reporting categories.

50. B – All options accounts must be sent the options disclosure document upon account opening.

51. C – 100 shares. This is one of those numbers you just need to memorize.

52. A – The option writer or seller receives the options premium. This must be paid by settlement date.

53. B - $75.00. When owning a call option, the owner does not make money when the call option is away from the money. For a call option, away from the money means that the market price is lower than the strike price. The strike price in this is example is $80.

54. C – The length of the Mayor's term is not likely relevant. The remaining items have a direct impact on the financial viability of the municipality and would likely be relevant to a rating agency.

55. A – These options will expire worthless. A put options owner makes money when the strike price is lower than the market price.

56. C – In order to be considered a fully covered position, the options and equity positions must be for the same underlying company in the equivalent number of shares.

57. A - A CD, or certificate of deposit, is considered a time deposit. CD's with a face value of less than $100,000 are considered non-negotiable.

58. C – The FDIC will cover up to $250,000 per eligible account.

59. D – Commercial paper is typically issued for periods less than nine months in maturity and is not backed by specific corporate assets. It is typically sold on a discount basis.

60. A – Since both bonds are otherwise equivalent, which would include bond rating, an investor would look for the higher yielding bond. An investor would typically pay federal taxes on corporate bond coupon payments, while an investor would not pay federal taxes on municipal bonds. An investor needs to take into consideration taxes and therefore demands a higher coupon payment from the corporate bond.

61. A – TANs are Tax Anticipation Notes. They are issued ahead of an expected and regular tax payment, like property taxes. GO bonds are general obligation bonds and supported by the taxing authority of the municipality. BAN's are Bond Anticipation Notes, and are similar to TANs, except they are issued in anticipation of a more formal bond issuance.

62. A – The FDIC will not cover safe deposit boxes, but will cover the remaining items.

63. D – Proceeds, or profits, are exempt if used for qualified education expenses. ESA's have an annual contribution limit of $2,000. 529's do not have an annual contribution limit. 529s are authorized by individual U.S. states.

64. B – Common stock typically has voting rights. Preferred stock does not typically have voting rights. Preferred stock has also first right of bankruptcy and dividends, ahead of common equity.

65. B – Secondary market. The primary market is the initial sale of shares from the issuer to the investor. A third market sale occurs when a listed stock is traded off of the listing exchange. The fourth market occurs directly between two investors.

66. D - Although there is no hard and fast definition for market capitalization, it is generally understood that this would be a microcap stock. For the SIE Exam, think in terms of big distinctions – a $10 billion market cap would be a large cap stock for instance.

67. B – Equity holders can at most, lose their entire ownership position in the company. Equity holders cannot be personally liable for company liabilities in liquidation.

68. C – When an investor holds an equity security in their account, they are considered long the position and own the security. Options gives the holder the right, but not the obligation to purchase a security in the future. Dividends are never fully guaranteed to receive future dividend payments.

69. D – Penny stocks are considered highly speculative investments. They are not typically listed on an exchange.

70. C – Lead manager, co-manager, syndicate member, selling group

71. A – Investors can only be solicited after the Registration Statement has been filed with the SEC. The remaining choices all may happen in a security offering, but do not drive when investors can be solicited.

72. B – U.S. Government securities are not typically issued privately, as the U.S. Government is the issuer in this case. All other security types listed may issue private offerings.

73. C – By decreasing the discount rate, there is more incentive to borrow money from the Federal Reserve by member banks, which increases the amount of money in the money supply. When the Fed purchases securities, the Fed puts money into the money supply (securities for cash). Increasing the reserve requirements takes money out of the money supply by requiring more money to be held, and not spent or loaned.

74. C – An increase in the discount rate gives less incentive to borrow money from the Federal Reserve, making it a contractionary indicator or factor.

75. C – The Fed Funds rate is the rate member firms charge each other for the use of funds, usually overnight. The discount rate is the rate which the Federal Reserve loans funds to member institutions.

76. B – The issuer sells a part or all of itself is considered the issuer. An underwriter might help with the sale of the issuer's stock, and the transfer agent might assist with transferring the ownership interest from one party to another.

77. D – SIPC has a max of $250,000 in cash, and a max of $500,000 total per account for cash + securities.

78. A – M2 is a store of value, and M1 is a medium of exchange. These are terms used by the Federal Reserve to help measure the money supply.

79. A – In the event of a bankruptcy, debt holders are paid first, then preferred, then equity. Equity holders take the most risk and receive the most potential for return.

80. B – A registered representative can hold mail for a period of 3 months without justification, and a total of 6 months with written justification from the customer.

81. A – In a reverse split, the investor owns fewer shares at a higher price, with the investor's overall financial position not changing. A 1-10 reverse split means you have 1/10th the number of shares, but 10x the share price.

82. A – The fact that the individual was found guilty of or pled to a felony, means that individual would be considered statutorily disqualified, whether it was financial related or not. Other choices may be required to be disclosed to the individual's employer and/or a regulator.

83. B – Associated persons are not permitted to purchase an IPO security under any circumstances. There are no conditions where that is permitted.

84. B – To use the de minimis exception to MSRB political contribution rules, the political contribution must be $250 or less per election and the contributor must be able to vote for the candidate. The political contribution rules apply to a subset of municipal office holders, or those seeking to hold a municipal office.

85. B – NYSE is considered a U.S. securities exchange. FINRA, SEC, and MSRB are all considered regulators.

Final Exam #2

1. You have just opened up an account at ABC Brokerage and would like to buy some stocks. You deposit $10,000 cash into the account and would like to use the maximum margin available to you. What is the total value of stocks you will be able to purchase in this account, assuming you use maximum amount of margin?
    a. $10,000
    b. $14,000
    c. $20,000
    d. $25,000

2. When evaluating KYC and CIP documents, which of the following would be considered non-documentary?
    a. Partnership agreement
    b. Trust documents
    c. Passport
    d. Name

3. Which of the following is considered a U.S. Exchange?
    a. SEC
    b. Fed
    c. CBOE
    d. IRS

4. Which of the following is TRUE regarding GNP and GDP?
    a. The primary driver for GDP is ownership.
    b. Geographic location is the focus of GNP calculations.
    c. GNP measurement includes GDP as a component.
    d. GDP includes activity by American Nationals all over the world.

5. Which of the following entities are exempt from CIP?
    a. Hospital
    b. Private company
    c. Municipality
    d. Charitable Foundation

6. Given the following account balances, which of the following statement about SIPC coverage is true?

    <u>Bob and Megan Joint Account</u>
    Cash balance - $200,000
    Stocks - $500,000

    <u>Megan Individual Account</u>
    Cash balance - $150,000
    Stocks - $300,000

    a. The Individual Account stocks are only covered up to $250,000, the Joint Account is covered up to $200,000 cash and $300,000 stocks.
    b. The Joint Account and Individual Account cash balances are only covered up to $250,000 combined.
    c. The Joint Account is fully covered for cash and securities.
    d. The Individual Account is fully covered and the Joint Account is covered up to $200,000 cash and $300,000 stocks.

7. Which of the following regulatory entities is most closely related to state laws and blue sky issues?
   a. NASAA
   b. SEC
   c. Department of Treasury
   d. SIPC

8. Which of the following is TRUE about ETFs and open-end (mutual) funds?
   a. Both can be bought or sold throughout the day.
   b. ETFs may charge fees to investors, while open end mutual funds may not charge a fee.
   c. Both are traded on an exchange.
   d. Both have professional management.

9. Of the following economic indicators, which is considered a leading indicator?
   a. Stock prices
   b. Average prime rate
   c. Average duration of employment
   d. Industrial production levels

10. Which of the following is a characteristic of a private securities offering?
    a. Only used for bonds
    b. Limited number of buyers
    c. Buyers are always restricted from selling for a period of time
    d. The size of the offering is less than $10m

11. Which type of risk mitigation technique is an investor using that has the following portfolio?

    Long 100 shares of ABCD   Long 1 ABCD April put
    Long 100 shares of EFGH   Long 1 EFGH April put

    a. Diversification
    b. Portfolio Rebalancing
    c. Hedging
    d. Liquidity

12. The syndicate manager of XYZ's IPO tells you that the offering is oversubscribed. What does this mean?
    a. The underwriter has received orders for more shares than what the issuer is willing to sell.
    b. The Lead Underwriter has sent out more than 200,000 prospectuses.
    c. The underwriters have decided to exercise their overallotment option.
    d. The Lead Underwriter has decided there are too many underwriters in the syndicate and has decided to remove one from the syndicate.

13. Which of the following regulatory bodies operates with a single commissioner or set of commissioners?
    a. IRS
    b. FINRA
    c. U.S. Treasury
    d. Nasdaq

14. Which of the following is typically found on a customer statement?
    a. Trade capacity
    b. Average price disclosure
    c. Customer net worth
    d. Total account value

15. Financial firms are permitted to call individuals who are on the Do Not Call registry:
    a. under no circumstances.
    b. that have inquired with the financial firm in the past 6 months about their available service offerings.
    c. that are former customers.
    d. that have inquired with the financial firm 12 months ago about their product offerings.

16. Which of the following is true regarding an annuity?
    a. Life annuity contract payments are not impacted by the age of the annuitant.
    b. Annuity contracts cannot be entered into by anyone under the age of 65.
    c. Payouts from a qualified annuity's investments are made free of income tax.
    d. Life annuity contract payments are not impacted by the sex of the annuitant.

17. Your grandmother and grandfather both would like to each contribute to your Educational Savings Account (ESA). What is the maximum amount they could both contribute in a calendar year, assuming no other contributions are made?
    a. $0
    b. $1,000
    c. $2,000
    d. $15,000

18. A trade in a security occurring directly between two institutions occurs in which market?
    a. Primary market
    b. Secondary market
    c. Third market
    d. Fourth market

19. Earnings Before Interest and Taxes (EBIT) is found on which of the following financial statements?
    a. Income statement
    b. Balance sheet
    c. Statement of Cash flows
    d. Statement of Owners Equity

20. If an underwriter exercises the **green shoe** what does this mean?
    a. The underwriter has received approval for the offering from the SEC.
    b. The underwriter has chosen to purchase additional shares from the issuer.
    c. The issuer must pay the underwriter their agreed upon fee.
    d. The issuer must provide the underwriter with a certain number of warrants.

21. The type of equity security that always allows existing shareholders to purchase additional shares at a predetermined price from the issuer are:
    a. Convertibles   c. Rights
    b. Preferred   d. Warrants

22. If interest rates have fallen since a bond was issued, which of the following is more likely to occur?
    a. Issuer calls the bonds   c. Issuer cancels the bonds
    b. Issuer puts the bonds   d. Issuer takes no action

23. Bonds that mature in 2 years are _____ sensitive to interest rate changes in comparison to bonds that mature in 20 years, which are _____ sensitive to interest rate changes.
    a. Less, more   c. Not, more
    b. More, less   d. Less, not

24. Which of the following is NOT considered part of the money markets?
    a. Treasury Notes   c. Commercial Paper
    b. Banker's Acceptance   d. Certificate of Deposit

25. Which of the following is TRUE regarding LEAPs?
    a. Available on fewer underlying securities in comparison to non-LEAP options
    b. Mature in less than one year from original creation
    c. More liquid than non-LEAP options
    d. Written only on indexes

26. You currently hold 10 ABC April 80 European style puts. When is the earliest you can exercise your option if it is in the money?
    a. Trade date   c. Expiration date
    b. Settlement date   d. Assignment date

27. A back-end load mutual fund means
    a. no fee is paid by the investor at purchase.
    b. upfront fees are paid by the investor.
    c. no dividends are paid by the mutual fund until the fee is paid.
    d. an annual fee is paid by the investor.

28. American Depositary Receipts allow investors to purchase indirect interests in
    a. convertible securities.
    b. foreign securities.
    c. preferred securities.
    d. control securities.

29. A convertible bond allows the holder to exchange the bond for which of the following?
    a. Common equity
    b. Return of principal
    c. Coupon payments
    d. Options

30. Which of the following types of preferreds requires the issuer to catch up on dividend payments first, before paying dividends out to other preferred stockholders?
    a. Participating
    b. Preference
    c. Convertible
    d. Cumulative

31. If the current year is 2020, which of the following bonds, all rated the same, has the least amount of interest rate risk?
    a. ABC bond maturing in 2022
    b. ABC bond maturing in 2024
    c. ABC bond maturing in 2026
    d. ABC bond maturing in 2030

32. Which of the following is TRUE about open-end funds?
    a. fixed number of shares
    b. a prospectus is available for 25 days after the IPO
    c. purchases and sales can be made during normal market hours
    d. bought and sold at NAV

33. Which of the following do closed and open end funds have in common?
    a. Pooling of investor resources to hire a manager
    b. Fixed number of shares available
    c. Can be bought and sold on an exchange
    d. Available for sale during normal market hours

34. If you are 50 year old employee you can contribute a maximum of _____ to a 401(k) and _____ to an IRA.
    a. $26,000, $6,000
    b. $19,500, $6,000
    c. $19,500, $7,000
    d. $26,000, $7,000

35. Class A shares in an open end mutual fund make the most sense for which of the following investors?
   a. Customer M, who wants to hold the shares for 10 years
   b. Customer Y, who would prefer to pay slightly higher ongoing fees instead of a higher upfront fee
   c. Customer G, who wants to trade these shares on an exchange
   d. Customer J, who would like to defer the charges until a later date

36. Which of the following mutual fund share classes has less invested at the time of initial purchase?
   a. Class A   c. Class C
   b. Class B   d. Class R

37. Which of the following is common characteristic between 529 Plans and Education Savings Accounts?
   a. Limit investments to those selected by the plan manager
   b. Authorized by individual U.S. states
   c. Both can be used for secondary (i.e. middle school and high school) and post-secondary educational expenses (i.e. college or university)
   d. Proceeds are exempt from federal taxes if used for any expense under $100,000 per calendar year

38. Your rich aunt has decided to contribute to your 529 plan as part of her estate planning strategy. If she wanted to condense her contributions from 5 years out to just one year, what is the maximum she could contribute this year?
   a. $15,000   c. $75,000
   b. $30,000   d. $150,000

39. Which of the following is TRUE about ETF's?
   a. The number of shares issued stays static
   b. New shares are issued through creation units
   c. The number of shares never decreases
   d. New shares are only issued annually

40. Which of the following is true about penny stocks?
   a. they are typically listed on either the NYSE or Nasdaq exchanges
   b. typically trade between $1.01 and $10.99
   c. must meet stringent listing requirements to be traded over the counter
   d. would not be suitable for investors seeking protection of principal

41. Which of the following is a common characteristic between common and preferred stock?
    a. Voting rights
    b. Pay dividends
    c. Always listed on an exchange
    d. Unlimited liability

42. If you own a bond that is currently selling above par, this means what about the current interest rate environment for comparable bonds?
    a. Not enough information
    b. Interest rates have increased
    c. Interest rates have decreased
    d. Interest rates are unchanged

43. Who has insider trading liability if the information about a public company is obtained and acted upon?
    a. Tipper only
    b. Tippee only
    c. Tipper and tippee
    d. Public company

44. Which of the following top off examinations allows an individual to act as principal trader?
    a. Series 57
    b. Series 79
    c. Series 7
    d. Series 52

45. An individual who is not registered would be able to perform which of the following duties?
    a. Provide a copy of a customer's recent trading activity
    b. Create a research report
    c. Accept an order
    d. Recommend a customer sell a bond from their portfolio

46. In exchange for providing a specific basket of underlying securities, an ETF Authorized Participant receives:
    a. Cash
    b. ETF shares
    c. Different underlying securities
    d. ETF Fees

47. Form U4 must be updated for which of the following events?
    a. Paid a late fee on your credit card
    b. Opened up a new checking account
    c. Moved to a new apartment
    d. Got a ticket from a police officer for speeding

48. Which of the following is a difference between ETF's and mutual funds?
    a. Only mutual funds are index-based
    b. Only ETF's can be actively managed
    c. Only ETF's can be traded during market hours
    d. Only mutual funds can be sector based

49. Diversification fails to mitigate which of the following risks?
   a. Non-systematic risk
   b. Systematic risk
   c. Credit risk
   d. Currency risk

50. Which of the following securities has the greatest reinvestment risk?
   a. ABC Bond maturing in 2028, 6% coupon
   b. XYZ Bond maturing in 2028, 5 % coupon
   c. Zero coupon municipal bond maturing in 2048
   d. Zero coupon municipal bond maturing in 2028

51. What is the annual contribution and gift limit for 529 plans per contributor?
   a. $2,000
   b. $5,500
   c. $30,000
   d. $15,000

52. A GTC order is a live order until which of the following occur?
   a. Order is represented in the market maker's quotation
   b. Order is cancelled
   c. Market closes for the day
   d. Order is routed to an exchange

53. On January 1, an investor's portfolio has the following components:
   Equities: 50%
   Municipal Bonds: 20%
   Corporate Bonds: 20%
   Cash/Money Markets: 10%

   Due to changes in the market and the growth of the overall portfolio over the course of the year, the investor's portfolio now looks like this on December 31 of the same year:

   Equities: 55%
   Municipal Bonds: 25%
   Corporate Bonds: 15%
   Cash/Money Markets: 5%

   If the investor wants to maintain the portfolio composition that they had on January 1, which of the following actions should they take to rebalance their portfolio?

   a. Buy equities, sell municipal bonds, sell corporate bonds
   b. Buy equities, sell municipal bonds, buy corporate bonds
   c. Sell equities, buy municipal bonds, buy corporate bonds
   d. Sell equities, sell municipal bonds, buy corporate bonds

54. The risk that the issuer will have to buy a security back from the security holder at a predetermined date and price is which of the following risks?
a. Put risk
b. Call risk
c. Reinvestment risk
d. Credit risk

55. Which of the following is NOT a factor in the amount of premium charged to purchase an option?
a. Listing exchange of the underlying security
b. Length of time to expiration
c. Volatility of the underlying security
d. Number of options contracts

56. You own the following positions in your individual account:
1000 shares of WXYZ
500 shares of ABCD
Short 10 WXYZ August calls

Your options position in WXYZ is considered:
a. Naked
b. Covered
c. Long
d. Bullish

57. As a bond's yield goes _____, the bond's price goes _____.
a. Up, down
b. Down, flat
c. Flat, up
d. Up, flat

58. Traditionally, listed options expire on what day each month?
a. Third Friday
b. Fourth Friday
c. Third Thursday
d. Fourth Thursday

59. Higher interest rates are typically:
a. Bearish for the economy
b. Represented by the PPI
c. Have no impact on the economy
d. Represented by the CPI

60. You currently hold 10 ABC April 80 American style puts. When is the earliest you can exercise your option if it is in the money?
a. Trade date
b. Settlement date
c. Expiration date
d. Assignment date

61. In your investment account, you currently hold the following:
     1 call option contract on ABC company; 100 shares of XYZ company

     Given these holdings, which of the following is true?

     a. This is considered a covered options position
     b. A fully covered options position would only exist if you held 100 ABC option contracts
     c. The options position and stock position have nothing to do with one another
     d. If the price of XYZ equity shares are volatile, the option will tend to be worth more.

62. Which of the following is a bullish indicator?
     a. Decrease in unemployment rate
     b. Decrease in durable goods orders
     c. Decrease in real GDP
     d. Decrease in retail sales

63. An investor is choosing between a 4.0% corporate bond and a 3.0% municipal tax-exempt bond. At what marginal tax rate would the investor be indifferent to choosing either bond?
     a. 15%
     b. 20%
     c. 25%
     d. 30%

64. Total return includes all of the following **except**:
     a. Sales of securities
     b. Purchases of securities
     c. unrealized gains
     d. realized gains

65. You own 75 shares of XYZ security which has just split 5-3. How many additional shares will you own after the split?
     a. 125 shares
     b. 75 shares
     c. 50 shares
     d. 45 shares

66. Which of the following is NOT required to be provided to FINRA by the issuer regarding corporate actions?
     a. with cash distributions, the amount to be paid per share
     b. for distribution of securities, generally the amount of the security outstanding immediately prior to and immediately following the dividend or distribution and the rate of the dividend or distribution
     c. details of any conditions that must be satisfied to enable the payment or distribution
     d. for cash distributions or securities distribution, the name of the listing exchange if applicable

67.   How does an issuer entice existing shareholders to purchase additional shares in the issuer's stock in a rights offering?
      a. Pay shareholders a special dividend
      b. Provide shareholders with a cash payment
      c. Offer a discount on the issuer's goods or services
      d. Sell the issuer stock below the market price

68.   At what age must an IRA holder begin to take required minimum distributions?
      a. 72   c. 55
      b. 65   d. 59 ½

69.   Which of the following is TRUE about U.S. National Debt?
      a. It is simply a different way to describe GDP
      b. Equal to the amount of federal government revenue – federal government expenses in a given year
      c. Amount of money the federal government owes in aggregate
      d. National debt includes dollars owed by U.S. consumers and businesses

70.   Which type of offering allows an underwriter to purchase as many shares that they can sell to investors (up to a limit), but are not liable for any unsold shares?
      a. Best efforts   c. Competitive
      b. Firm commitment   d. Stock rights

71.   At what age can a 401k owner withdrawals funds from their 401k without incurring any penalties if you no longer work for your employer?
      a. 72   c. 55
      b. 65   d. 59 ½

72.   If both of your grandparents decided to contribute to your 529 plan, what is the maximum amount they could give to you in any one year?
      a. $2,000   c. $15,000
      b. $5,500   d. $30,000

73.   Financial institutions would be required to report which of the following to AML regulators?
      a. $7,500 wire from your individual account to your joint account
      b. Three separate $3,000 third party wires on the same day to the same entity
      c. Five separate $2,500 third party wires on the same day to the same entity
      d. $9,800 wire from your bank account to your brokerage account

74. In discussing a potential investment with a customer, which of the following is the registered representative not permitted to do?
    a. Agree to share in any future losses if the investment performs poorly
    b. Point out potential risks to the investment
    c. Send a research report about the investment and other companies in the same industry
    d. Recommend against purchasing the investment

75. Ingrid Investor recently purchased 100,000 shares XYZ stock at $.52 per share. She would like to sell her shares at a higher price and make some money on the trade. To do this, she starts a social media campaign on her own indicating that XYZ is about to announce a big drug approval from the U.S. FDA (Food and Drug Administration). After a few hours, the stock trades up around $2.56 per share and she sells her entire position. What best describes this type of activity?

    a. Pump and dump
    b. Wash trading
    c. Insider trading
    d. Backing away

76. How often is Firm Element training required to be conducted?
    a. 2 years after first registered
    b. 3 years after first registered
    c. Annually
    d. Once every two years

77. Please review the following selected bonds, rating, and yields.
    - State of New York Municipal Bond, BBB rated: 4.20%
    - State of Georgia Municipal Bond, BB- rated: 4.40%
    - ABC Corporate Bond, BBB rated: 5.58%
    - XYZ Corporate Bond, BB- rated: 5.88%

    Assuming a 30% marginal tax rate, which bond has the highest after-tax yield?
    a. New York Municipal Bond
    b. Georgia Municipal Bond
    c. ABC Corporate Bond
    d. XYZ Corporate Bond

78. Which of the following represents a short term capital loss if you buy 100 XYZ on 1/3/18 at $99 and
    a. sell 100 XYZ 1/2/19 at $110
    b. sell 100 XYZ 7/3/18 at $89
    c. buy 100 XYZ 1/5/19 at $109
    d. sell 100 XYZ 1/5/19 at $102

79. Which of the following is NOT required to be provided to FINRA by the issuer regarding corporate actions?
    a. date of declaration by the issuer's Board of Directors
    b. record date
    c. payment or distribution date
    d. date of corporate action decision by the issuer's Board of Directors

80. Which of the following is required for a political contribution to be considered de minimis under MSRB rules?
    a. The political contribution is less than $500 per election
    b. The person making the contribution is eligible to vote for the candidate
    c. The political contribution must be for an incumbent office holder
    d. The person making the contribution works in the same jurisdiction of the upcoming election

81. Failure to disclosure an Outside Business Activity on your U4 may result in which of the following actions by FINRA?
    a. Charged with a felony
    b. Charged with a misdemeanor
    c. Suspension from the industry
    d. Prohibition on making political contributions

82. What is the maximum amount of cash the SIPC will insure in a bank account if the bank becomes insolvent?
    a. $0
    b. $200,000
    c. $250,000
    d. $500,000

83. Which of the following would not be a permissible gift under FINRA's gift and entertainment rule?
    a. Cash in the amount of $75
    b. Set of personalized golfs balls valued at $50
    c. Attending a college football game with your client with tickets that cost $150/each
    d. Set of picture frames valued at $100

84. Which of the following best describes a Yankee bond?
    a. Pay interest in U.S. dollars, principal in the foreign currency
    b. Require a put option to be included
    c. Issued outside of the U.S.
    d. Registered in the U.S. after SEC approval

85. What is the typical maturity of a banker's acceptance?
    a. 1-30 days
    b. 30-180 days
    c. 180-250 days
    d. 250-365 days

Final Exam #2 – Answer Sheet (First Attempt)

Place your answer in the space below that corresponds to each question. When you complete the Final Exam, check your answers against the answer key that follows.

1 _____	30 _____	58 _____	
2 _____	31 _____	59 _____	
3 _____	32 _____	60 _____	
4 _____	33 _____	61 _____	
5 _____	34 _____	62 _____	
6 _____	35 _____	63 _____	
7 _____	36 _____	64 _____	
8 _____	37 _____	65 _____	
9 _____	38 _____	66 _____	
10 _____	39 _____	67 _____	
11 _____	40 _____	68 _____	
12 _____	41 _____	69 _____	
13 _____	42 _____	70 _____	
14 _____	43 _____	71 _____	
15 _____	44 _____	72 _____	
16 _____	45 _____	73 _____	
17 _____	46 _____	74 _____	
18 _____	47 _____	75 _____	
19 _____	48 _____	76 _____	
20 _____	49 _____	77 _____	
21 _____	50 _____	78 _____	
22 _____	51 _____	79 _____	
23 _____	52 _____	80 _____	
24 _____	53 _____	81 _____	
25 _____	54 _____	82 _____	
26 _____	55 _____	83 _____	
27 _____	56 _____	84 _____	
28 _____	57 _____	85 _____	
29 _____			

Final Exam #2 – Answer Sheet (Second Attempt)

Place your answer in the space below that corresponds to each question. When you complete the Final Exam, check your answers against the answer key that follows.

1	_____	30	_____	58	_____
2	_____	31	_____	59	_____
3	_____	32	_____	60	_____
4	_____	33	_____	61	_____
5	_____	34	_____	62	_____
6	_____	35	_____	63	_____
7	_____	36	_____	64	_____
8	_____	37	_____	65	_____
9	_____	38	_____	66	_____
10	_____	39	_____	67	_____
11	_____	40	_____	68	_____
12	_____	41	_____	69	_____
13	_____	42	_____	70	_____
14	_____	43	_____	71	_____
15	_____	44	_____	72	_____
16	_____	45	_____	73	_____
17	_____	46	_____	74	_____
18	_____	47	_____	75	_____
19	_____	48	_____	76	_____
20	_____	49	_____	77	_____
21	_____	50	_____	78	_____
22	_____	51	_____	79	_____
23	_____	52	_____	80	_____
24	_____	53	_____	81	_____
25	_____	54	_____	82	_____
26	_____	55	_____	83	_____
27	_____	56	_____	84	_____
28	_____	57	_____	85	_____
29	_____				

Final Exam #2 – Correct Answers

Grading time! Check your answers against the answer key below.

First attempt score: _____   **Second attempt score:** _____

1	c	30	d	58	a
2	d	31	a	59	a
3	c	32	d	60	a
4	c	33	a	61	c
5	c	34	d	62	a
6	d	35	a	63	c
7	a	36	a	64	b
8	d	37	c	65	c
9	a	38	c	66	d
10	b	39	b	67	d
11	c	40	d	68	a
12	a	41	b	69	c
13	a	42	c	70	a
14	d	43	c	71	c
15	b	44	a	72	d
16	c	45	a	73	c
17	b	46	b	74	a
18	d	47	c	75	a
19	a	48	c	76	c
20	b	49	b	77	b
21	c	50	a	78	b
22	a	51	d	79	d
23	a	52	b	80	b
24	a	53	d	81	c
25	a	54	a	82	a
26	c	55	a	83	a
27	a	56	b	84	d
28	b	57	a	85	b
29	a				

Final Exam #2 – Correct Answers with Explanations

1. C – The maximum margin permitted by the Federal Reserve under Regulation T is 50%. Since you have $10,000 in cash, you would be able to purchase another $10,000 on margin, for a total purchase of $20,000.

2. D – A name would not be considered documentary evidence. The remaining choices are all some form of written document, providing evidence of the entity or individual legal existence.

3. C – CBOE is considered a U.S. securities exchange. FINRA, SEC, and MSRB are all considered regulators.

4. C – Recall the formula GNP = GDP + income from foreign sources – income paid to foreign sources. The primary driver for GDP is geographic location, for GNP – ownership.

5. C – Municipal entities are exempt from CIP requirements. The remaining entities would all be required to follow industry rules pertaining to CIP when opening up or maintaining a securities trading account with a broker dealer.

6. D – Recall that SIPC coverage applies separately to accounts that have different ownership, so the joint and individual accounts in this case would be subject to separate limits. This is true even through Megan is listed on both accounts. Knowing this, apply the cash limit of $250,000 and total account value limit of $500,000 to each account.

7. A – NASAA is comprised of U.S. states and seeks to combine the voices of all states to protect investors and regulate firm activities. The remaining choices would normally be considered federal regulators.

8. D – Only ETF's are traded on an exchange and can be bought/sold throughout the day. Both ETFs and mutual funds may charge fees to investors.

9. A – Stock prices are considered a leading indicator. Average prime rate and average duration of unemployment are lagging indicators. Industrial production levels are considered a coincident indicator.

10. B – Private securities offerings are used for all types of securities. There are no specific limits for all security types for size of a private securities offering, nor are there always restrictions that prevent the resale within a specific period of time. In many private securities offerings, there are often resale and size restrictions.

11. C – This investor is fully hedged because the investor has an equal number of put options against their long equity shares. The investor is protected on the downside if the price of either equity security decreases, because the put option then becomes more valuable, as the equity position decreases in value.

12. A – If an offering is oversubscribed, it means more investors want to purchase more shares than what the issuer is offering to sell.

13. A – Only the IRS operates with a commissioner or set of commissioners of the choices provided. FINRA has a board and CEO/president, U.S. Treasury has a secretary appointed by the U.S. President and approved by the U.S. Senate, and Nasdaq has a CEO.

14. D – Trade capacity and average price disclosure would be found on a customer confirmation of a trade. Customer net worth would exist on neither customer confirmation or statement, as net worth would be combination of all a customer's assets and liabilities, not all available to the firm holding the customer's account.

15. B – The Do Not Call registry limits firms from call customers or potential under certain circumstances. Firms are permitted to call individuals that have inquired with the financial firm in the past 6 months about their available service offerings.

16. C – Annuity payments are often impacted by the age and sex of the annuitant and can be entered into by those under the age of 65. The tax benefits of annuities are often the reason why annuities are purchased.

17. B – The overall ESA contribution limit of $2,000 applies, regardless of the number of individuals contributing to an ESA during a calendar year.

18. D - The primary market is the initial sale of shares from the issuer to the investor. The secondary market sale occurs in a listed security on that listed securities listing exchange. A third market sale occurs when a listed stock is traded off of the listing exchange. The fourth market occurs directly between two investors.

19. A – EBIT deals with earnings, so it would be found on the Income Statement. The Balance Sheet is a snapshot in time of assets, liabilities, and owner's equity. Statement of Cash Flows shows the flow of cash in and out of the entity. Statement of Owner's equity shows how the ownership equity changes over a period of time.

20. B – The green shoe allows the underwriter to purchase additional shares within a certain period of time from the issuer at the offering price. Registration statements are approved by the SEC, but offerings are not approved per se by the SEC. The underwriter's fee is typically a contractual agreement between the underwriter and the issuer.

21. C – Convertible securities change from one security type to another. For instance, bonds or preferreds convert to common equity. Preferred shareholders often have preferential dividend payments, but do not typically give the preferred shareholder the right to purchase shares. Rights are issued to shareholders of record, while this is not always true for warrants.

22. A – Falling interest rates benefit issuers, as they can issue new debt to replace existing debt at lower interest rates, saving them money. Issuers are not permitted to outright cancel bonds. Calling bonds means the issuer pays back the investors at a contractually agreed upon price. Issuers don't normally put bonds, as this is a bond feature usually available to investors.

23. A – All things being equal like credit rating, coupon payment, etc..., a shorter term to maturity bond is less sensitive to interest rate changes than a longer term to maturity bond would be. This is simply because there is less time to maturity, and more certainty that the remaining interest and principal payments will be made.

24. A – Treasury Bills would be considered part of the money markets, but not Treasury Bonds.

25. A – LEAPs usually mature more than one year from original creation and can be written on a variety of underlying securities or indices.

26. C – European options, unlike American options, are only traded on expiration date.

27. A – A back end load mutual fund means that fees are paid at sale, not at purchase.

28. B – ADRs allow investors to purchase indirect interest in foreign securities. One share of a foreign security, also known as an ordinary security, is worth one or more ADR securities.

29. A – Convertible bonds allow the owner to convert the bond into equity or preferred shares in most scenarios. A return of principal occurs when a bond is called or when it reaches maturity. Coupon payments are received by the bondholder at predetermined intervals as payment for loaning the issuer money.

30. D – Cumulative preferreds require the issuer to catch up on any missed dividends before paying dividends to common equity or other preferred stockholders. A Preference Preferred gets paid ahead of all preferred issuances, with the exception of the Senior Preferred. Participating Preferred Securities have an 'upside' feature built into them that allows the stockholder to be paid more than normal based upon the issuer passing a key metric, like profitability level, or gross revenue. Convertible bonds allow the owner to convert the bond into equity or preferred shares in most scenarios.

31. A - All things being equal like credit rating, coupon payment, etc..., a shorter term to maturity bond is less sensitive to interest rate changes than a longer term to maturity bond would be. This is simply because there is less time to maturity, and more certainty that the remaining interest and principal payments will be made.

32. D – Open end funds do not have a fixed number of shares nor can they be bought and sold during market hours. Open end funds also have a prospectus, which is available continuously while the mutual fund is available to investors.

33. A - Open end funds do not have a fixed number of shares nor can they be bought and sold during market hours. The opposite is true for closed end funds. Closed end funds can also be bought and sold on an exchange.

34. D - The contribution limits for an individual under 50 years old are $19,500 per year to the 401k and $6,000 to the IRA. Since the individual is older than 50, they could make **additional catch up** contributions of $6,500 per year to their 401k and $1,000 to their IRA.

35. A – Since Customer G wants to trade the shares on an exchange, this customer would be better suited to purchase close end mutual funds. Customers who want to defer charges or pay higher ongoing fees would not want to purchase a mutual fund that charges fees upfront like Class A shares typically do. Holding the shares for a long period of time makes the Class A shares the best fit for Customer M.

36. A – Class A shares have an upfront load charged, so there would be less investible funds at the time of initial purchase.

37. C – ESAs can invest in most securities and are not limited by those choices from the plan manager. 529s are authorized by individual states.

38. C – The federal annual gift limit is $15,000 per year. For 529's, 5 years' worth of contributions can be consolidated in one year. $15,000 x 5 years = $75,000.

39. B – New shares are issued through creation units. The number of shares in an ETF do change over time based on supply and demand and are issued when needed.

40. D – Penny stocks are not typically listed on exchanges nor are able to meet listing requirements. They usually trade at less than $5, but often of pennies per share.

41. B – Only common stock has voting rights. Common and preferred stock can be listed on an exchange, but they do not need to be listed on an exchange. Liability ends for common and preferred stockholders when their investment is worth $0, nothing more.

42. C – Interest rates and bond prices move in opposite directions, so if the price of bond has increased, interest rates have likely decreased.

43. C – Both the tipper and tippee have insider trading liability if the information is acted upon. The tipper is the individual you passes along the inside information, while the tippee is the individual who receives the inside information. Passing or receiving the information is not enough to trigger insider trading laws – the information must be acted on in some way to be considered illegal.

44. A – Principal trader's exam is the Series 57. The Series 79 is for Investment Bankers, Series 7 is General Securities, and Series 52 is for Municipal Securities.

45. A – An unregistered individual would be able to provide a copy of a customer's recent trading activities. There remaining items would all require some form of registration.

46. B – This is how the ETF is able to sell the ETF shares to the public. The Authorized Participant acquires shares that make up the ETF and in exchange, they receive shares in the actual ETF.

47. C – A change of address would require an update to your U4.

48. C – Mutual funds are only traded and priced after normal market hours end each day (4pm ET). ETF's can be trade continuously during market hours. The remaining choices are all commonalities between mutual funds and ETFs.

49. B – Diversification is the risk mitigation technique of spreading out your investments across the market and type of security. No one single investment can bankrupt your entire portfolio. Diversification however fails to mitigate systematic risk, as this type of risk mitigation only helps eliminate systematic risk, or the risk of holding an individual security.

50. A – Zero coupon bonds do not have reinvest risk, as they do not have coupon payments to investors. ABC bond has the most reinvestment risk, given it has the highest coupon and greatest time to maturity.

51. D – 529 plans technically do not have an annual contribution limit, but the annual gift limit of $15,000 is often used to limit contributions from individuals. Contributions about the $15,000 limit are taxable.

52. B – GTC means good-til-cancelled. The order is live until it is cancelled.

53. D – The equities and municipal bond portion of the portfolio has grown, so in order to balance the portfolio, some of the equities and municipal bonds must be sold. On the other side, the investor must buy additional corporate bonds and have some of the proceeds from the sale of equities and municipal bonds remain in cash.

54. A – Put risk usually resides with the issuer. A put gives the owner of the put the right, but not the obligation to sell the investment to another party (in this case the issuer) at a predetermined price. Call risk is the opposite, and this risk resides with the owner of the investment. Reinvestment risk exists when a security owner has to invest dividends or coupon payments. Credit risk is the risk an investor takes whenever they make an investment – they could lose their entire investment.

55. A – The listing exchange of the underlying security has no impact on the amount of the premium charged to purchase an option. All of the other choices do have an impact on the premium charged.

56. B – This is considered a covered options position because the options are for the same underlying security, in the same proportional amount – 1000 shares worth of equity and 1000 shares worth of options. Recall that 10 options are worth 1000 equity shares. Long equity and short calls are also on opposite sides of the market.

57.   A – A bond's price and yield move in opposite directions, or are inversely related.

58. A – Listed options traditionally expire on the third Friday of each month.

59. A – Higher interest rates are more bearish than bullish, as the cost of money increases as interest rates increase. The CPI and PPI are price indices and measure the movement of prices, not interest rates.

60. A – American style options can be exercised immediately. The earliest you could exercise would be today, or trade date. European style options can only be exercised on expiration date.

61. C – Given that options contracts are on a different underlying security when compared to the equity shares, these positions have nothing to do with one another.

62. A – A drop in the unemployment rate would mean more people are employed. More people employed means they have the ability to spend and save money – bullish for the economy. Drops in durable goods orders, real GDP, and retail sales would all be bearish.

63. C – Recall that municipal bonds provide coupon payments that are free of federal income tax. To determine the break-even point, apply each of the tax rates against the corporate bond coupon rate. 4.0% x (1-25%) = 3.0%, so this is the breakeven point where an investor would be indifferent to either bond, assuming all else is equal.

64. B – The sale of securities, unrealized gains, and realized gains are all aspects of total return. The purchase of securities is not part of total return by itself. In order to determine total return, it would need to be paired with a sale of securities, or a change in price of the security owned.

65. C – To determine the total shares you own after the split in a standard stock split, multiply the number of shares times the split. In this case, 75 shares x 5 / 3 = 125 shares. However, the question asks for **additional** shares, so take 125 total shares – 75 starting shares = 50 **additional** shares.

66. D – This is a NOT question, so three of the answers are actually items that FINRA requires from issuers in corporate actions. FINRA does not need the name of the listing exchange of the issuer, as this would already be known to FINRA.

67. D – To entice existing shareholders to purchase additional ownership interest in the company through a stock purchase, the issuer offers shares at a discount from market price. The Board of Directors of the issuer may decide to pay cash or stock dividends, but this would not require the investor to purchase additional shares.

68. A – RMDs, or Required Minimum Distributions must begin at age 72.

69. C – The U.S. National Debt is the amount of money owed by the U.S. government. It does not include debt owed by U.S. consumers or businesses. It does not used interchangeably with GDP. The U.S. government budget deficit is the amount of federal government revenue – federal government expenses in a given year.

70. A – This best describes a best efforts underwriting. Firm commitment underwriting allows the underwriter to solicit investors and take orders on behalf of the issuer, but the underwriter in this case is liable for any unsold balances. A competitive underwriting is bid on by several underwriters, with the highest bid receiving the securities to sell to investors..

71. C – Age 72 is the age Required Minimum Distributions must begin in Regular IRAs. Age 65 is often considered normal retirement age. At age 55, 401k owners can withdrawal funds from their 401k without penalty if they are still work at the 401k employer. If they do not work for their 401k employer any longer, the age to withdrawal funds from their 401k without penalty is 59 ½.

72. D – The federal gift tax limit is $15,000, so each grandparent could give $15,000 for a total of $30,000.

73. C – Although each separate wire is below the $10,000 reporting threshold, the combination of wires adds up to greater than $10,000. Any single wire about $10,000 or a combination in excess of $10,000 would be reported to FINCEN using Form CTR.

74. A – Sharing in losses or gains with customers is strictly prohibited under FINRA rules. The remaining items would all be permissible activity.

75. A – This is a basic description of a classic pump and dump scheme. First the investment is purchased, then the social media campaign helps generate interest in the stock and pumps up the price, followed by the quick investor sale to capture the profit, the dump.

76. C – Firm Element must be completed annually. Regulatory Element must be completed 2 years after first being registered, then every 3 years thereafter.

77. B – To determine after tax yield, take the corporate bond yield x (1 – tax rate). Corporate bond coupon payments are subject to income taxes. In this example, take 5.88 x (1-.30) = 4.116%. Since this is the highest paying coupon bond, and the after tax yield is already less than the highest yielding municipal bond, the 4.40% coupon bond has the highest after tax yield.

78. B – The only choice where the investor has a short term capital loss is buying at $99 and selling at $89. A loss occurs when the investment is sold for less than the price it was purchased.

79. D – The issuer would not be required to inform FINRA about the date of the recent issuer Board of Director's meeting. The remaining choices are all information that FINRA has no way of knowing independently and are key pieces of information to make sure the corporate action is recorded successfully.

80. B – In order to be considered a deminimis political contribution, the contribution must be for less than $250 per election and the contributor must be able to vote for the candidate.

81. C – For individuals that have a U4 filed with FINRA, updating your U4 with information pertaining to an Outside Business is required. Failing to do so could result in a fine, suspension, or termination from the industry.

82. A – SIPC provides no coverage for cash in a bank account. In a securities account, the cash limit is $250,000.

83. A – Although the gift limit is $100, cash is not an acceptable gift and is prohibited.

84. D - A Yankee bond becomes registered in the U.S. after SEC approval

85. B – Banker's acceptance is a short term instrument, usually lasting anywhere from 30-180 days in length.

FINRA Final Exam

After you have read all of the course material, taken the End of Chapter quizzes, reviewed the Table of Figures, watched our YouTube videos, and taken the Final Exams, you need to take FINRA's Final Practice Exam located on their website, here:

https://www.finra.org/industry/sie-practice-test

Good Luck!

Endnotes

[1] https://www.sec.gov/spotlight/jobs-act.shtml
[2] http://www.sec.gov/about/whatwedo.shtml
[3] https://investor.gov/introduction-markets/role-sec
[4] http://www.finra.org/about
[5] http://www.finra.org/about
[6] http://www.msrb.org/About-MSRB.aspx
[7] http://www.msrb.org/About-MSRB/About-the-MSRB/Mission-Statement.aspx
[8] https://www.irs.gov/uac/The-Agency,-its-Mission-and-Statutory-Authority
[9] http://www.nasaa.org/about-us/our-role/
[10] https://www.stlouisfed.org/in-plain-english
[11] http://www.sipc.org/about-sipc/sipc-mission
[12] https://www.fdic.gov/deposit/covered/
[13] https://www.fdic.gov/deposit/covered/categories.html
[14] https://www.sec.gov/files/ib_accreditedinvestors.pdf

[15] https://www.sec.gov/fast-answers/answersinvadvhtm.html
[16] https://www.sec.gov/divisions/marketreg/mrtransfer.shtml
[17] https://www.conference-board.org/data/bci/index.cfm?id=2160
[18] http://www.cnbc.com/2016/06/13/microsoft-to-buy-linkedin.html
[19] https://www.msrb.org/EducationCenter/Municipal-Market/Lifecycle/Disclosure/Official-Statements.aspx
[20] https://www.sec.gov/reportspubs/investor-publications/investorpubsrule144htm.html

[21] https://www.sec.gov/fast-answers/answerspennyhtm.html
[22] https://www.sec.gov/reportspubs/investor-publications/investorpubsmicrocapstockhtm.html
[23] https://www.sec.gov/fast-answers/answersadrshtm.html

[24] https://www.sec.gov/investor/alerts/adr-bulletin.pdf
[25] https://www.treasurydirect.gov/instit/auctfund/work/work.htm
[26] https://www.treasury.gov/resource-center/faqs/Markets/Pages/fixedfederal.aspx
[27] This data set has been simplified for ease of understanding. The first day of each year was selected to represent the entire year, intending to show the relative differences between each of three types of Treasury securities.
[28] http://gfoa.org/local-government-investment-pools
[29] http://www.msrb.org/msrb1/pdfs/About-Municipal-Variable-Rate-Securities.pdf

[30] https://www.sec.gov/answers/mfclose.htm
[31] https://www.sec.gov/oiea/investor-alerts-bulletins/ib_mfprospectus1.html
[32] http://www.finra.org/industry/breakpoints
[33] https://www.irs.gov/uac/Tax-Benefits-for-Education:-Information-Center
[34] https://www.irs.gov/taxtopics/tc310.html
[35] https://www.sec.gov/reportspubs/investor-publications/investorpubsintro529htm.html
[36] https://www.irs.gov/uac/529-plans-questions-and-answers
[37] https://www.sec.gov/fast-answers/answersreitshtm.html
[38] https://www.sec.gov/investor/pubs/sec-guide-to-mutual-funds.pdf
[39] http://www.sec.gov/investor/alerts/trading101basics.pdf
[40] http://www.finra.org/investors/key-economic-indicators-every-investor-should-know
[41] http://www.coca-colacompany.com/press-center/press-releases/the-board-of-directors-of-the-coca-cola-company-declares-regular-quarterly-dividend0/

42 http://www.finra.org/investors/highlights/tax-time-topics-cost-basis-what-you-need-know
43 http://www.msrb.org/msrb1/pdfs/MSRB-Indices-Defined-Report_FINAL.pdf

44 https://www.sec.gov/answers/tender.htm
45 http://www.finra.org/investors/what-expect-when-you-open-brokerage-account
46 https://www.fdic.gov/consumers/community/aei/regional/other-resources/baei-fact-sheet-cip.pdf

47 http://www.finra.org/industry/business-continuity-planning
48 https://www.sec.gov/fast-answers/answersfreeridehtm.html

49 http://www.sec.gov/answers/churning.htm
50 http://www.finra.org/industry/breakpoints
51http://www.finra.org/industry/statutory-disqualification-process#sthash.hfzhDQdW.dpuf

52 https://www.finra.org/sites/default/files/AppSupportDoc/p015111.pdf
https://www.finra.org/sites/default/files/form-u4.pdf
53 https://www.finra.org/sites/default/files/AppSupportDoc/p015113.pdf
https://www.finra.org/sites/default/files/form-u5.pdf

CPSIA information can be obtained
at www.ICGtesting.com
Printed in the USA
BVHW060850240721
612638BV00007B/564